An introduction to international economics

Chris Milner and **David Greenaway**

Longman
London and New York

Longman Group Limited London

*Associated companies, branches and representatives
throughout the world*

*Published in the United States of America
by Longman Inc., New York*

© Longman Group Limited 1979

First published 1979

British Library Cataloguing in Publication Data

Milner, C R
  An introduction to international economics.
  1. International economic relations
  I. Title II. Greenaway, D
  382.1   HF1411   78-40512

  ISBN 0-582-45576-6

Printed in Great Britain by
Richard Clay (The Chaucer Press) Ltd, Bungay, Suffolk

Contents

Preface

An introduction to international economics was conceived of as a text which would do justice to the main corpus of international trade (theory and empirical evidence), and international monetary economics within the space of around 100 000 words. In addition it was conceived of as a text which would be manageable enough to provide a genuine 'introduction' to the subject area to any second-year undergraduate with a grounding in basic economic theory; whilst at the same time proving sufficiently rigorous to provide the basis for study for any third-year undergraduate specialising in International Economics, at any university or polytechnic in just about any country. Furthermore, we also hoped that the text could act as a useful introduction to any graduate student following specialist studies in International Economics.

Maximising (subject to such constraints) did not prove straightforward. Clearly, no text can be all things to all men. However, we are hopeful, and confident in ourselves, that these aims have been met as far as possible. Specifically we would make the following observations.

First, the techniques employed are primarily of a geometric nature, mathematical exposition being deliberately kept to a bare minimum in order to cater for the non-specialist and less numerate student. This nevertheless, does not detract from the overall rigour of the book since many of the geometrical tools employed, and many of the topics analysed, do require a considerable amount of sophistication on the part of the reader.

Second, we have consciously allocated a larger proportion of space to empirical work than is usual, feeling that this is a frequently neglected aspect of the subject area. Thus all sections on trade theory, as well as the chapters on international monetary economics, contain a review of the salient empirical work, and within the text itself a carefully prepared guide to further work. This should prove of value to specialist students and of interest to non-specialist students.

Third, we have provided an up to date and detailed compilation of references intended to guide the student at any level of study. The length of our reference section is partly indicative of the fact that the subject matter of International Economics is such a richly documented area; and partly due to a deliberate policy decision that the prerequisites to further study should be provided. Thus, the student hoping to pursue any topic further should find the bibliography both helpful and challenging.

Fourth, we aimed to make the text itself as up to date as possible by including treatment of recent theoretical developments (e.g. the modern monetary approach to balance of payments analysis) and recent empirical and policy issues (e.g. the allocation of an entire section to monetary disorder and reform). This should make available to undergraduates many issues which were previously only to be found in journal literature.

Finally, we managed to complete the work within the intended space. This we hope is one of the main strengths of the book, that it is considerably shorter than many other treatises on the subject. We are none the less confident that within this space we have given adequate coverage to the vast majority of theoretical and empirical issues which form the basis to any courses in International Trade, International Monetary Economics or International Economics.

Clearly, any textbook writers must acknowledge a debt to previous textbook writers both 'ancient' and 'modern' (as well as the more obvious and more lasting debt to journal literature). In general, the majority of texts written in any branch of economic science are to some extent or other derivative, drawing consciously or unconsciously on the stock of previously amassed knowledge. This no doubt is also the case with the current text. It is probably also fair to say, however, that each new text adds something to the existing stock of knowledge. We also hope that this is true of *An introduction to international economics*.

More specifically we would like to gratefully acknowledge the assistance of a number of people whose comments proved invaluable in the preparation of the final manuscript. In particular we would like to thank R. Shone of Stirling University for his careful reading of the entire text and for his detailed and constructive comments. In addition, a number of other individuals offered valuable criticism on various sections of the text. We would therefore also express our gratitude (and in some cases intellectual debt) to K. W. Elliott (Liverpool Polytechnic), Professor D. Swann, W. P. Maunder, Dr J. R. Presley (Loughborough University), J. S. Metcalfe (Liverpool University) and D. R. Sapsford (ESRI, Dublin). Furthermore, we would like to acknowledge the assistance and encouragement of Professor D. W. Pearce (Aberdeen University) in the initial conception of this text. Last, but not least, our wives Ruth and Susan deserve our warmest appreciation for their passive acceptance of endless conversations dominated by the subject matter of *An introduction to international economics*, and for their unquestioning encouragement to our preoccupation with more abstract matters.

We sincerely hope that students using this text gain a fraction of the benefits we have gained in writing it. If so, our efforts will not have been in vain. No doubt errors and omissions still remain, any such failings are the authors' sole responsibility.

C. R. Milner
Loughborough
P. Greenaway
Buckingham

Acknowledgements

We are grateful to the following for permission to reproduce copyright material:

The Brookings Institution for adapted tables from pp. 165 and 168 *Nontariff Distortions of International Trade* by R. Baldwin © 1971 by the Brookings Institution; Cambridge University Press for an adapted figure from p. 703 by G. D. MacDougal from *Economic Journal* Vol. 61, 1951; The European Free Trade Association for an adapted table from tables 6 and 11 pp. 26 and 38 *The Trade Effects of EFTA and the EEC* 1959–1967; the author, Professor G. K. Helleiner for table 12 p. 79 from *International Trade and Economic Development* by G. K. Helleiner 1972; Her Majesty's Stationery Office for an adapted table from tables 15.1, 15.2 and 15.3, pp. 128–9 from *Monthly Digest of Statistics* January 1978, used with the permission of the Controller of Her Majesty's Stationery Office; The International Monetary Fund for extracts from *IMF Annual Report* 1969, 1974, 1976 and 1977, *International Financial Statistics, IMF Papers 9* and *Finance and Development*; The Johns Hopkins University Press for Table 1.1 from *The Structure of Protection in Developing Countries* by Bela Balassa; Oxford University Press for an adapted table from p. 338 Table 3 by J. Williamson and A. Bottrill *Oxford Economic Papers* Vol. 23 1971; a table from p. 174 and a table from p. 60 *Industry and Trade in Some Developing Countries* by Little, Scitovsky and Scott, published by Oxford University Press, 1970; Pakistan Institute of Development for figure 7.4 p. 21 by H. G. Johnson from *Pakistan Development Review* Vol. 7, 1967; the author, Professor T. W. Swan for Diagram 1 from the article 'Longer Run Problems of the Balance of Payments' in *The Australian Economy* Vol. 1 edited by H. W. Arndt and W. M. Corden; The United Nations, The World Bank and the International Monetary Fund for a table compiled from data from *The United Nations World Economic Survey* 1975, *The United Nations Statistical Yearbook* 1975, *The World Bank Atlas* 1976 and *International Financial Statistics* December 1976; The University of Chicago Press for an adapted figure from figure 7.2 p. 371 by P. B. Clark from *Journal of Political Economy* Vol. 78 1970.

Chapter 1

The genesis of trade

1.1 Introduction

From time immemorial, individuals have traded with one another. Different personal skills and specialisms result in differing propensities to produce. The hunter does not attempt to make his own shoes. Instead he concentrates on hunting, trading part of his capture with the cobbler. Such specialisation of function is an accepted part of life, even in the most primitive of economies, and provides the basis for exchange or trade.

As economies become more sophisticated, and production more capital intensive, the scope for specialisation increases. So too does the scope for trade, until eventually communities and geographical areas, rather than merely individuals, may specialise in a particular line of production. The development of international trade is similar. Different countries may concentrate on the production of different commodities, exchanging their surpluses with each other.

The immediate purpose of this chapter will be to investigate precisely why nations specialise in production and why nations trade with each other, rather than producing all their requirements themselves. This examination of the genesis of trade will involve a consideration of both demand- and supply-based factors. As we shall see, several theorems, some accepted wisdom for a considerable length of time, others more recent and more contentious, attempt to explain why nations engage in trade.

This seems the logical starting point for any text on international economics. The remainder of the book will occupy us in building refinements and elaborations to the basic, essentially very simple, theory of the origins of trade. In Chapter 2 we will ask the question: What happens when we distort free trade flows with government-imposed tariffs, or with government-financed subsidies? Chapter 3 will take this a stage further by examining discriminatory trade barriers, i.e. by looking at the situation when countries form trading groups within which free trade prevails between members, but where trade barriers discriminate specifically against outsiders. In Chapter 4 we will then attempt to see whether the conclusions reached must be altered substantially when allowance is made for the fact that economies grow through time and, furthermore, grow at different rates.

Throughout Chapters 1 to 4 we are conducting our analysis within a non-money, i.e. barter, framework. Chapters 5 to 8 relax this simplification, in considering the implications and consequences of, and the problems created by, trade flows in a monetary framework.

1.2 Why do nations engage in international trade?

Essentially, nations trade for precisely the same reason as do individuals. If a nation can obtain a particular commodity for less than it would cost to produce it itself, then clearly it would benefit by doing so. This basic principle of exchange has of course been recognised for centuries. Like so many embryonic principles of economics, however, it was not formalised until fairly recently.

Absolute advantage
The beginnings of modern trade theory are generally traced to Adam Smith's momentous work, *The Wealth of Nations,* first published in 1976. Smith's important contribution is usually referred to as 'the principle of absolute advantage'. This principle can be demonstrated by reference to a simple two-country model.

As with most of Chapters 1 to 4 of this text, we will assume that there are only two countries in the world. For purposes of exposition we will refer to them as Britain and America. Both countries have a given labour force, which can be employed in producing either pottery or grain. In the classical world of Adam Smith, the labour theory of value was presumed to hold. In accordance with this we will initially assume that commodities gain value only from their labour input. We will also assume that conditions of perfect competition prevail, in both the pottery and grain industries, in Britain and America. Prior to the opening up of trade (a situation we will refer to as *autarky*) both countries produce pottery and grain. We can see in the following example how much of each commodity can be produced by one unit of labour in a week. In this example, America has an *absolute advantage*

	Output of one unit of labour (units per week)	
	Pottery	Grain
Britain	9	6
America	8	12

over Britain in the production of grain. Using one unit of labour for a week, she can produce twelve units of grain, whereas Britain can only produce six units, with the same labour input. With regard to pottery manufacture however, America faces an absolute cost *dis*advantage. One unit of labour produces only eight units of pottery per week, compared with an output of nine units in Britain. If these production requirements are translated into price differences (which following from the labour theory of value they would), then clearly it will benefit both countries to engage in trade. Rather than employing scarce labour units in grain production, where one man produces only six units in a week, Britain could obtain the same amount of grain from America, where only half the labour input is required for the same output. In exchange, Britain could export pottery, the commodity in which she has an absolute cost advantage. Thus, contrary to prevailing mercantilist philosophy, this simple principle established that trade could benefit both partners, and need not serve to benefit just one.[1]

Comparative advantage
Despite its obvious deficiencies, such a simple model is useful as a first approximation of the gains from trade. Later economists, however, took the argument a step further. Torrens and Ricardo addressed themselves to the situation where one country has an absolute cost advantage in the production of both commodities. In these circumstances, is it still possible for both countries to gain from trade? Consider the following example. Here, American labour is absolutely

	Output of one unit of labour (units per week)	
	Pottery	Grain
Britain	6	3
America	9	12

more productive in producing both grain and pottery. But, as Ricardo demonstrated (Ricardo, 1817), trade may still be mutually beneficial. Take the domestic, pre-trade, price ratios in each country.

In autarky, 1 unit of grain will exchange for $\frac{3}{4}$ unit of pottery in America. In other words, since the economy can produce either grain or pottery, the opportunity cost of 1 unit of grain is $\frac{3}{4}$ unit of pottery. Given that conditions of perfect competition prevail, the goods will exchange in this ratio. The comparable autarkic rate of exchange in Britain will be 1 grain for 2 pottery. Ignoring transport costs, it would therefore profit American grain producers to export grain to Britain, where they will receive in exchange up to 2 units of pottery. This will not be a unilateral transfer, since British pottery producers will have the incentive to export pottery to America, where they can receive more than $\frac{1}{2}$ unit of grain in exchange for 1 unit of pottery. In fact, they will receive up to $1\frac{1}{3}$ units of grain. Thus, despite the fact that America can produce more of both grain and pottery, trade can take place to the possible mutual benefit of both countries.

The reason for this is that although America has an absolute advantage in the production of both commodities, she has a *comparative advantage* in the production of only one. The comparative cost of pottery production, in terms of grain, is less in Britain than in America. America has, on the other hand, a comparative cost advantage in the production of grain. Thus, despite Britain's absolute disadvantage, she will nevertheless export pottery to America in exchange for grain.

This then is the so-called comparative cost principle, credit for which is most often given to Ricardo. According to this principle it is not absolute cost differences which are important in determining trade flows, but rather comparative cost differences. The principle can also be easily demonstrated geometrically.

Suppose Britain and America both have 100 workers each. We

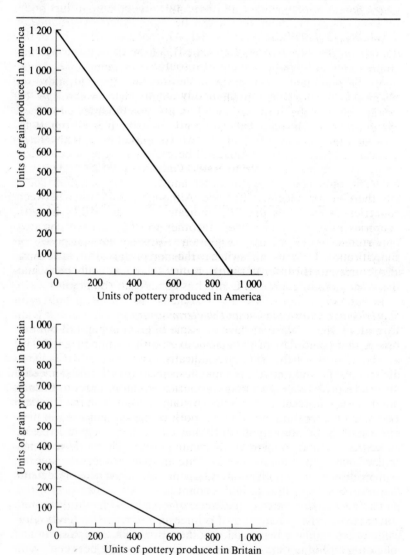

Fig. 1.1 Production possibility curves for America and Britain

already know the relative productivities of labour in each industry in both countries, and since we assume these productivities are constant, over the relevant range of output, we can construct production possibility tables for each country. If, for example, America employs all its labour in the production of grain, total output would be 1 200 units per week (100 workers each producing 12 units). Alternatively, all of the 100 workers could be employed in pottery production, in which case 900 units can be produced. The labour force could then be employed producing either of these two limits, or various combinations between them, which can be represented by *production possibility curves* (PPCs), as in Fig. 1.1. Any point on the curve (or the *production frontier* as it is often called) can be chosen since this is consistent with full employment of resources.

The PPC is also often referred to as the *transformation curve,* since it shows the rate at which one commodity can be 'transformed' into the other. The slope of this curve therefore gives us the *marginal rate of transformation* (MRT). When MRTs are the same in both countries, relative costs of production of the two commodities, and therefore domestic pre-trade price ratios, will be the same in both countries. There will be no incentive to trade. Only when MRTs differ will domestic, pre-trade, price ratios differ, and only in these circumstances will there be any incentive to trade. Although MRTs differ between countries, linearity of the PPC indicates that the MRTs in both countries have constant values. In other words, we have constant opportunity costs. (This assumption is made for purposes of simplification. Later we will switch to the more usual case of increasing opportunity costs of transforming production of one commodity into the other, which yields a PPC which is concave to the origin.)

Specialisation in production and the terms of trade

Consider Fig. 1.2. Here we have the same PPCs as in Fig. 1.1, but this time we have placed them on the same axes, with a common origin. The different slopes of the PPCs are indicative of differing MRTs. This difference in comparative costs manifests itself in differing domestic, pre-trade, price ratios. In autarky, America produces and consumes at point A on her production frontier; Britain at point B on her frontier. Following the opening up of trade, both countries specialise in production of the commodity in which they enjoy their comparative cost advantage – America in grain, Britain in pottery. The terms at which the two countries will trade (i.e. the rate at which grain exchanges for pottery internationally) ultimately depends on the impact of demand factors. These we will take into account later. All we can say for the moment is that the international *terms of trade* (TOT), must lie somewhere between the limits set by the domestic pre-trade price ratios for trade to be mutually beneficial. In other words, on the international market, a unit of pottery will exchange for somewhere between $\frac{1}{2}$ unit of grain and $1\frac{1}{3}$ units of grain. (Conversely, 1 unit of grain will exchange for between $\frac{3}{4}$ unit and 2 units of pottery.) Since the slopes of the

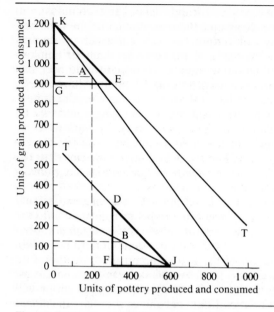

Fig. 1.2 Production possibility curves, and American and British trade triangles

respective PPCs reflect these autarkic price ratios, the international price line must lie somewhere between them.

Suppose the international TOT settles at 1 unit of pottery exchanging for 1 unit of grain. This is of course the international price ratio faced by both countries, and the condition is depicted by the lines TJ and KT being parallel. Faced with this terms of trade, Britain reallocates her resources from the production of grain and specialises in pottery production, at point J. America runs down pottery production, using the resources released to expand grain production, until she is specialised at K. Several important observations can be made regarding the consequences of these shifts. First, *commodity price equalisation* has occurred, i.e. the post-trade price of pottery and grain is the same in Britain and America. Second, both countries have completely specialised in the production of that commodity in which they enjoy their comparative advantage. As a result of specialisation, the total world output of both goods has increased. In autarky, with America producing at point A, and Britain at point B, the total amount of grain produced would be 1 060 units (130 units in Britain and 930 units in America) and total pottery production of 550 units (350 in Britain and 200 in America). Following specialisation, 1 200 units of grain and 600 units of pottery are produced. This increased output must clearly enhance consumption possibilities, and we may find that America and Britain now consume at points E and D respectively. At these post-trade consumption points, both countries have increased their consumption of **both** commodities.

If we now combine the production and consumption points for both countries, we can derive their *trade triangles*. Since Britain produces OJ of pottery, but only consumes OJ minus FJ, the difference must represent exports to America. Analogously, although Britain produces no grain, she still consumes an amount equal to FD. FD must therefore have been imported from America, in exchange for pottery. The British trade triangle is then, DJF with FD representing imports and FJ exports. The same reasoning can be followed in deriving the American trade triangle KEG.

One final point, which the observant student may have already noted, the trade triangles DJF and KEG, are congruent triangles. This is not coincidental. In a two-country world, where barter prevails, British exports (imports) must of necessity equal American imports (exports) for trade to balance. If volumes do not balance initially, relative prices will adjust, i.e. the international terms of trade will alter, until equilibrium is achieved. (The process of balancing trade when money is taken into account, is very much more complex, and will be the subject of Chapters 5 to 7.)

Thus, through the medium of a relatively simple piece of analysis, we have demonstrated the principle of comparative advantage, or how when comparative cost ratios differ, trade can be mutually beneficial. It is important to bear in mind, however, that the analysis is based on a number of very restrictive assumptions. This does not of course make it erroneous, but it may mean that once we relax these assumptions, we will have to alter our conclusions.

Our next task will therefore be to progressively relax some of the conditions on which we built our simple comparative advantage model. For instance, we can allow for more than one factor of production. Thus we can then investigate the implications of differences in the quantity of factors between countries, not simply differences in the quality, or productivity of factors (which formed the basis to the simple Ricardian comparative costs model). In addition, we must consider the impact of demand factors. As every student soon learns in economics, relative prices and quantities are not just the outcome of supply-based factors, but of the interaction of supply and demand. Finally, we may attempt to consider the validity of our analysis in a dynamic, multilateral framework rather than a completely static, bilateral framework.

1.3 Comparative advantage elaborated

Factor intensities and factor endowments
One of the most glaring deficiencies of the basic, Ricardian-type model is that only one factor of production is assumed, namely labour. Differing labour productivities resulted in different production conditions, which were the direct cause of trade. We will now become a little more realistic, and allow for a second factor of production,

capital, which can be 'mixed' with labour in the production process.[2]

We will continue with our same two countries (America and Britain), and our same two goods (grain and pottery), both of which use labour and capital in production. For analytical purposes, we initially assume that production functions (i.e. the purely technological relationships between factor inputs and commodity outputs) differ between commodities but are the same for each commodity in the different countries. We can depict these production relationships by reference to Fig. 1.3. Units of capital input are 'measured' along the

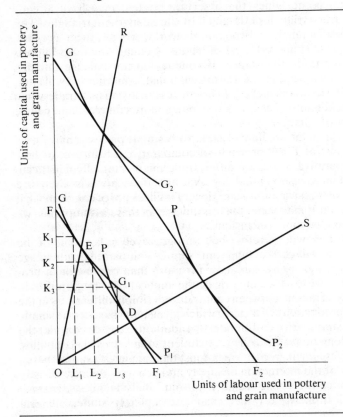

Fig. 1.3 Production relationships with two factors

vertical axis, units of labour along the horizontal axis. GG_1 and PP_1 are *isoquants* for the production of grain and pottery respectively. These isoquants, or equal output lines, show how the same output of a particular commodity can be produced, using different combinations of inputs. For instance, GG_1 of grain can be produced combining K_1 of capital with L_1 of labour, or K_2 of capital and L_2 of labour, or K_3 capital and L_3 labour, and so on. The isoquants for each commodity are in sets, isoquants above and to the right reflecting higher levels of output.

Both sets of isoquants are convex to the origin. This convexity is a consequence of the fact that capital and labour are imperfect substitutes for each other. Thus, as we move around GG_1, reducing the number of units of capital used, increasing amounts of labour have to be substituted to maintain the same level of output. We refer to this phenomenon as a *diminishing marginal rate of substitution* (DMRS), between the two factor inputs.

Production can take place at any point on the isoquant. In order to ascertain precisely which point, we introduce *isocost lines* such as FF_1 and FF_2. These isocost lines (or budget lines) tell us several things. The **slope** of the isocost line is determined by the relative prices of the two factors, or the factor price ratio. The steeper this slope, the lower the price of capital inputs relative to labour. Conversely, if the slope becomes shallower, it indicates that labour inputs are becoming cheaper relative to capital. The **situation** of the isocost lines relative to the origin is determined by the amount of expenditure available for the purchase of inputs. The greater the available expenditure, the greater the amount of inputs which can be hired, and the further from the origin will the isocost line lie. Thus FF_2 represents a greater outlay than FF_1. Since producers are assumed to produce the maximum quantity of output from a given outlay on inputs, production will take place at a point of tangency between an isocost line and an isoquant. In terms of Fig. 1.3, production of grain and pottery will take place at E and D respectively. At these points, the maximum possible output (PP_1 and GG_1) is being obtained for a given outlay on capital and labour denoted by the isocost line FF_1.

We can also note that the isoquants PP_1 and GG_1 are tangential to the isocost lines at different points. Were they tangential at the same point, both commodities would use capital and labour in precisely the same proportion. The fact that they differ, however, tells us that pottery and grain production have different requirements in terms of capital and labour. These differing requirements, or differing *factor intensities*, can be depicted by tracing a ray, from the origin, to the point on the isoquant where production takes place. Thus OE and OD are *factor intensity rays*, for grain and pottery respectively, their different slopes reflecting the differing proportions in which capital and labour are used in grain and pottery production; grain production being more capital intensive, pottery more labour intensive.

The final relationship we must note, for the time being, is that between the scale of inputs and level of output. Initially, we will assume that all production functions exhibit constant returns to scale. Therefore, as long as relative factor prices remain unchanged, a doubling of all inputs will result in a doubling of output. This is often referred to as 'homogeneity to degree one' of the production function. We can portray this condition by ensuring that all factor intensity rays are linear (so the two factors of production are used in unchanged proportions) and that isoquants are equally spaced from the origin.

To many readers, all that we have said so far in Section 1.3 is really just a revision of basic production theory. It is imperative that the student has a thorough understanding of the techniques and concepts discussed, as they are essential tools of trade theory and will be used time and time again (useful résumés of price theory can be found in Laidler, 1974 and Mansfield, 1970).

The next step in our model building is to link the production relationships so far discussed with the total quantities of factors available. To do so, we must now introduce the *Edgeworth Box* diagram, shown in the upper section of Fig. 1.4. The sides of the Box

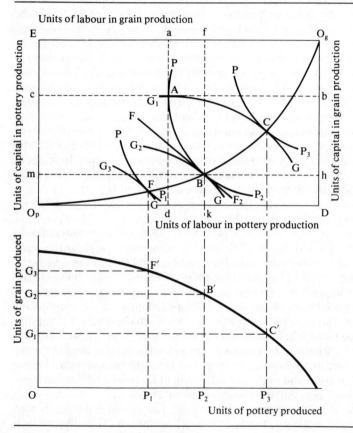

Fig. 1.4 The Edgeworth Box and the PPC

diagram represent the total endowment of each factor of production. Thus, total labour available for employment is O_pD (= O_gE), total capital O_pE (= O_gD). As before, production of pottery is viewed from the O_p origin, with pottery isoquants PP_1, PP_2, PP_3, and so on. Rather than viewing grain production from the same origin, however, we invert the grain isoquant map, and reverse its sides, so that grain production is now viewed from the O_g origin. Thus, grain isoquants GG_1, GG_2 and GG_3 represent increasing production of grain. By employing this technique, we can readily see how any economy's total resources are deployed between pottery and grain production.

For instance, point A is a feasible production point. Here, all of the economy's resources are fully employed. O_pc of capital is combined with O_pd of labour to produce PP_2 units of pottery. The remainder of the country's factor endowments are employed producing GG_1 units of grain (O_gb of capital, O_ga of labour). Is this the 'best' that the economy can do, given its available labour and capital? Closer inspection reveals that it is not. In actual fact, total output can be further increased, simply by reallocating the same resources. If capital were transferred from pottery production to grain production, and conversely, labour from grain to pottery, we could shift from A to B. As before, all resources are fully employed, and the total endowment of labour and capital remains unchanged. Because of the reallocation, however, total output is greater at B than A. PP_2 of pottery is still produced, but grain production has increased from GG_1 to GG_2. A reallocation of factors has allowed us to move on to a higher grain isoquant, whilst remaining on the same pottery isoquant. At B we have a point of efficiency, in the sense that no further reallocation could increase the output of one of the two commodities without decreasing the output of the other (this the reader ought to check for his/herself).

Since the slope of an isoquant reflects the marginal rate of substitution of labour for capital (MRS_{LK}), whenever isoquants are tangential to each other, as at B, the MRS_{LK} is the same in the production of both commodities. Furthermore, both isoquants are also tangential to an isocost line (FF_2), the slope of which reflects the factor price ratio. Thus, for equilibrium, MRS_{LK} (pottery) $= -P_L/P_K = MRS_{LK}$ (grain). When this condition holds, the allocation of resources is Pareto optimal, inasmuch as further reallocation between industries can only increase the output of one good, if output of the other is decreased. Alternatively viewed, at B the maximum possible output of pottery and grain is being produced, **given** the distribution of capital and labour. In this sense, point B has a corresponding point on the production possibility curve (B' on the lower part of Fig. 1.4).

Point B is not unique. Points such as F and C are also tangency solutions where maximum output of the two goods is produced for a given combination of inputs. As such, these also have their corresponding points on the PPC (i.e. F' and C'). The relationship between the Edgeworth Box and the PPC should by now be clear. The Box depicts how a given endowment of inputs can be deployed in producing outputs of grain and pottery. The points within the Box where maximum output is being produced for a given mix of inputs form the points on the production frontier. (For a formal derivation of the PPC from the Edgeworth Box, see Grubel, 1977.)

When all points of tangency in the Edgeworth Box are joined, we end up with a *contract curve* or *efficiency locus* (O_PO_g), the latter term being applied for the obvious reason that all points on the curve are points of optimal efficiency. The curvilinear shape of the contract curve serves to confirm our assumption that the two goods have differing factor intensities in production. If the contract curve were a straight line between the origins, factor intensity would be the same in pottery and grain production. Since the curve lies below the diagonal, it is obvious that pottery is the labour intensive commodity, grain being capital intensive. If the curve lay wholly above the diagonal, factor intensities would be the opposite.

Having developed these essential tools, we are now in a position to consider more fully what is often referred to as the 'Modern Theory of International Trade'. We will consider first the supply side, since this is merely an extension of comparative advantage, and then the demand side.[3]

The Heckscher–Ohlin theorem

Credit for the development of modern trade theorising is most often ascribed to Eli Heckscher (1919), Bertil Ohlin (1933) and latterly Paul Samuelson (1948, 1949). We have already seen that the Ricardian-type model was based on only one factor of production. Heckscher and Ohlin addressed themselves to the situation where more than one factor was available. Their analysis ran along the following lines.

Again assume there to be only two countries, Britain and America; two factors of production, labour and capital; two commodities, pottery, production of which is labour intensive, and grain, production of which is capital intensive. We will recall that the essence of the Ricardian model was that production functions differed between countries. In the Heckscher–Ohlin model (H–O), we will assume that although production functions differ between commodities they are in fact identical in all countries. All production takes place under conditions of perfect competition, and consumption patterns are assumed similar between countries. This is quite a stringent set of assumptions. It does however permit us to analyse the situation where the only difference between the two countries is a difference in their factor endowments. Britain, we will assume, is relatively better endowed with labour than capital, whereas America finds itself more abundantly endowed with capital than labour. Therefore labour (capital) is relatively cheap in Britain (America), whilst capital (labour) is relatively expensive.

When these conditions hold, the H–O theorem postulates that both countries will specialise in the production of that commodity which uses its abundant factor more intensively. Since it will enjoy a comparative cost advantage in the production of this commodity, it will export quantities of it in exchange for the commodity which uses its relatively scarce factor more intensively. In terms of our example,

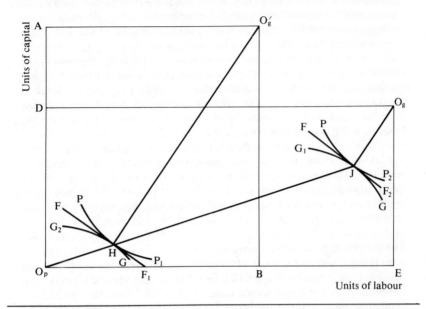

Fig. 1.5 Production with two factors in Britain and America

America should therefore export grain to Britain in exchange for pottery. Consider Fig. 1.5. $O_PAO_g'B$ represents America's factor endowments, with O_PA of capital, and O_PB of labour. Britain's factor endowments are delineated by the box O_PDO_gE. Labour is clearly her abundant factor (O_PE), capital her scarce factor (O_PD). In order to ascertain the output mix for each country, we simply recall the assumptions made earlier. Since the production technique for pottery is assumed to be the same in both countries, and since both countries share a common origin for pottery production (O_P), production of pottery in both countries must take place on a factor intensity ray from the O_P origin (O_PJ). To depict identical factor intensity in grain production, we must trace parallel factor intensity rays from the separate grain origins (O_g and O_g'). (For a fuller development of this analysis see Lancaster, 1957.)

As the H–O theorem predicts, each country is specialising in the production of that commodity which uses its abundant factor more intensively. Britain settles at point J, with total output comprising PP_2 pottery and GG_1 grain. America, on the other hand, produces PP_1 pottery and GG_2 grain at point H. Since pottery production is labour intensive, and since labour is Britain's relatively abundant (and relatively cheaper) factor, Britain will enjoy a comparative cost advantage in the production of pottery. In America, capital is the relatively cheaper factor, and therefore America enjoys a comparative advantage in grain production. As long as factors are internationally immobile, i.e. so long as British labour cannot emigrate to America, where labour is the scarce factor, in search of greater rewards, these comparative cost differences will result in the opening up of trade. If factors of production were internationally mobile, British labour would emigrate to America, whilst American capital would flow into Britain. Factor prices would ultimately be equalised, and there would be no basis for trade. (As we will see in Chapter 2, even when factors are internationally immobile, commodity flows may eventually establish factor price equalisation.)

The H–O theorem therefore points to an alternative basis for comparative cost differences. It argues that differences in comparative costs may not necessarily be due to differences in factor quality, but may also be due to differences in factor quantity. Different factor endowments result in different factor rewards, and in turn, comparative cost differences. The labour-rich country will have a comparative cost advantage in the production of the labour-intensive good, whilst the capital-rich country will enjoy a comparative advantage in the production of the capital-intensive good. Once trade opens, each country will tend to specialise in that commodity which uses its abundant factor more intensively.

The formal proof of the H–O theorem, whilst interesting, is beyond the scope of this text (see for instance Lancaster, 1957). It is worth noting, however, that the proof can vary in accordance with how we define factor abundance and factor scarcity. It is possible to define factor abundance in purely physical terms. Alternatively one can define it by reference to factor prices. As Södersten (1970) demonstrates, the proofs may not be identical (see also Shone, 1972).

Thus far then we have focused almost entirely on supply-based reasons for the opening of trade; either differences in factor quality, or differences in factor quantity between countries. We have ignored the possibility that different tastes and preferences may generate trade flows. For this reason, we must now attempt to take some account of demand. We must also try to incorporate demand in a more general equilibrium framework in order to comment on the international terms of trade, and therefore, on the distribution of the gains from trade.

Demand factors and the opening of trade
When discussing demand in basic price theory, one of the first techniques we familiarise ourselves with is indifference analysis. In analysing demand factors in international trade theory we introduce an extension of this technique with the derivation, and use, of *community indifference curves* (see Leontief, 1933 and Meade, 1952).

Individual indifference curves are relatively straightforward to derive, and exhibit certain unique properties. We usually conceive of an indifference map as reflecting individual preferences between the consumption of alternative bundles of two goods. Indifference curves are, as a rule, downward sloping, implying that increased consumption of one good is only possible with decreased consumption of the other. Furthermore, they are convex to the origin, reflecting a diminishing marginal rate of substitution (MRS) in consumption between the two goods. Any indifference curve which lies wholly above another, reflects a higher level of satisfaction. Indifference curves can only lie wholly above, or below, each other since they cannot intersect. Intersection would mean that consistent and rational choices by the consumer could not be guaranteed.

Some of these properties follow automatically for community indifference curves (CICs), which are simply indifference curves for the community as a whole. For others to follow, however, we have to make some very strong assumptions. Perhaps we can illustrate by example.

For illustrative purposes, we will assume that there are only two individuals (X and Y), and that both consume quantities of two commodities, grain and pottery. In Fig. 1.6, individual X's indifference

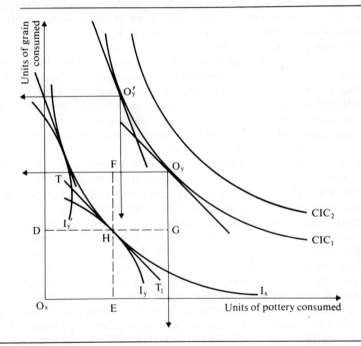

Fig. 1.6 Derivation of the community indifference curve

map is viewed from the O_x origin, whilst Y's is viewed from the O_y origin. By assumption, X consumes O_xD of grain and O_xE of pottery, to reach his highest possible indifference curve (I_x). At point H, individual Y consumes O_yG of grain (= HF) and O_yF of pottery (= HG), thus reaching his highest possible indifference curve, I_y. The indifference curves are tangential to each other at H, thus individual X's MRS between the two commodities is equal to Y's MRS. Furthermore, both indifference curves are tangential to the commodity price line TT_1. Point H is therefore Pareto optimal since, given the existing distribution of grain and pottery, each individual is as well off as he can be. No reallocation of grain and pottery could make one individual better without making the other worse off. Point H has its corresponding point on the CIC. This is denoted by the O_y origin, and represents total consumption of X and Y, at the initial commodity price ratio. At O_y, the slope of the CIC will be the same as the slopes of the indifference curves I_x and I_y, at H.

In order to find the remaining points on the CIC, we must discover the alternative commodity combinations between which the two individuals are indifferent, i.e. those other commodity combinations where both individuals enjoy an unchanged level of welfare. Thus, we shift Y's indifference curve around X's, whilst keeping the coordinate axes parallel. In so doing, the shifting O_y origin traces out the CIC. Effectively then, the CIC denotes how both individuals change their consumption patterns while maintaining a constant level of satisfaction, or welfare.

The use of CICs, however, presents certain conceptual difficulties. When using individual indifference curves, we can usually say, quite unreservedly, that if an individual moves from one indifference curve to one that lies wholly above it, his utility (or welfare) has increased. Higher indifference curves always represent higher levels of welfare. When considering a movement from one CIC to another, however, we cannot be quite as definite.

If, for instance, our 'community' of X and Y moved from point O_y, on CIC_1 to a point on CIC_2, we could not say unambiguously that community welfare had increased. The reason for this is that we would have to know first the distribution of the gains from the change. Do the gains from the change accrue to one individual, to both, or is one made absolutely better off and the other worse off? If the latter, are there any redistribution policies?

Paretian welfare economics restricts the comments we can make. Our welfare criteria permit us to conclude only that the community is better off, if one person cannot be made better off, without the other being made worse off, or that in the situation where one gains whilst the other loses, the community can still be made better off if the gainer compensates the loser. Thus if the shift from CIC_1 to CIC_2 resulted in both X and Y increasing their consumption of pottery and grain, it would seem in order to claim that the community's welfare had increased. Providing utility functions were independent, such an inference would indeed be in order. If, however, X and Y gain in unequal amounts, and if their utility functions are interdependent (i.e.

their welfare depends, not only on their own 'income', or command over resources, but also on the other person's), we would be hard pressed to draw any unqualified conclusions. This inability to make interpersonal utility comparisons is the principal constraint on the use of CICs. The only means of circumventing this difficulty is to make some very heroic assumptions. We could, for example, treat the CIC 'as if' it were an individual indifference curve, if we assume there is only one individual in the community: or by assuming that the community's tastes are determined by the metaphorical 'benevolent dictator'; or by assuming that all individuals have the same income and tastes; or by assuming that there are suitable redistribution policies to compensate 'losers' from any change. Really, it is immaterial which rationalisation is adopted, so long as we are aware that it is no more than a rationalisation, made for the purposes of using CICs.

Once CICs are introduced, it is much easier to analyse 'the gains from trade'. Figure 1.7 brings together the PPC and the CIC. (The student will note that again, as in Fig. 1.4, we will continue to use a PPC which is concave to the origin. This is the more usually assumed case, consistent with increasing, rather than constant, opportunity costs.)

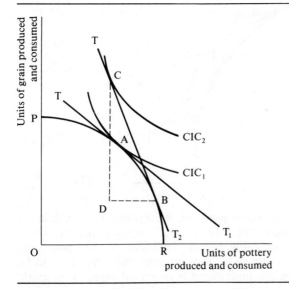

Fig. 1.7 The gains from trade

Prior to the opening up of trade, production and consumption take place at A, where the PPC is tangential to a CIC, at the domestic, pre-trade price ratio (TT_1). Following the opening of trade, the country specialises in the production of the commodity in which it enjoys a comparative cost advantage. Production shifts from A to B, where the international price ratio, or terms-of-trade line TT_2 is tangential to the PPC. Consumption shifts from A to C where a CIC is tangential to TT$_2$. Thus following specialisation, BD of pottery is exported in exchange for DC of grain, and trade has enabled this country to achieve a higher level of economic welfare (denoted by the shift from CIC$_1$ to CIC$_2$). Since the international price ratio is tangential to both CIC$_2$ and the PPC, the marginal rate of substitution in consumption, between pottery and grain, is equivalent to the price ratio between the two commodities, which in turn, matches the MRT in production. We have then an equilibrium situation.

It is also possible to illustrate, via the use of CICs, how differing demand patterns between countries can result in gainful trade. Take the situation portrayed in Fig. 1.8. In order to focus specifically on the

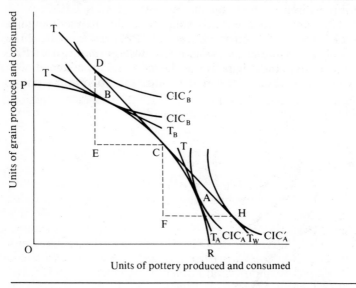

Fig. 1.8 The impact of differing demand conditions when supply conditions are identical

impact of different demand patterns, we assume that Britain and America have identical PPCs, i.e. supply conditions are exactly the same in both countries. PR is then the common PPC. Although both countries have similar supply conditions, taste patterns differ. In Fig. 1.8 we can see from the position of Britain's indifference map, that British consumers prefer grain to pottery. Therefore, production and consumption are at point B, where a CIC (CIC$_B$) is tangential to both the PPC and to the autarkic price ratio (TT$_B$).

American consumers, on the other hand, have a preference for pottery. This is reflected by the fact that production and consumption take place at A. At A, an American CIC (CIC$_A$), is tangential to the PPC and to the American autarkic price ratio (TT$_A$).

As we can readily see, despite their common PPC, the different position of the two countries' CICs results in differing marginal rates of transformation. Consequently, trade between Britain and America opens up and the international terms of trade TTw is established. Faced with these terms, Britain increases her production of pottery and decreases her production of grain, settling at C. She now exports quantities of pottery (CE), in exchange for grain (ED), and point D on CICƄ is attained. America also produces at C on the new international price line. She, however, has clearly specialised more in grain production, exporting CF units of grain, in exchange for FH units of pottery.

Clearly the trade triangles, CFH and DEC, are congruent. Trade volumes balance. Close inspection reveals that MRSs, MRTs and the international price ratio are all equalised; yielding an equilibrium situation.

It is of course far from likely that supply conditions ever would be identical between two countries. Nevertheless, extension of our simple trade model effectively demonstrates how differing demand patterns can serve to provide the basis for trade.

As we will see presently, CICs have other uses in trade theory. At this stage, however, we will combine both halves of our price/quantity equation, in order to examine the interaction of demand and supply.

1.4 General equilibrium analysis

Trade indifference curves and trade offer curves
Equilibrium price and output are not determined by demand or supply in isolation, but by the interaction of both. So far, we have concentrated on considering demand and supply separately within a partial equilibrium framework. The technique used to simultaneously consider both is the *trade offer curve* or *reciprocal demand curve,* a mode of analysis developed and refined by John Stuart Mill, Alfred Marshall and James Meade (see Meade, 1952). We can derive the trade offer curve by reference to Fig. 1.9. The curve PR in quadrant IV is Britain's PPC. Pre-trade equilibrium is at A, where the PPC is tangential to a CIC (CIC₃). If we now take the production block OPR, and move it bodily, keeping it tangential at all times to CIC₃, whilst keeping the axes parallel, we find that the origin of OPR traces out a completely new curve, TIC₃. This curve we refer to as a *trade indifference curve* (TIC). What precisely does the TIC tell us?

As we shift the production block, OPR, around CIC₃, consumption and production patterns do not remain consistent. Take for instance point B. At B, production of grain amounts to BD, yet consumption is BE. The difference between the two, DE, must of course be imports. Similarly with pottery, BF is produced, of which only BG is consumed domestically. GF must therefore be exported abroad. We could repeat this exercise for other situations where domestic production and con-

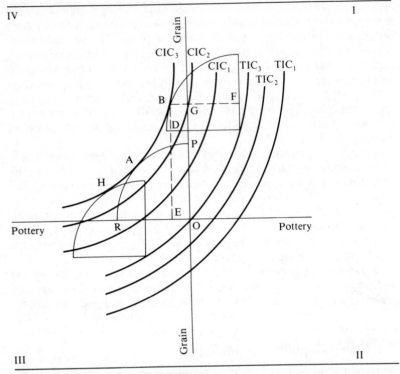

Fig. 1.9 Derivation of the trade indifference curve

sumption are only balanced by imports and exports. (The student may find it valuable to trace through the level of imports and exports at point H, for example.)

By shifting the PPC around CIC₃, we are tracing a locus of points, along which the country engages in foreign trade, and still attains the same level of welfare, as denoted by CIC₃. Therefore, the TIC shows us how, with a given PPC, a certain level of welfare can be achieved, with different combinations of imports and exports. Alternatively, we could say that it shows us how a given, pre-trade, level of welfare can be maintained by engaging in foreign trade.

We can, in fact, trace a complete family of TICs simply by repeating the above analysis for different CICs. Such a family is represented by TIC₁, TIC₂, TIC₃, etc., with higher TICs representing higher levels of welfare. Figure 1.10 reproduces quadrant I of Fig. 1.9, with the TIC set just derived. In Fig. 1.10, we also include some relative price rays, such as TOT₁, TOT₂, TOT₃ and TOT₄. These denote the relative price of pottery, in terms of grain. The steeper such a ray is, the more expensive pottery is, in terms of grain. These TOT rays therefore tell us the terms on which pottery will exchange for grain or, for brevity, the terms of trade. If the TOT ray is relatively steeply sloped, like TOT₄, the terms

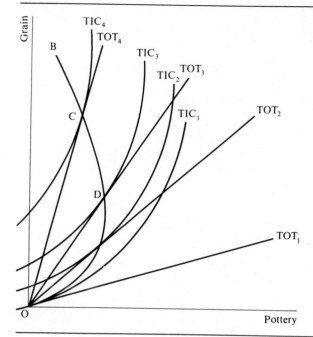

Fig. 1.10 Derivation of the trade offer curve

of trade are moving in favour of pottery since more grain must be exchanged for a given quantity of pottery. Conversely, if the TOT line becomes relatively shallow, like TOT₁, the terms of trade are shifting in favour of grain (and therefore, grain producers).

When we combine TICs with TOT rays, we can ascertain what Britain's optimal trade pattern will be at different relative prices for the two commodities. Thus if the terms of trade were TOT₄, the highest level of welfare attainable is at point C, where TIC₄ is tangential to TOT₄. If the terms of trade were to alter, say to TOT₃, the highest level of welfare attainable would be that denoted by D on TIC₃. When all points of tangency between TICs and TOT rays are connected, a curve OB is traced. This is Britain's *trade offer curve* which shows us how much of her exportable commodity (pottery) Britain will be able to offer in exchange for importables (grain) at different relative prices.

In order to complete our general equilibrium system, America's trade offer curve must be derived. The process for so doing is precisely the same as with Britain's except we would start with America's production block in quadrant II of Fig. 1.9, ultimately tracing the trade offer curve OA in quadrant I, as in Fig. 1.11.

The equilibrium terms of trade

Figure 1.11 shows the equilibrium trading position for Britain and

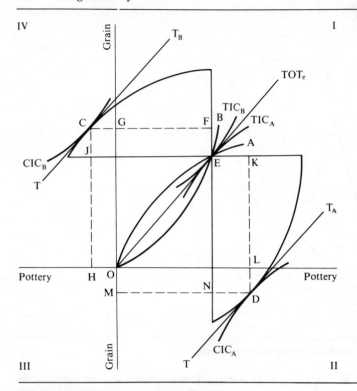

Fig. 1.11 Equilibrium in international trade

America, conveying information about both countries' production, consumption, imports and exports. Equilibrium is at point E. At E, both countries' trade offer curves intersect the international terms-of-trade line (TOTₑ). Britain produces and consumes at C, on CICв. CF units of pottery are produced, of which GF are exported to America. Although Britain only produces CJ units of grain, her total grain consumption amounts to CH. JH units of grain are therefore imported from America.

Analogously, America settles at D on CICА. Here, domestic grain production is DK, of which DL is retained for domestic consumption, and LK exported to Britain. Pottery production is DN, with NM being imported to satisfy domestic consumption.

The intersection of the offer curves, with the international terms of trade, indicates that relative prices are 'correct', in the sense that the market is cleared, and trade volumes balance. Thus, American grain exports, LK, are equal to British grain imports, JH; and British pottery exports, GF, are equivalent to American pottery imports, MN. If these 'offers' of grain and pottery for export did not balance, excess demands (supplies) would cause changes in relative prices (the terms of trade) which would lead to consumers and producers making adjustments, until equilibrium were re-established. We can illustrate this by reference to Fig. 1.12. Suppose, initially, the terms of trade were

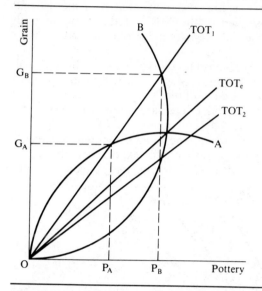

Fig. 1.12 Adjustments in the terms of trade

TOT₁. Given the terms of trade, America would like to export OG_A units of grain in exchange for OP_A units of pottery. With terms of trade of TOT₁, however, Britain offers OP_B of pottery in exchange for OG_B of grain. Clearly there is an excess demand for grain and an excess supply of pottery. To eliminate these excess demands (supplies) relative prices must change. Grain becomes more expensive relative to pottery (which, conversely, becomes cheaper in relation to grain) and these changes are depicted by a rightward movement in the terms of trade, until equilibrium is established at TOTₑ. Here, demand and supply for both grain and pottery are in balance. (The student might like to consider what adjustments will be made when the terms of trade are TOT₂.)

Through the medium of offer curve analysis, then, we can depict both demand and supply, in both countries, on the same plane. This, in turn, enables us to derive the equilibrium terms of trade, i.e. that set of relative prices where exports balance imports, and both countries are attaining the highest level of welfare possible. The latter condition is portrayed by the tangency of both countries' trade indifference curves, and the terms-of-trade line, at point E in Fig. 1.11. Further examination of Fig. 1.11 reveals why E is a point of **general** equilibrium. Commodity price equalisation has taken place, therefore TOTₑ is parallel to TT_A and TT_B, the domestic price ratios in America and

Britain respectively. TTA and TTB are in turn tangential to CICA and CICB respectively. Therefore, the MRS of pottery for grain is the same in both countries, and is equal to the international price ratio. Furthermore, TTA and TTB are also tangential to America and Britain's PPCs. In consequence, the MRT is the same in both countries, and is the same as the international price ratio, **and** the MRS in consumption.

Offer curves then, are very important tools of analysis. Since we will be using them repeatedly in future chapters, it will probably be of benefit to stay with the topic a little longer and examine the consequences of shifts in the underlying parameters, i.e. to consider the impact of shifts in demand and/or supply.

Suppose British demand for her exportable commodity increased. Since she now has less pottery available for export, her offer curve would bend leftward from OB to OB', in Fig. 1.13. Given the initial

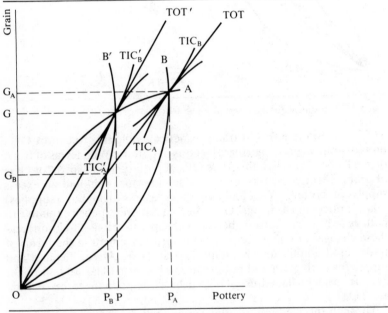

Fig. 1.13 The effect of demand changes on the terms of trade

price ratio, TOT, Britain now offers only OPB of pottery, and demands OGB of grain. America, on the other hand, still offers OGA of grain and demands OPA of pottery. Clearly, at terms of trade TOT, there is an excess demand for pottery and an excess supply of grain. As a result of this, the price of pottery rises relative to grain. The change in relative prices generates an increased supply of pottery for export from Britain (OPB to OP) and stimulates increased consumption of grain (OGB to OG). Equilibrium is re-established at TOT'. The movement in the terms of trade has clearly favoured Britain (the pottery exporter) at the expense of America. The movement results in Britain progressing to a higher level of welfare (TIC_B to TIC'_B) whilst America moves on to a lower trade indifference curve (TIC_A to TIC'_A). From this simple piece of analysis, it would seem that an increase in the domestic demand for a country's exportable good will cause a favourable shift in the terms of trade.

Consider now the situation when, perhaps due to some technological breakthrough, Britain increases her supply of pottery on to the world market. We can see from Fig. 1.14 that the initial response is a rightward shift of the offer curve from OB to OB'. It is immediately apparent that this shift in the offer curve generates an excess supply of pottery ($P_B - P_A$) and an excess demand for grain ($G_B - G_A$) at the initial terms of trade. Clearly the adjustment in the terms of trade on this occasion must favour the grain exporter. Thus, the movement from TOT to TOT', results in America reaching a higher trade indifference curve, but Britain moving on to a lower one.

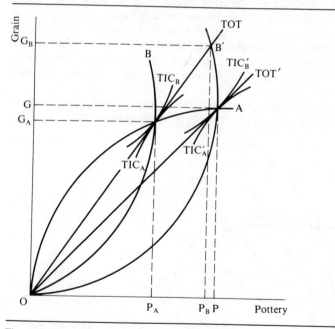

Fig. 1.14 The effect of supply changes on the terms of trade

Thus, it appears that an increased supply of a country's exportable good can turn the terms of trade against it.[4] To reinforce his/her understanding of this analysis, the student should now consider the effects of changes in demand and supply conditions on America's offer curve.

The stability of equilibrium

Underlying all of the foregoing analysis has been the implicit assumption that where offer curves intersect, we not only have an equilibrium, we have a stable equilibrium. We are thinking of stability in the sense that any movements away from equilibrium are 'corrected' by adjustments in relative prices, and there is an inherent tendency for equilibrium to be restored. It is worth noting here that this need not always be the case. Where offer curves intersect more than once we have the phenomenon of multiple equilibria, not all of which are stable. Let us elaborate further on this point.

We can see, from Figs 1.10 to 1.14, that offer curves are generally constructed so that they become backward-bending after a point, i.e. they become relatively inelastic. This is due to both demand and supply factors. If we construe the offer curve as a supply curve, the backward-bending, inelastic section can be seen as being due to increasing opportunity costs in production. The exportable good is becoming so expensive to produce, that absolutely fewer units are offered in exchange for increasing amounts of the importable good. Viewed from the demand side, inelasticity can be seen as the result of consumers experiencing strongly diminishing marginal rates of substitution in their consumption of the imported good. In other words, they have so much of the imported good that the only way they can be induced to accept more is if fewer units of the exportable are offered in exchange.

Multiple equilibria occur when both offer curves bend back so sharply that they intersect each other more than once, as in Fig. 1.15.

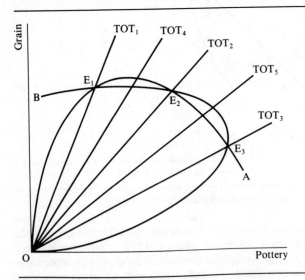

Fig. 1.15 Multiple equilibria in the terms of trade

Here, three different terms of trade equate demand and supply in both countries, TOT_1, TOT_2 and TOT_3. Consequently we have three possible equilibrium situations, E_1, E_2 and E_3. Of these three, however, only E_1 and E_3 are stable equilibria. If, for any reason, there was a movement away from E_1 or E_3, towards TOT_4 or TOT_5, forces would be set in motion which would tend to re-establish the terms of trade TOT_1 or TOT_3 respectively. E_2 on the other hand, is an unstable equilibrium. Any movement from E_2 would not result in a tendency towards equilibrium being re-established at E_2. In fact, forces would be set in motion which would drive further away from, rather than back towards E_2. The analysis to demonstrate this instability is simply an extension of the excess demand/supply process considered in Figs. 1.12 to 1.14. The student should therefore apply the expertise so far acquired, and satisfy him/herself that he/she understands precisely why there is an inherent tendency for equilibrium to be re-established at E_1 and E_3 but not at E_2.

A shorthand method of identifying stability/instability is to look at where the offer curves cut each other. If they intersect each other from below, as drawn from the origin, equilibrium will be stable. Where, however, they cut each other from above, again as drawn from the origin, we find an unstable equilibrium (see Meade, 1952; Mundell, 1960a).[5]

We have dwelt at length on the derivation, properties and use of offer curves. This will prove a valuable 'investment' for the developments we will consider in Chapters 2, 3 and 4. Meantime, however, we will return to the principal area of study in this chapter, the genesis of trade. It is now time to devote our attention to a consideration of some of the empirical work on this area.

1.5 Some empirical evidence

In this section, we will briefly consider some of the empirical work which has aimed at testing the Ricardian and Heckscher–Ohlin theorems of the genesis of trade.

Tests of the Ricardian comparative cost theorem
A number of attempts have been made at verifying the Ricardian comparative cost postulate. Most notable is the work of MacDougall (1951), Stern (1962), Balassa (1963) and Bhagwati (1964).

MacDougall's seminal contribution in 1951 is widely regarded as the standard source of reference for empirical work on the Ricardian theorem. MacDougall examined data for the US and the UK for the year 1937. Since tariff walls greatly distorted bilateral trade between the two countries, MacDougall considered British and American export performance in third markets.[6] As a proxy for labour productivity, he used the ratio of output per worker in the US to the ratio of output per worker in the UK. MacDougall argued that each country will export those goods for which the ratio of its output per worker, to that of the other, exceeds the ratio of its money wage rate to that of the other.

Since pre-war US money wages were approximately twice British money wages, for those products where American output per worker was more than twice British output per worker, the US should have the larger share of the export market. Where, however, US output per worker was less than twice UK output per worker, Britain should enjoy the advantage. Out of his sample of 25 product groups, 20 were consistent with this *a priori* expectation (these comprised 97% by value of the total sample). The results are plotted in the form of a regression line in Fig. 1.16. The approximately linear relationship appears to

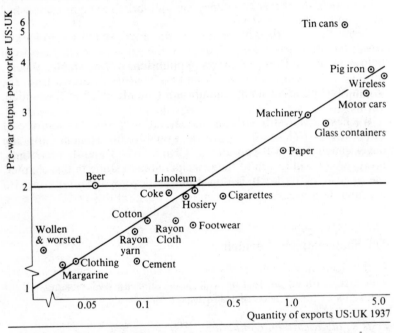

Fig. 1.16 US and UK productivity and exports (Adapted from MacDougall, 1951, p. 703)

provide convincing support for the hypothesis that the greater a country's output per worker, the more of a comparative advantage it will enjoy, and hence the better it will do in export markets. Follow-up studies by Stern and Balassa, using similar samples, but different years, seemed to confirm MacDougall's results.

Stern took three different samples, one of which was MacDougall's 1937 sample, for the year 1950. Balassa examined a sample of 28 industries, for the years 1950 and 1951. The countries under consideration were again the US and the UK, and results which corroborated MacDougall's seemed to provide an almost irrefutable case in favour of the comparative cost doctrine.

In a valuable survey of the literature, however, Bhagwati (1964), provides a careful critique of these findings. He questions both the proxies employed and the method of analysis and proceeds himself to recast their data in a more sophisticated statistical framework. Bhagwati's findings, which suggest that there is no statistically significant relationship, are '. . . seriously prejudicial to the usefulness of the Ricardian approach' (Bhagwati, 1964, p. 21).

In summary then, there is some conflict over the empirical verification of the Ricardian comparative cost theorem. Inconclusiveness still remains, despite more recent empirical work (see for example, Agarwal, Askari and Corson, 1975).

Tests of the Heckscher–Ohlin theorem
We will recall that the crucial postulate of the H–O theorem is that differences in factor endowments between countries are the sole determinant of differences in comparative costs. A country will enjoy a comparative advantage in the production of a commodity, when that commodity uses its abundant factor more intensively, and economises on its scarce factor. Perhaps the best-known attempt at empirically testing this theorem is that of Wassily Leontief (1953).

Leontief commenced from the widely accepted, though unproven, premise that the United States was capital-abundant relative to the rest of the world. Accordingly, one would expect the US's exports to be capital intensive, her imports labour intensive. To test this proposition, Leontief used input–output tables for 1947, and computed capital and labour requirements for average aggregate exports. Since he lacked the requisite data to repeat the exercise for imports, he computed capital and labour requirements for average aggregate 'import replacements', or import substitutes. His findings were as follows:

Domestic capital and labour requirements per $1 000 000 of US exports and competitive import replacements

	Exports	Import replacements
Capital (US, $ at 1947 prices)	2 550 780	3 091 339
Labour (man years)	182 313	170 004
$\frac{\text{Capital}}{\text{Labour}}$ ($ per man-year)	13 991	18 184

According to these figures, US exports embody less capital and more labour than her import replacements, contrary to *a priori* expectation. Because these findings appear inconsistent to what the H–O theorem would predict, they became known as the 'Leontief paradox'.

Leontief's study can be easily criticised, on the grounds of the possibly unrepresentative year selected, his aggregation, and the implicit assumption that production functions for imports are identical to those for import substitutes.[7] Rather than dwelling on methodological points, however, quite a number of researchers followed up Leontief's study. Of these, a number have confirmed Leontief's apparently perverse findings. Tatemoto and Ichimura (1959) for Japan; Wahl (1961) for Canada, and Baldwin (1971a) for the US, all confirm the 'Leontief paradox'. On the other hand, some studies have been conducted whose findings seem consistent with the H–O theorem. For example, Stolper and Roskamp's (1961) study of East Germany's trade with her Eastern European neighbours; Tarshis's (1954) work on US exports; and Bharadwaj's (1962a) study of India's trade with the rest of the world.[8]

Is it possible to explain these findings? Some support can be adduced for the H–O hypothesis but even more evidence can be found which would appear to refute the hypothesis. Do these studies indeed refute what Leontief calls the 'common-sense' appeal of the H–O hypothesis, or is it possible to provide some explanation which will reconcile empirical evidence and theory?

Leontief himself suggested a possible explanation. He postulated that American labour is more productive than that abroad, and argued that if a suitable adjustment were made for this greater productivity, the paradox would be resolved. Specifically, Leontief suggested that American labour was three times more productive than foreign labour. Thus, if the labour force were multiplied by 3, it would be possible to ascertain a figure of 'equivalent foreign man-years'. This Leontief does and reaches the conclusion:

In terms of the relative production possibilities here and abroad, the US is rich in man power and poor in capital. This country resorts to foreign trade to save its capital and to dispose of its relative surplus labour.

(Leontief, 1953, p. 24)

Although Leontief may be justified in his claim that American workers are more productive than foreign labour (for whatever reason) the choice of the multiplicative factor of 3, does seem something of an *ex post* rationalisation.

Most efforts at explaining the 'paradox' have been directed at questioning the assumptions on which the H–O theorem is constructed. For instance, if one relaxes the assumption of identical tastes between the two countries, a plausible explanation suggests itself. Factor endowments may be such that America is relatively well endowed with capital. When trade opens, according to the H–O theorem, America should export the capital-intensive good. It may well be, however, that American consumers have a distinct preference for the capital-intensive good. So much so, that when trade opens the labour-intensive good is exported, in exchange for imports of the capital-intensive good. In this manner, demand conditions may offset the effect of factor endowments.

Despite the plausibility of this argument, it is as yet unsupported by empirical evidence. Few studies relate specifically to consumption patterns. Those that do suggest that tastes exhibit considerable similarity between countries.

A second assumption which might be relaxed is that of identical production functions. When building the H–O model, we assumed that production functions differed between commodities but were identical internationally for a given commodity. Clearly it is quite possible that different production techniques can be used for the same commodity, in different countries. This possibility might be even more feasible (as Leontief appreciated) when one allows for more than just two factors of production. If land is introduced, and is assumed to be a substitute for capital but, like capital, is a complement to labour, the same commodity could be capital intensive, land intensive or even labour intensive in different countries.

This argument is in the same spirit as the possibility of *factor intensity reversals*. Again this emerges when we relax one of the H–O assumptions. Originally, we assumed that isoquants intersected only once. Consider the situation depicted in Fig. 1.17, where the grain and

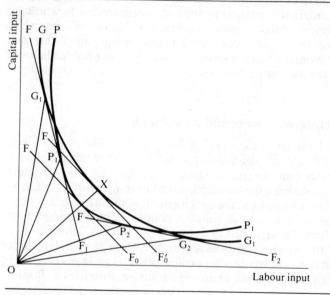

Fig. 1.17 Factor intensity reversals

pottery isoquants intersect more than once. Initially, the factor price ratio is FF_0. At this set of factor prices, factor intensities in both grain and pottery production are exactly the same. Thus, they have a common factor intensity ray, OX. Consider what happens when capital becomes relatively cheaper. Clearly, the factor price line becomes steeper at FF_1. Faced with this new set of factor prices, both industries substitute capital for labour. The resultant factor intensity rays indicate that grain is the capital-intensive commodity (OG_1) whilst pottery production is more labour intensive (OP_1). Now suppose labour becomes relatively cheaper, so that the factor price line shifts to FF_2. Because labour is now cheaper, relative to capital, both grain and pottery producers substitute labour for capital, but in differing proportions. When we examine the new factor intensity rays we find that grain production is now more labour intensive than pottery production.

This phenomenon we refer to as factor intensity reversal. It occurs because of the differing possibilities for substitution in the two industries. The greater convexity of the pottery isoquant is indicative of the fact that capital and labour are more easily substituted for each other in grain production than pottery production.

Therefore, when factor prices change, substitution takes place more quickly, and to a greater extent, in grain production compared with pottery production. We will have occasion to refer to factor intensity reversals again, in Chapter 2, when we examine the factor price equalisation theorem. In the present context, however, its value is that it provides another possible explanation of the Leontief paradox. If the American situation is typified by the factor price ratio FF_1 whilst the ratio FF_2 prevails abroad, the US may find itself importing goods which would have been produced domestically using capital-intensive methods (Leontief's 'import replacements') but are produced abroad using labour-intensive techniques.

1.6 Recent developments and elaborations

Following Leontief's discovery of his paradox, there was a considerable amount of attention devoted to both testing the H–O theorem further and in endeavouring to 'explain' Leontief's findings mainly by questioning the assumptions of the H–O theorem. A further reaction to his findings was the development of the other, less general, explanations of the genesis and commodity composition of trade (Kravis, 1956; Posner, 1961; Linder, 1961; Vernon, 1966).

Two of the more significant recent developments are worthy of specific note: the incorporation of transport costs and the existence of non-traded goods; and the existence of intra-industry trade flows.

Transport costs and non-traded goods
Allowance for transport costs is not itself a recent development, and integration into the basic model presents no real difficulties. Clearly where transport costs exist, and are of course positive, any divergence between comparative cost ratios will be narrowed, commodity price equalisation will be prevented, and the volume of trade will be reduced. The conclusions of our basic model will not therefore be

altered substantially. Of greater significance is the situation where transport costs are prohibitive, i.e. where transport costs are sufficiently high to prevent trade in a particular commodity.

The introduction of a *non-traded good* into the model, for example, because of prohibitive transport costs, can be problematic since we now have to take account of a further set of price relations. It is no longer the case that the only relevant price ratios are the autarkic and post-trade prices of the two traded goods. We now have to allow for a 'terms of trade' between traded and non-traded goods. As one would imagine, this has far-ranging implications since it provides opportunities for substitution between traded and non-traded goods as price relations differ. Once Chapters 2 and 4 have been read, it will also be clear that the existence of non-traded goods must affect tariff structures, and the analysis of economic growth. The former because non-traded goods may also be intermediate goods and substitution between traded and non-traded inputs may influence the degree of effective protection given to import substitutes by a tariff structure; the latter because economic growth may take place in the non-traded good sector as well as in the tradeable goods sector.

A more detailed consideration of the full implications of non-traded goods is beyond the scope of this text. An introduction to the subject can however be found in Pearce (1970).

Intra-industry trade
An important recent development has been the growing attention given to intra-industry trade. See, for instance, Grubel and Lloyd's pioneering text on the subject (Grubel and Lloyd, 1975).

All of our analysis so far (and most of the remaining trade theory we will consider) has been concerned with the generation of *inter*-industry trade flows, i.e. where the products of one industry are exported in exchange for the products of a different industry. Thus, Britain exported pottery in exchange for grain. *Intra*-industry trade on the other hand deals with 'international trade in differentiated products which are close substitutes for each other' (Grubel and Lloyd, 1975). In contrast to inter-industry trade then, we need to explain situations where a country both imports and exports the products of the same industry. For example, the UK exports and imports furniture and televisions; West Germany imports and exports coal and steel; the USA imports and exports cars and cigarettes, and so on.

The empirical work of Grubel and Lloyd (and others) suggests that this phenomenon is a relatively common characteristic of the commodity composition of trade among advanced industrial nations. Indeed, Grubel and Lloyd's work suggests that as much as half of the total trade of the major industrial countries might be of an intra-industry type. (See Greenaway, 1979.)

How can we explain these trade flows? In a tautological sense their existence does not contradict the basic tenets of our model since presumably they must be generated by comparative advantage. The difference is, that comparative advantage in this case cannot be explained by reference to factor endowments. This does not mean that we must abandon the H–O model as our theoretical foundation: we can follow Grubel and Lloyd in explaining the phenomenon by relaxing some of the H–O assumptions.

Thus, transport costs might again be relevant. Because of the sheer physical dimensions of its geographical frontiers, a country may simultaneously import and export high-bulk–low-value commodities where transport costs increase markedly with distance covered. For example, steel is exported from France to Germany at the southern end of the Franco–German border; whilst at the northern extremity of the frontier, France imports steel from Germany.

Similarly, if we relax the assumptions of homogenous products, and homothetic tastes, we may have a basis for intra-industry trade. Both the UK and the USA simultaneously import and export cars, but the actual cars traded are differentiated in that they have different attributes which appeal to different consumers. It would seem that the majority of American consumers have a preference for larger cars, compared with British consumers whose preference is for relatively smaller models. Some American consumers may however prefer smaller cars, some British consumers larger cars. To satisfy these minority tastes, Britain may end up exporting some small cars to America whilst importing larger models from America. Similar considerations may apply to the simultaneous export (import) of barley (rye) whisky; or Axminster (Persian) carpets, etc.

Differentiated products and differences in tastes are usually necessary but not sufficient to generate trade flows. The sufficiency condition may well be the existence of decreasing costs of production. Thus a further assumption (of constant costs) of the H–O model is relaxed. Given the existence of economies of scale, resources are better allocated if Britain specialises in the production of 'small' cars and imports 'large' cars; or specialises in the production of barley whisky and imports rye whisky. Factor endowments do not dictate that 'large' cars or rye whisky cannot be produced in Britain, but the existence of scale economies does mean that domestic production to cater for minority tastes will result in prohibitively high unit costs.

Grubel and Lloyd do consider other explanations of intra-industry trade flows (in Chs 5–7). The sources we have considered so far are sufficient to demonstrate that intra-industry trade does not contradict the basic H–O model. Many of the explanations of the phenomenon are those same explanations which were invoked to explain the Leontief paradox. As before, they serve to complement and enrich the H–O model as do other attempts at elaboration, such as the more explicit allowance for differences in technological development (Vernon, 1970); heterogenous capital (Metcalfe and Steedman, 1973); or the existence of migrant labour (Krauss, 1976).

The H–O model, in its crudest form, does make many simplifying assumptions but its analytical precision makes it an extremely powerful mode of analysis. Its acceptability, as well as its 'common-sense' appeal (Leontief) are behind the longevity and persistence of the model. As we will now see, most of the theoretical developments in Chapters 2, 3 and 4 build directly on the H–O foundations considered here in Chapter 1.

Notes

1. A basic tenet of mercantilist philosophy was that the principal objective of international trade was the achievement of a balance-of-payments surplus and the accumulation of gold reserves. According to mercantilist philosophy, therefore, only the surplus country could gain from trade.
2. The use of 'capital' as the second factor of production makes the implicit and heroic assumption that not only can capital be conceived of as homogenous, in some sense, but it is also in some way measurable. As students of advanced economic theory will very well appreciate, considerable controversy exists over precisely what constitutes 'capital', and the validity of assuming homogeneity for analytical purposes. See for instance Harcourt (1969).
3. Chronologically this is in reverse order, since work on demand factors under the auspices of John S. Mill and Alfred Marshall predated the work of Eli Heckscher and Bertil Ohlin.
4. This interesting possibility, that economic growth can turn the terms of trade against the growing country, will be developed further in Chapter 4. The possibility is of particular interest for the developing countries.
5. The conditions for stability are analogous to the conditions for stability in the foreign exchange market (see pp. 172). For an equilibrium to be stable, both countries' price elasticities of demand for imports must exceed unity. Thus the equilibria E_1 and E_3 are stable since the sum of the elasticities is greater than 1. At E_2 both offer curves are so inelastic that they intersect each other from above, i.e. the elasticities sum to less than 1, and equilibrium is unstable.
6. On the range of goods considered by MacDougall, the average unweighted British tariff on American goods was 24 per cent. The American average on British goods was 45 per cent.
7. In response to methodological criticisms, Leontief produced another paper (Leontief, 1956). This confirmed the findings of his earlier work.
8. When, however, Bharadwaj considered Indo–US trade, his results provided further support for the 'paradox' (Bharadwaj, 1962b).

Chapter 2

Free trade and restricted trade

2.1 Introduction

In Chapter 1 we devoted our attention to considering the reasons why nations engage in international trade, and in the process we developed a number of important techniques of analysis, which will be further employed in this and subsequent chapters.

Our first task in Chapter 2 will be to take our previous analysis a stage further by reconsidering in more detail how a particular country gains from trade. This was a subject touched upon early in Chapter 1. Here we will elaborate our previous thoughts by considering not only the gains which accrue to a particular country, but also how those gains or benefits are distributed among the residents of that country.

In conducting this analysis we will provide further justification for free trade. Inevitably, however, the question will be begged, 'If free trade appears to maximise world welfare, why at various times during this century have we seen such a prevalence and plethora of trade restrictions?' In attempting to provide an answer to this question, we will see that quite a number of 'economic arguments', 'non-economic arguments', and 'non-arguments' (Johnson, 1971) can be advanced as justification for intervention in free trade flows.

The theory of tariff imposition will then occupy us for some time. We will examine precisely how tariffs affect production, consumption and economic welfare. Once we have analysed tariffs in a theoretical framework, we can become more empirically oriented. We will examine the issues involved in government commercial policy, and consider some of the problems involved in distinguishing between nominal and effective tariff rates.

2.2 Further effects of free trade

In a simplified 2 × 2 × 2 trade model, differences in the relative costs of producing two commodities provides the incentive to trade internationally. According to the H–O theorem, differences in factor endowments between countries are the immediate cause of differences in comparative costs.

We have already analysed the proximate consequences of the

opening of trade. A glance back at Fig. 1.2 reminds us that following commodity price equalisation (at the international terms of trade), a rearrangement of production takes place in both countries. Because of differences in marginal rates of transformation in the two countries, total world output increases after specialisation, and consumption possibilities increase in both countries. Hence we saw how in a two-country world unrestricted trade serves to benefit the world as a whole.

Having acquired an expertise in more sophisticated techniques since then, we are now in a position to take the analysis a stage further. We will persist with our basic H–O model, and for the moment we retain the assumptions which underpin that model. Since we will be discussing the gains from trade, we will continue with the use of community indifference curves as indicators of welfare.

The gains from free trade reconsidered

Let us take one of the countries from Fig. 1.2 (say America), and consider its 'gains' specifically. In Fig. 2.1 PR denotes the American PPC. (We have not reproduced the simple linear PPC of Fig. 1.2, but have adopted the more usual increasing costs, concave PPC.) In autarky the relative prices of grain and pottery are represented by TT_0, production and consumption taking place at A. A is a point of tangency of the PPC with a CIC (CIC_1), and the domestic price ratio. Tangency of course indicates that the MRS of consumers is equal to the price ratio of the two goods and the marginal rate of transformation in production; our conditions for equilibrium are satisfied.

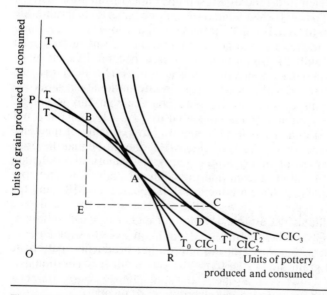

Fig. 2.1 The gains from exchange and specialisation

America as assumed has a relative abundance of capital. Capital is therefore her relatively cheaper factor, and since grain production is capital intensive, America enjoys a comparative advantage in the production of grain. This comparative advantage (combined with a comparative disadvantage in the production of pottery), provides the basis for trade. When trade opens, the relative price of grain rises in America (because of increased demand), whilst the relative price of pottery falls (as a result of cheaper imports). Resources are switched from pottery production into grain production until equilibrium is reestablished at B on the production frontier, where PR is tangential to TT_2, the international price ratio.

America thus increases her grain production, trading her surplus requirements for pottery. Because trade has widened consumption possibilities America can consume at point C. The trade triangle indicates that BE of grain is exported in exchange for EC of imported pottery. Again all of our conditions for equilibrium hold since B and C are points of tangency (of the PPC and CIC respectively), with the international terms of trade.

The gain from trade is immediately obvious. In autarky America was confined to CIC_1. Following the opening of trade, specialisation, and the widening of consumption possibilities, a higher level of welfare as denoted by CIC_3 is attainable.

Conceptually we can break this gain from trade (A–C), into two components, a *gain from exchange,* and a *gain from specialisation.* The gain from exchange derives purely from the ability of the country to engage in foreign trade and as a result alter her consumption pattern accordingly. To isolate this element we confine America to its autarkic production point, A in Fig. 2.1. At the same time, however, we assume it is possible to trade at the going international terms of trade. To depict this we shift TT_2 back parallel to itself to become TT_1, and as we see point D on CIC_2 is attainable. This gain of A–D is therefore due entirely to America's ability to engage in international exchange.

On closer inspection, however, we can see that this is not an equilibrium situation. CIC_2 is tangential to TT_1 at D, but PR is not tangential to TT_1 at A. Thus although we have equality of the MRS with the international price ratio, the MRT does not equal the price ratio. In order to obtain this latter equality, the American production pattern must be altered from that prevailing at point A to that consistent with point B. This production shift equates the MRS and the price ratio at point C, and the MRT and the price ratio at B, and thereby facilitates the attainment of a yet higher level of welfare as denoted by CIC_3. The progression, from D on CIC_2 to C on CIC_3, is due to the fact that America has altered her production pattern to specialise in grain, hence the term 'the gain from specialisation'.

Free trade and the intranational distribution of income

This relatively straightforward piece of analysis demonstrates then how a country gains from trade. The next stage is to ascertain precisely who benefits from these gains. Are they equally distributed among all members of the community, do some gain more than others, or do some even gain at the expense of others? To answer this question we will continue with the example developed above, where following the opening of trade America specialises in production of grain. On this occasion though we will transfer the information contained in Fig. 2.1 into the Edgeworth Box in Fig. 2.2.

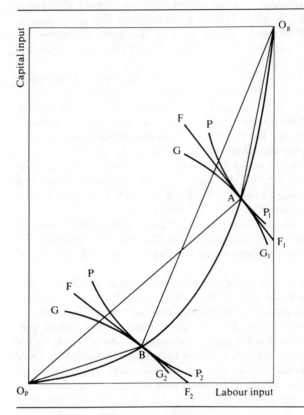

Fig. 2.2 Free trade and factor rewards

In autarky, GG_1 of grain and PP_1 of pottery are produced at A, given the relative factor prices of capital and labour, FF_1. When trade opens, pottery production is run down, grain production expanded, and post-trade equilibrium is at point B on the contract curve. Total output now comprises GG_2 of grain and PP_2 of pottery. We note that at this new equilibrium the factor price line FF_2 is shallower, indicating that rewards to capital have increased relative to labour. What adjustments have taken place to bring about the change in factor rewards?

We already know that once trade opens we have commodity price equalisation. In terms of our example the post-trade price of grain will be higher whilst the post-trade price of pottery will be lower than under autarky. Pottery production will contract in the face of foreign competition and grain production will expand to satisfy foreign demand. In order to facilitate expansion, grain producers require additional capital and labour. Since full employment prevailed prior to trade the only source of additional capital and labour will be from the contracting pottery sector. But capital and labour are released from pottery production in unequal proportions. Specifically, more labour than capital is released. Grain production is, however, capital intensive. Thus at the initial factor intensity, there is a deficiency of capital inputs and an excess of labour. This will tend to depress the price of labour, whilst the returns to capital increase as producers bid the price up against each other.

As this is happening there in an incentive for both industries to become more labour intensive in order to economise on (relatively expensive) capital. This tendency is depicted in Fig. 2.2 by the changing slopes of the factor intensity rays, O_PA and O_PB for pottery, O_gA and O_gB for grain. The change in factor intensities must of course have implications for the relative productivities of capital and labour. Since labour has less capital to work with in both industries, the marginal product of labour is lowered. Conversely, the fact that each unit of capital has more labour to work with tends to raise its marginal productivity. In accordance with our assumption of perfectly competitive markets, these changes in marginal productivity will be reflected in changes in rewards, thus reinforcing the tendency for rewards to labour to decrease whilst the payment received by capital increases.

The conclusion of this piece of analysis is that the factor of production used most intensively in the production of that good in which a country enjoys a comparative advantage, will gain as a result of unrestricted international trade. On the other hand, the factor of production used intensively in the import substitute sector will tend to find its reward decreasing. We can see then that the gains from free trade are not equally distributed. In general, the relatively abundant factor gains at the expense of the relatively scarce factor as a result of free trade.

Factor price equalisation
This line of thought was pursued further by Samuelson in developing the factor price equalisation theorem (Samuelson, 1948; 1949). In our discussion so far we have concentrated on the effect of free trade on factor prices in America alone. In a two-country model British factor prices would be similarly affected. Since Britain would be specialising in pottery production, labour, her relatively abundant factor, would find its rewards increasing, whereas capital, her relatively scarce factor, would find its rewards decreasing.

When factor prices are being simultaneously affected in both countries in this manner, some very important implications follow.

Since in autarky, capital (labour), is relatively cheap and labour (capital), relatively dear in America (Britain), trade in commodities serves to narrow these differentials. What Samuelson demonstrates is that when the usual (fairly stringent) H–O assumptions hold, factor price differences between countries will not merely narrow, they will equalise.[1] The factor price equalisation theorem therefore specifies the conditions under which trade in commodities acts as a substitute for international factor mobility.

If the reader refers back to Fig. 1.5 on p. 13 it can be seen that we have already implicitly encountered the possibility of factor price equalisation. As we can see, at the post-trade equilibrium points H and J, factor intensities are identical in both countries, and since production functions are linear homogenous in both countries we find that the factor price lines FF_1 and FF_2 must be parallel, indicating that relative factor prices are equalised. Consider a more elaborate method of demonstrating the process, by reference to Fig. 2.3.

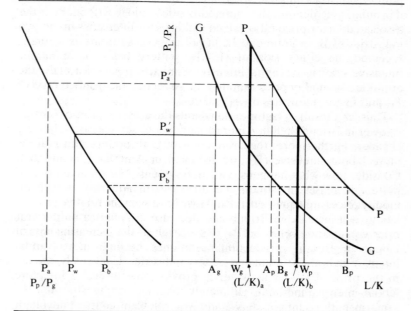

Fig. 2.3 Factor price equalisation

The left-hand quadrant depicts the relationship between the commodity price ratio (P_p/P_g) and the factor price ratio (P_L/P_K). They are positively related since, as we already know, the higher the relative price of pottery, the higher the relative price of the factor used most intensively in its production, i.e. labour. The right-hand quadrant shows the relationship between the factor price ratio, and the ratio of labour to capital, i.e. factor intensity. The negatively sloped functions

PP and GG indicate that the higher the relative price of labour the more capital intensive will production techniques be (as producers substitute capital for labour), and vice versa. We have two functions in this quadrant indicating that at any set of factor prices pottery production (PP) will **always** employ more labour-intensive techniques, (conversely grain will **always** be relatively more capital intensive). This follows because by assumption, factor intensity reversal is ruled out of the model.

$(L/K)_a$ and $(L/K)_b$ denote the overall ratios of labour to capital for America and Britain respectively. $(L/K)_b > (L/K)_a$ since by assumption Britain is relatively better endowed with labour than capital. These overall factor ratios are no more than a weighted average of the factor ratios in all sectors of the economy. Since our model is a simple $2 \times 2 \times 2$ model, then each ratio is a weighted average of factor ratios (factor intensities) of the grain and pottery sectors. Geometrically therefore, factor intensities in the grain and pottery industries must be either side of the overall factor ratios. Thus, if in autarky, P_b denotes the commodity price ratio in Britain, P_b' is the associated factor price ratio, which yields factor intensities in the two industries of B_g in grain and B_p in pottery. These ratios as we have specified, lie either side of $(L/K)_b$; pottery being more labour intensive, grain more capital intensive. Similarly in America where the autarkic commodity price ratio has an associated factor price ratio of P_a' and factor intensities of A_g and A_p.

Thus, as a result of factor endowments the autarkic price of pottery is lower in Britain than in America, and labour services are relatively cheaper. Furthermore, the production of both pottery and grain is more labour intensive (B_p and B_g) than in America (A_p and A_g). Consider now what happens once trade opens. The relative price of pottery increases in Britain and decreases in America, until commodity prices are equalised at P_w. As we have seen the relative price of labour will increase in Britain and decrease in America until factor price equalisation occurs at P_w'. As a result of the increasing cost of labour in Britain, production techniques become more capital intensive in both the grain and pottery industries. Conversely, the fall in the price of labour in America provides the incentive for more labour-intensive methods. Ultimately then, factor intensities are the same in both countries, at W_g and W_p. (Note of course that factor intensities still differ between commodities.)[2]

The system is therefore complete. When factor intensities are the same, marginal products are the same, factor prices are equalised, as are commodity prices. Clearly the implications of this theorem are far-reaching. It asserts in effect that even where factors of production are internationally immobile, it is nevertheless possible for their real earnings to be equalised via trade in commodities. Unsurprisingly perhaps, we are a long way from complete factor price equalisation in the real world. To speculate why, we need only recast our thoughts to the assumptions which underlie the theorem, and consider the effects of relaxing them. Clearly, the existence of government-imposed tariffs, or transport costs, would prevent commodity price equalisation and therefore complete factor price equalisation. In addition the influence of imperfect competition in factor markets; non-constant returns to scale; the possibility of factor intensity reversals, etc., all place obstacles in the way of complete factor price equalisation. As Samuelson himself said of the theorem:

. . . it would be folly to come to any startling conclusions on the basis of so simplified a model; but, on the other hand, strong simple cases often point the way to an element of truth present in a complex situation.
(Samuelson, 1949, p. 181)

Given the number and diversity of market imperfections and trade obstructions associated with modern trade flows, one would indeed be fortunate to observe any strong tendency to factor price equalisation.

Free trade and welfare

We have seen then some of the more important international and intranational effects of free trade. What kind of comments can we make by way of conclusion on the welfare implications of free trade? We have already seen how free trade increases the welfare of the world as a whole, and of the individual country. It is this proposition, that free trade leads to a maximisation of world welfare, which provides the classic case for unrestricted trade flows. This however is far from the 'be-all and end-all' of trade and welfare theory, for two related reasons. First, countries may gain from free trade in unequal proportions. When this is the case, given the tenets of Paretian welfare economics, it becomes difficult to comment meaningfully on gains and losses. Furthermore, as we will see in Section 2.3 the 'best' policy for any trading nation **acting in isolation** might not in fact be to engage in free trade but rather to impose an 'optimum tariff' on its trading partner. The second complication in considering the welfare effects of trade is that different income groups within a country gain unequally from trade. The relatively abundant factor will generally gain from free trade at the expense of the relatively scarce factor. Again, given the foundations of Paretian welfare economics, it is difficult (though not impossible) to comment on the net effects of trade. As Samuelson (1962) showed though, in a situation where some gain and some lose, it is still possible to show that **everyone** can be better off as a result of free trade, providing the gainers can compensate the losers.[3] We will however defer a final consideration of this issue until such time as we have considered the effects of tariff imposition and contrasted them with the effects of free trade.

2.3 The effects of barriers to free trade

A number of barriers can be erected which distort free trade flows. Government-imposed taxes and subsidies are perhaps the most common form of intervention. By convention it is the effects of these restrictions which receive most detailed treatment. Initially we will be following convention by focusing almost entirely on the effects of tariff imposition. We must at all times be aware, however, that there is a range of other (increasingly more common) non-tariff barriers. Physical quotas (whether voluntary or mandatory), export subsidies, and restrictive administrative and technical regulations are examples. These we will return to in Section 2.5.

Tariff imposition

A tariff is a tax on trade in a particular commodity. Tariffs may be specific, in which case a fixed amount is levied irrespective of the volumes of goods traded; or they may be *ad valorem*, in which case a percentage of the value of the goods traded is levied. A tariff can be imposed on an export good or an importable (see Lerner, 1936). Most often they are imposed on the latter. As we will see in Section 2.4, quite a range of arguments can be cited in favour of tariff protection. What we are interested in initially, however, are the precise economic effects of tariff imposition, both in the tariff-levying country and in the country facing the tariff. We can analyse these effects with the aid of Fig. 2.4. (For a much more comprehensive treatment see Corden, 1971.)

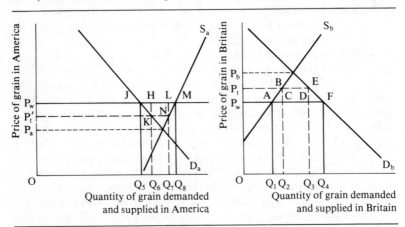

Fig. 2.4 The effects of tariff imposition

D_bS_b and D_aS_a are the domestic demand and supply curves for grain in Britain and America respectively. P_a and P_b are the autarkic prices of the commodity, whilst P_w is the world price following the opening of trade and commodity price equalisation. Consider the situation when Britain imposes a tariff on the import of American grain.

Clearly the tariff must be paid. Several alternatives are possible. It could be, for instance, that the whole burden of the tariff is 'passed on' to domestic consumers, in which case the price of grain in Britain would rise by the full amount of the tariff rate. Alternatively, American grain producers may absorb the burden of the tariff by reducing the export price of grain, again by the full tariff rate. A further possibility is that the burden will be shared between domestic consumers and foreign producers. Here the internal British price of grain will rise whilst the price which American exporters charge decreases, the difference going to the tariff-levying authority. This latter possibility is analysed in Fig. 2.4 where the tariff rate (t) results in the price of grain in Britain increasing from P_w to P_t whilst in America the price falls from P_w to P_t'.

The increased price of grain in Britain has several predictable effects. On the consumption side it causes consumers to contract their demand for grain from OQ_4 to OQ_3. On the supply side, domestic grain producers are induced to expand their supply from OQ_1 to OQ_2. Now, an increased proportion of the (shrunken) British market is supplied by domestic (high-cost) producers at the expense of foreign (low-cost) producers. Accordingly, total revenue of British grain producers increases from OP_wAQ_1 to OP_tBQ_2. Of this total, Q_1ABQ_2 represents increased costs, P_wP_tBA increased profit.

Because of the higher post-tariff price of grain there is an observable change in the welfare of British grain consumers. This change can be approximated by the overall reduction in consumers' surplus of P_wP_tEF.[4] This is not, however, a total welfare loss to Britain. As we have already seen, domestic grain producers' profits increase by P_wP_tBA. This is therefore a redistribution of income from domestic grain consumers to domestic producers of the import substitute as a direct consequence of the tariff. Furthermore, since tariff revenue collected goes directly from grain consumers to the government, CBED represents a redistribution of income from domestic consumers to the tariff-levying authority (i.e. the share of the tariff rate which falls on British consumers CB ($= P_wP_t$) multiplied by the amount of grain imported CD ($= Q_2Q_3$).

The net change to British residents as a result of the tariff is the sum of the areas ABC and DEF. The latter is the net loss in consumer surplus, whilst ABC is the welfare loss due to the higher costs of domestic grain producers. Tariff imposition would seem then to result in a welfare loss in the tariff-imposing country. This, however, is not the total welfare effect of the tariff. We must not forget that there will be production and consumption changes in the country facing the tariff. These too can be analysed by reference to Fig. 2.4.

As a result of the lower post-tariff price of grain in America, and reduced demand in Britain, American grain producers contract their supply from OQ_8 to OQ_7. On the other hand, demand from American grain consumers expands from OQ_5 to OQ_6. As we can see, the total revenue of American grain producers decreases from OP_wMQ_8 to $OP_t'NQ_7$. Of this, Q_7NMQ_8 represents the change in costs. Of the remainder, $P_t'P_wJK$ is redistributed to American grain consumers in the form of increased consumer surplus. KHLN is redistributed to the British tariff-levying authorities. The residual areas JHK and NLM are the net losses to American grain producers due to the tariff.

The size of these net losses will vary as the relative share of the tariff burden varies, and as the slopes of the various demand and supply curves alters. A useful and instructive exercise for the student would be to alter the slopes of the domestic and foreign demand and supply curves, to evaluate the impact this has on the gains and losses of tariff imposition.

Tariffs, employment and income distribution

The implications of tariff imposition for domestic employment and the domestic distribution of income ought to be clear by now. If tariff protection results in the import-substitute sector being insulated against foreign competition, clearly expansion of that industry is facilitated. Employment prospects at home therefore improve at the expense of employment prospects in the competing industry abroad. In terms of Fig. 2.4, this is depicted by the expansion of British grain production from OQ_1 to OQ_2, and the run-down of American grain production from OQ_8 to OQ_7. Since, because of tariff imposition the price of grain rises in Britain, the factor of production used relatively intensively in grain production (capital) must gain at the expense of the factor used less intensively. (The reasoning behind this assertion is exactly analogous to that on p. 39.) Thus, whereas free trade raises the reward to a country's relatively abundant factor, restricted trade via tariff imposition raises the reward of the country's scarce factor. This proposition is often referred to as the Stolper–Samuelson theorem (Stolper and Samuelson, 1941).

As we will see below, these implications of protection for employment and factor rewards provide some of the more persuasive arguments in favour of tariff imposition. It is not uncommon to find sectors of the economy vigorously pressing their claims for protection, arguing that domestic employment is more important than foreign employment (see Milner, 1977). These, and the more applied aspects of commercial policy, we will consider in due course. Meantime, however, we must consider the question of tariff imposition within a general equilibrium framework.

Tariff imposition and the offer curve

In Fig. 2.5, OA and OB are America and Britain's respective trade offer curves. Free trade equilibrium is at point E with terms of trade TOT_1. We will analyse again the effect of a British tariff on the import of American grain. The initial impact is described by a shift in the British offer curve, from OB to the tariff-distorted OB_t. We can see from this that for a given amount of pottery exports offered, more grain is required in exchange. Thus when free trade prevailed and OF pottery was offered, FG grain was demanded in exchange. Now because of the tariff, FH of grain is demanded in exchange for OF exports of pottery. The additional units of grain (GH) are equivalent to the tariff levy.[5]

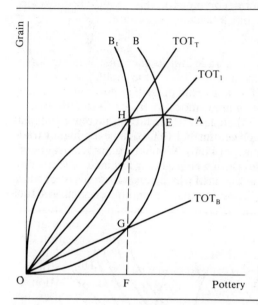

Fig. 2.5 The effects of tariff imposition: offer curve analysis

We can see that the tariff-distorted terms of trade TOT_1 have shifted in favour of Britain, the tariff-imposing country (albeit at a reduced volume of trade), and against America. If we reflect for a moment on our partial equilibrium analysis of Fig. 2.4 we will see that this movement in the terms of trade was to be expected, since a consequence of tariff imposition was a fall in the American export price of grain. Remember also from Fig. 2.4 that when the tariff was imposed, despite the fact that the **international** price of grain had fallen, domestic residents in Britain found themselves paying a higher price for grain than under free trade. This too is depicted in Fig. 2.5. The tariff-distorted terms of trade TOT_T have shifted in favour of Britain, but the internal price ratio which UK residents face is given by TOT_B. Although grain is entering Britain relatively cheaper than under free trade, domestic grain consumers find themselves paying a higher price than under free trade, because they must pay the tariff-distorted price.

We have seen there to be conflicting tendencies from tariff imposition. Some gain, some lose. More specifically there tends to be a redistribution from domestic consumers to domestic producers and to the tariff-levying authority. Also there tends to be a redistribution away from the tariff-imposing country's abundant factor towards its scarce factor. The relative magnitude of these opposing effects will depend on a number of factors, in particular the elasticity of the tariff-imposing and the tariff-facing countries' offer curves. Is it at all possible, however, to say in general what the total effect of tariff imposition will be? In order to comment on this we must re-introduce trade indifference curves, our 'measure' of welfare.

The optimum tariff

Once we superimpose Britain's trade indifference map as in Fig. 2.6, it is immediately apparent that it is possible for the country as a whole to attain a higher level of welfare as a result of tariff imposition. In fact, by levying a tariff and displacing her offer curve from OB to OB_t, Britain is able to reach TIB_3 rather than TIB_1. If the tariff is increased, so that Britain's offer curve is displaced further to OB_0, an even higher trade indifference curve is attainable (TIB_4). Would further increases in the tariff result in yet higher levels of welfare being attained? Clearly not. Any subsequent increase in the tariff which bends Britain's offer curve further merely serves to take her on to lower indifference curves, thus

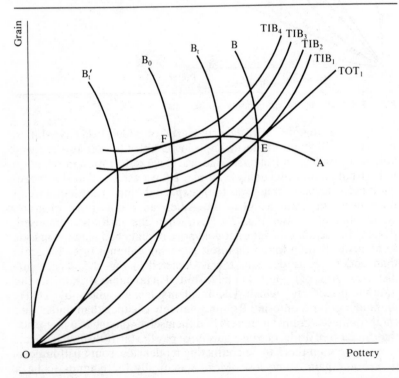

Fig. 2.6 The optimum tariff

OB$'_t$ takes Britain back on to TIB$_3$. The highest possible indifference curve is attainable when the tariff rate is such that Britain's offer curve is OB$_0$. Consequently, we refer to that tariff which maximises welfare as the *optimum tariff*. The optimum tariff rate can easily be identified as that rate which results in one of the tariff-imposing country's trade indifference curves being tangential to the tariff-facing country's offer curve (as OB$_0$ is as F).

It seems therefore that it may be possible via tariff imposition to attain levels of welfare higher than was possible under free trade. In fact, national welfare is maximised when a country acting in isolation imposes an optimum tariff. These conclusions clearly have important implications for the conduct of trade policy. They seem in fact to provide a sound rationale for protectionist policies. Several crucially important caveats are however in order.

First, all of the foregoing analysis applies to one country **acting in isolation.** Implicit in the analysis is the assumption that the country

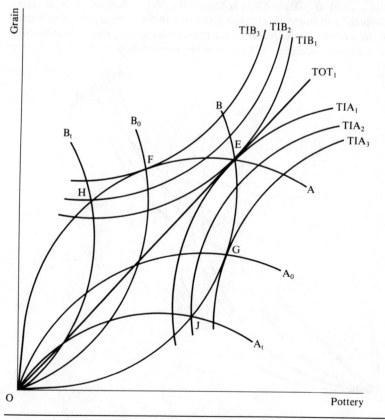

Fig. 2.7 Competitive tariff imposition

facing the tariff takes no retaliatory action. This is far from a realistic assumption. Indeed it is quite likely that a country faced with the sudden imposition of a tariff on its primary exportable (irrespective of any arguments based on the other country's policy being 'optimal'), would be more than tempted to reciprocate. The situation could ultimately resemble that portrayed in Fig. 2.7, where retaliation and counter-retaliation serve merely to take both countries on to lower levels of welfare, whilst simultaneously reducing the total volume of trade. Thus, although an optimum tariff policy may raise the welfare of the country imposing it if she acts in isolation, our initial proposition still holds, i.e. free trade maximises **world welfare.**

A second qualification is that it is not always possible to levy an optimum tariff. As we can see in Fig. 2.8, because America's offer curve (OA) is infinitely elastic it is impossible for Britain to turn the terms of trade in her favour by tariff imposition. All that tariff imposition serves to accomplish is a lower volume of trade at the same terms of trade. At the initial free-trade terms of trade, a British trade indifference curve TIB₃ is already tangential to the American offer curve. No tariff can improve on this situation. In fact any tariff takes Britain on to a lower trade indifference curve. Therefore, faced with an offer

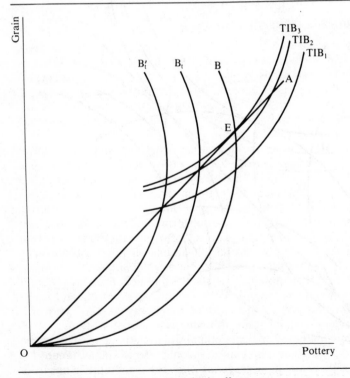

Fig. 2.8 Tariff imposition against an elastic offer curve

curve of infinite elasticity, a country cannot improve on her free-trade position by imposing a tariff.

A third factor is that we have deliberately avoided the question of what happens to the tariff revenue raised. If it is simply stored in government coffers we have no problems. More realistically, however, if the government enters the world market to 'spend' the tariff proceeds, this increase in demand will affect the terms of trade and will alter our conclusions accordingly. Similarly, if the proceeds from the tariff are distributed to domestic residents, this too will inevitably affect demand and ultimately relative prices. Once relative prices alter, the tariff will no longer be optimal. (A much more detailed and comprehensive analysis of the dynamic effects of tariff imposition can be found in Corden, 1974.)

This then completes our initial review of the economic effects of free trade and tariffs (the latter being the most widely documented form of protection). Further implications will be explored as we extend our analysis to consider in more detail the various arguments which can be advanced in support of protectionist trade policies (see also Milner and Greenaway, 1979).

2.4 Arguments for trade restriction

The analysis of the consequences of unrestricted trade was in terms of Paretian welfare economics. Gains and losses were measured in income and output terms. The criteria therefore for prescribing that trade liberalisation raises welfare, is based on two important assumptions. First, the competitive market is assumed to function perfectly. Second, the policy prescription is made possible by the use of the 'potential compensation' concept.

Perfectly functioning markets satisfy what we might describe as 'first-best assumptions'. Perfectly competitive markets, where private and social valuations do not diverge, operate so as to produce optimal resource allocation. Under such circumstances the price ratio of any two goods will equal both the marginal rate of consumer substitution and the marginal social rate of transformation between those two goods. Where, however, distortions occur and therefore first-best assumptions do not apply, optimal allocations will not be produced by free market forces. In the presence of monopoly influences in factor and product markets, or of external costs and benefits which are not reflected in private valuations, we can identify a case for government intervention. Our present task must be to identify what form government intervention should take to restore optimal allocations.

In any movement towards an optimal situation there are likely to be some losers, and some who gain in income terms. The argument for free trade is therefore an aggregative one. The community gains from trade in so much as the gainers are **able** to compensate the losers.

Given that the compensation may not actually take place, then policy-makers may be reluctant to adopt such criteria with which to reach decisions. They may for instance prefer to use a social-welfare function which places more importance on 'income protection' (Corden, 1974), i.e. on the prevention of income falls, rather than on increases of income. Corden (1975) describes this as a 'conservative social-welfare function'. Such an interpretation of policy-makers' motives may well be consistent with pressure-group politics and the protection of sectional interests, but in terms of our own analysis, calls for trade restriction based on these arguments must be viewed as 'non-economic' in motivation. 'Economic' arguments focus on the 'community's' welfare.

But to what does the 'community' refer? The analysis of free trade and of the optimum tariff has produced an apparent paradox. On the one hand, if countries are on lower welfare relative to free trade then both can increase welfare by liberalising trade. On the other, it is possible for one country to gain by moving away from the unrestricted trade equilibrium, by applying an 'optimal' tariff. What therefore is the appropriate level of aggregation for making prescriptions?

The optimum tariff reconsidered
Bhagwati (1968) argues that the optimum tariff cannot be viewed as a first-best solution because first-best assumptions do not apply. A country can only move the terms of trade in its own favour through the application of a tariff if the world market is not perfectly competitive. In a perfectly competitive world market an individual country's participation in the market is insufficient to influence or distort world prices. The optimum-tariff solution is only possible where there is an international distortion generated by a country's monopsony influence.

In any case the threat of retaliation can serve to make everybody worse off in welfare terms, and to reduce the attractiveness of the optimum tariff to the imposing country, although it is possible to reach a tariff-distorted equilibrium in which one country is still better off. This solution is possible if an optimum-tariff strategy is reacted to by another optimum-tariff strategy, and if the offer curve elasticities are appropriate. In Fig. 2.9 the imposition of an optimum tariff by America moves the equilibrium from E to F; reducing Britain's welfare by raising its own welfare from trade indifference curve TIA_1 to TIA_3. If Britain now adopts an optimal strategy in relation to tariff-distorted offer curve AO_0, it will shift its own offer curve until it cuts OA_0 at the point where its own trade indifference curve TIB_1 is tangential to OA_0 (i.e. at point G). Although this retaliatory action lowers America's welfare, America is still on a higher trade indifference curve at G (i.e. TIA_2) than at the free-trade equilibrium at E (i.e. TIA_1). Britain is of course at a lower level of welfare than at the free-trade equilibrium. However, if Britain were to try to push the terms of trade further in its own favour, the improvement would no longer compensate for the declining volume of trade, and it would as a result lower its own welfare.

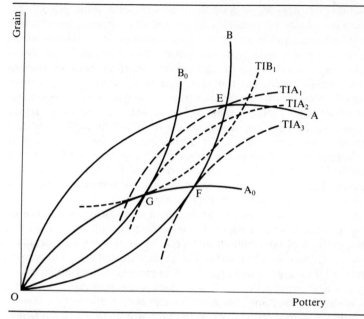

Fig. 2.9 Welfare-raising tariff with retaliation

Most countries are not, however, in a position to exploit national monopsony power, and would find it extremely difficult to devise an optimum tariff structure if they were. In any case the global policy prescription is that free trade maximises global welfare (subject to the provision that the potential gainers from tariff imposition are able to pay compensation to the potential losers). Nevertheless, national self-interest may best be served by pursuing an optimum-tariff strategy if the country is in a position to exploit distortions in international markets.

Optimal policies towards domestic distortions
We have already suggested that there may also be imperfections (distortions) in domestic markets which will produce non-optimal situations in the absence of government intervention. Traditionally, deviations from ideal domestic conditions (or first-best assumptions) formed the basis of arguments for divergence from free-trade policy on economic grounds (Haberler, 1950). Subsequent analysis[6] has shown, however, that correction for domestic distortions requires a tax or subsidy (or a combination of both) on either domestic consumption, production or factor use (depending where the distortion exists), not on international trade.

If, for example, pottery production in Britain imposes an external cost on grain production, the marginal costs of production as they appear to producers would diverge from marginal social costs. In the absence of trade, pottery production would be encouraged and grain production discouraged, because the relative price of pottery would be less than its social-opportunity cost. If with the opening up of trade between America and Britain the international price ratio (in relation to the distorted, domestic price ratio in Britain) indicated a comparative advantage in pottery production in Britain, then grain production in Britain would be further reduced. This equilibrium would be non-optimal. Clearly a tariff on imports of grain would help to encourage the production of grain in Britain, but at the expense of a further distortion on the consumption side as a result of the higher price of imported grain. Although the tariff may improve the situation, it is possible that the consumption losses from imposing a tariff would exceed the benefits from the reallocation of resources between pottery and grain. Trade restriction in the presence of domestic distortions may therefore lower rather than raise welfare.

If the aim is to reallocate resources in order to restore or maintain a level of production for a particular good at a certain level, then the optimal method of government intervention would take the form of a production subsidy on the good suffering the external cost. This can be illustrated by reference to Fig. 2.10. The external diseconomy raises the cost of grain production so that the domestic supply curve is pushed from S_b^* to S_b. Assuming that America can supply grain at a constant price, then without the distortion Britain would produce OQ_2 and import Q_2Q_4 of grain from America. The impact of the distortion has been to reduce domestic production by Q_1Q_2, and increase imports to Q_1Q_4. Certainly the government could increase domestic production to OQ_2 again by means of a tariff (T), but only by raising the price to the consumer to P_a^t. (Consumption would fall to OQ_3 and imports to Q_2Q_3.) The loss in consumer surplus resulting from the imposition of

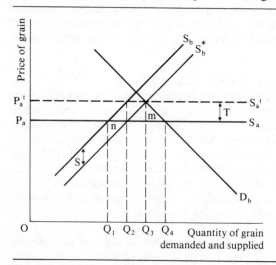

Fig. 2.10 Alternative policies towards distortions

the tariff would be equivalent to the triangle m in Fig. 2.10. A comparable subsidy S, which serves to shift the supply curve back to S_b* could however restore full allocative efficiency. Marginal production costs which now reflected social costs would again be in line with domestic and foreign prices. The price to the consumer would be P_a and domestic production would equal OQ_2 and imports Q_2Q_4.

The optimal solution is therefore a domestic production subsidy on the good suffering from the external cost, while the second-best solution may not be a tax on trade. The production loss resulting from the distortion can be represented by the area n in Fig. 2.10 (i.e. the fall in production from OQ_2 to OQ_1). Given appropriate elasticities of domestic supply and demand, it is possible that the loss in consumer surplus (m) from tariff imposition will be greater than the production loss (n) from domestic distortion.

This analysis serves to emphasise the need to distinguish between the case for government intervention and the case for the restriction of trade. Of course if the objective was to increase self-sufficiency, i.e. to reduce imports rather than just increase domestic production, then a tariff would be the more efficient means of achieving this (non-economic) objective. (Reduction of import dependence may be sought for strategic or political reasons, as in the case of military or agricultural products.) In Fig. 2.11 a tariff on imports from America (raising the supply curve from S_a to S_a^t) serves to reduce imports from Q_1Q_5 to Q_2Q_4. Our earlier analysis of the 'static' costs of protection has demonstrated that the production and consumption losses resulting from such a policy are measured by the triangles u and x respectively. To achieve

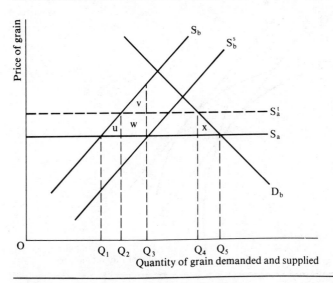

Fig. 2.11 Optimal policy for increased self-sufficiency

the same reduction in imports by means of a subsidy it would be necessary to increase domestic production to OQ_3, (i.e. so that Q_3Q_5 imports with a subsidy applied to domestic supply S_b^s was equal to Q_2Q_4 imports with a tariff). The production loss from subsidising domestic industry would however be equivalent to the enlarged triangle $u + v + w$. Since the area $u + v + w$ is larger than the area $u + x$, it is clear that a tariff is the more efficient means of achieving a reduction in imports.

Competition and intervention

The conclusion that government intervention may be justified where first-best assumptions do not apply, but that restriction of international trade may not be justified on economic grounds, can be illustrated by reference to the traditional 'infant-industry' argument for trade restriction. This doctrine claims that if new industries are small in relation to their optimal size, then initial lack of international competitiveness will disappear if potential economies of scale can be reaped. Temporary tariff imposition would therefore allow a country and the world to benefit from future cost advantages, and increased competitive and productive capacity.

These ideas can be represented in Fig. 2.12. The imposition of a tariff on imports of pottery shifts the domestic price ratio from TT to T'T', and raises domestic pottery production from A to A'. The claim is then that because of protection, economies of scale can be reaped in

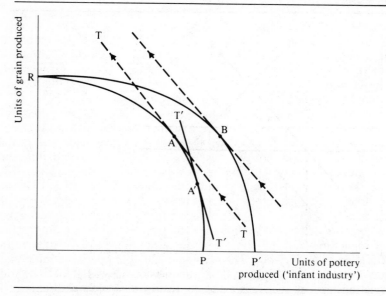

Fig. 2.12 'Infant-industry' argument for tariff protection

the pottery industry (raising the production possibility frontier from RP to RP'). With the removal of tariff protection the industry will produce at point B, which is above the free-trade production level A in the absence of scale economies.

If the short-term production and consumption losses generated by trade protection are likely to be offset by future gains, one might ask why the market would not invest in the new industry on the required scale. There is no *a priori* reason for believing that the government's foresight and ability to assess future risks is superior to that of the market. The government may in fact give protection to an industry that has no potential for growth, or may remove the incentive to innovate and reduce costs. Alternatively, we might argue that restriction on foreign competition will help to maintain profits at levels which will permit expenditure on research and development, or encourage risk-taking. Similarly, if businessmen in practice are excessively short-sighted and adopt a discount rate which exceeds the social rate, then a case for government intervention may be made. Our earlier analysis has shown, however, that where market distortions exist then the optimal form of government intervention would take the form of production subsidies, rather than the restriction of trade.

Of course our earlier analysis did not rule out the possibility that restricted trade was a superior solution where the market functions imperfectly. The dynamics of free trade and restricted trade is a contentious area in economics (Corden, 1970). The protection of infant or ageing industries is usually rejected on static criteria for allocative efficiency, because it results in the replacement of lower-cost foreign producers by higher-cost domestic producers. On the basis of such reasoning we reject the use of 'scientific' tariffs against imports from cheap labour countries. It is seen as a 'non-argument' because it contradicts the comparative-advantage motive for trade. (Of course there may be non-economic justifications for protecting incomes and employment in certain sectors, but again an employment subsidy would be a more efficient instrument of protection.)

If this unfair competition argument is fallacious, why then do countries worry about the 'dumping' of imports[7] at below-average production costs? Obtaining relatively cheaper goods from abroad is after all the aim of trade. However, where dumping is erratic and domestic resources are not highly mobile, then the result may be excessive 'market disruption'. Such uncertainty, underinvestment and labour conflict may also be produced by rapid import penetration of genuinely cheaper foreign products. In fact modern protectionist arguments are based on the view that the dynamic conditions for efficiency may diverge from the continual application of the static rules for allocative efficiency. The argument is that industrialisation based upon stable and protected domestic markets may alter behavioural relationships in such a way as to justify the trade restriction on economic grounds in the long run. 'Science policies' which seek to protect high-technology industries have similarly been justified in terms of the long-term benefits of industrial diversification.

However, when industrial strategy is based on trade restriction, domestic industry may become 'locked' into home markets where the potential for scale economies may be limited. Indeed, the main theme of the empirical work on dynamic or growth effects has been the benefits of economies of scale from the liberalisation of trade. (For the liberalisation of European trade see Balassa, 1967a; and for the Canadian experience see Eastman and Stykolt, 1967.) As a result a 'revitalising', industrial strategy may be better based on the subsidisation of export activities whose potential markets are greater, rather than on the protection of import substitutes, that is, on a policy of promotion rather than protection. In any case, whatever the relative merits of government intervention as opposed to reliance on market forces, the optimal method of protection is not the restriction of trade.

Trade restriction for development

Nevertheless, a considerable amount of trade policy literature has been directed towards the case for assisting import-substituting manufacturing industries in the less developed countries (LDCs) (see Diaz-Alejandro, 1975). The arguments usually centre around the infant-industry and wage-differential arguments.

We have already given some attention to the infant-industry arguments. It may well be that these have particular relevance for the LDCs, where poorly developed capital markets may result in underinvestment and high discount rates. Becker (1964) considers also the problems of human–capital market imperfections in the LDCs. 'Social' constraints may act as barriers to the retraining of labour and the growth of entrepreneurialism. Johnson (1970) provides an alternative basis for the infant-industry case. He suggests that the external benefits provided by the pioneering firms in a new industry, by retraining labour and diffusing knowledge, will be unrewarded by the market. This is of course a justification, as we have established, for government subsidisation rather than trade restriction.

The wage-differential argument on the other hand suggests that the excess of average incomes in the industrialised sector over those in the subsistence sector, places a constraint on the growth of the industrialised sector (Little and Mirrlees, 1969). The argument is dubious, however, because the differential may not exist (Harris and Todaro, 1970) and a tariff would not be the first-best solution. Little, Scitovsky and Scott (1970) see wage subsidies as preferable.

The relationship between trade, growth and development will be returned to in Chapter 4. At this stage we might point out that if the industrial nations enjoy a monopsony influence over primary-producing LDCs which distorts trade in such a way as to discourage industrialisation in the developing countries, then there may be a case for the application of an optimum tariff which pushes the terms of trade back in the LDCs' favour. It would of course be dependent on the LDCs being able to influence their terms of trade through 'collective' action.

Such 'collective' action may at a minimum serve as an important bargaining tool in the negotiation of trade liberalisation. Tariff structures generally tend to escalate with later stages of production. Lower tariffs on imports of raw materials bias trade towards raw materials and capital goods, rather than consumer goods; whilst trade in consumer goods tends to be biased towards luxury, or technically superior goods which are more likely to overcome tariff barriers. Johnson argues that these escalated structures:

... create serious barriers to the development of the underdeveloped countries on the basis of their resources of relatively cheap labour, and instead bias the opportunities for the development of the underdeveloped countries through international trade towards dependence on the exploitation of natural resources.

(H. G. Johnson, 1971, p. 321)

This escalation of tariff structures is particularly important when we consider effective, rather than nominal rates of tariff protection.

2.5 Measuring trade restriction

Our analysis of the impact of trade barriers on trade volumes has thus far been based on some simplifying assumptions. In order that the divergence between the domestic and world price of an importable good was accounted for fully by the **nominal** tariff on the final good, we made certain assumptions. First, no intermediate inputs were used to produce this good domestically; second, there were no non-tariff restrictions on the import of this particular good; and third, domestic producers priced up to the level permitted by the degree of protection provided (i.e. the domestic price equalled the world price plus the tariff). In terms of the partial analysis of nominal tariff imposition developed in Fig. 2.4, p. 44, a tariff reduces trade from Q_1Q_4 to Q_2Q_3. This trade restriction is composed of two elements; increased domestic production (Q_1Q_2) and reduced domestic consumption (Q_3Q_4). The latter is determined by the extent of the rise in the domestic price ($P_t - P_w$) and the elasticity of domestic demand; the former by the *effective protective rate* and the elasticity of domestic supply. The domestic demand and supply elasticities present no conceptual difficulties for this calculation. The measurement of actual trade restriction provided by the tariff structure is, however, complex. The consumption effect can be identified from nominal prices, but the production effect cannot. For this we need to examine the effective protective rate (see Corden, 1971).

The effective tariff rate

If we relax the assumption that no intermediate inputs are used in the domestic production of importables, then the total impact of a tariff structure on an importable is determined by the tariff on imports of the final good, and by any tariffs on the inputs into that process. The effective tariff rate seeks to measure the total impact of the tariff structure throughout the production process, on a particular stage of that process. If, for example, all imported inputs are subject to zero or low duties, while the final product is subject to a high tariff, then the result will be a relatively high effective tariff rate. On the other hand, if nominal tariffs on imported inputs are raised, whilst the nominal tariff on the final product remains unchanged, then the effective tariff rate on the final product will be lowered. In the extreme, where imported inputs into a process are heavily protected but imports of the final product of the process are subject to low or zero nominal tariffs, the effective tariff rate may become negative.

If we envisage a product's final value as the sum of the cost of intermediate inputs (Σa_i) and of primary production costs or value added (V), i.e. $1 = V + \Sigma a_i$, then the effective tariff rate measures the difference between the changes in intermediate inputs generated by tariffs (t_i) and the change in the good's final value generated by a tariff (t_n), in relation to the free-trade situation. Algebraically:

$$1 + t_n = V' + \Sigma a_i(1 + t_i)$$

where V' = value added at tariff-distorted prices. We can in fact measure the effective tariff rate (t_e) by measuring the percentage change in value added for this final stage of production produced by the tariff structure:

$$t_e = \left(\frac{V' - V}{V} \right) \times 100 \text{ per cent}$$

Alternatively expressed, the effective tariff rate measures the maximum percentage increase in value added on this stage of the process made possible by the tariff structure. By substitution:

$$t_e = \frac{1 + t_n - \Sigma a_i (1 + t_i) - 1 + \Sigma a_i}{V}$$

Rearranged:

$$t_e = \frac{t_n - \Sigma a_i t_i}{V}$$

From this formula we can illustrate our previous claims that the effective tariff rate varies directly with the nominal rate on the final product, and indirectly with the tariffs on intermediate inputs.

Consider for example an importable good which is produced domestically for £100 from one imported input, whose cost accounts for 50 per cent of the final value under free trade conditions. If tariffs are imposed on imports at the rate of 5 per cent on the input and 10 per cent on the final good, then the domestic value of the importable is increased to £110 and the cost of the input rises to £52.5. The tariff-distorted value added (V′) equals £57.5, i.e. £110 − £52.5, and the free-trade value added (V) equals £50, i.e. £100 − £50. Value added can increase by £7.50 as a result of the imposition of the tariff structure. The effective tariff is therefore:

$$\frac{57.5 - 50}{50} \times 100 = 15 \text{ per cent}$$

Thus even with a tariff on the imported input, the effective tariff rate exceeds the nominal rate on the final product. Though in the absence of a tariff on the imported input the effective rate would have been even higher:

i.e. $t_e = \dfrac{60 - 50}{50} \times 100 = 20$ per cent

This value indicates the extent of protection offered by the tariff structure to domestic producers on this final stage of the production process. In other words, primary production costs or value added on this stage of production could rise by up to 20 per cent, without reducing the competitiveness of domestically produced goods relative to imports of this final good. That is, the value of 20 per cent indicates the effective protective rate. The actual protective or production effect will of course depend upon the actual changes in primary production costs, if any, which occur, and upon the ability of the domestic producers to respond to the effective protection offered, i.e. upon the elasticity of domestic supply.

In practice of course the effective tariff rate is a more complex concept than we have so far suggested. Our analysis has been in partial terms, and it ignores therefore inter-industry relationships and the existence of indirect and feedback effects of trade restrictions from other industries. We have also assumed that input–output relationships in an industry are fixed. But changes in relative prices induced by tariffs may encourage substitution between traded and non-traded inputs and between intermediate and factor inputs, and may therefore make physical input coefficients variable. If for example a tariff increases domestic production, then the accompanying rise in demand for imported inputs may increase the price of inputs, unless their supply is infinitely elastic; in which case the actual change in value added resulting from tariff imposition upon the final good, i.e. the effective protection, will be less than the maximum possible change in value added. (For a more rigorous examination of effective protection, see Michaely, 1977.)

Non-tariff distortion

Attention has focused increasingly in recent years on measures other than tariffs as sources of international trade distortion. It is in fact possible to extend the concept of effective protection or restriction to include the effects of so-called non-tariff trade barriers. Such barriers include quotas and other quantitative restrictions such as voluntary export restraint, export subsidies, discriminatory buying campaigns, and restrictive technical and administrative regulations. (For a detailed consideration of non-tariff barriers, see Baldwin, 1971b.)

Since many of these measures will affect input and final prices in the same way as tariffs do, it is possible in principle to estimate the effective protection provided by non-tariff distortions. A quota can, by raising prices for example, provide the same effective protection as an equivalent tariff.[8] If a quota is imposed on a final product, it will increase the effective protective rate; if on an intermediate input, it will decrease the effective rate. Conversely, an export subsidy increases the effective rate of protection because it shifts sales from the home market, and therefore raises domestic prices. On the other hand, if the subsidised product is an input into another productive process, the higher cost of inputs will reduce the effective protective rate for the later-stage process. Similarly, if indirect taxes on final goods are uniform and general and imposed at destination, then both imports and domestically produced goods are affected equally, and value added is unaffected. (If the good is exported then there will be border adjustment for the tax.) However, if a selective indirect tax is imposed on a traded or non-traded input into another process, then the effective protective rate on that process will be reduced.

Some empirical evidence
Since the pioneering work of Balassa (1965) and Basevi (1966), investigations of the protective effects of trade distortions have multiplied. As Corden argues, the attraction of the effective rate concept is that:

. . . it allows a single figure to sum up the net result of various trade and other taxes and subsidies affecting any particular activity.
(Corden, 1975, p. 61)

As we have seen, however, the method is not without its problems (see also Grubel and Johnson, 1971), and results concerning the impact of protective structures are subject to considerable variation (see Balassa, 1971). The results are sensitive to the treatment of non-traded goods and domestic indirect taxes, for instance. Nevertheless, in general it has been found that effective rates considerably exceed nominal rates of protection in both developed and developing countries. Some nominal and effective rates for the UK and the US are provided in Table 2.1. In the case of industrial products, the greater value for effective rates is due to the phenomenon of tariff 'escalation' that we described in Section 2.4. This structure of protection in the less developed countries has favoured import-substitution activities rather than export-oriented industries. Table 2.2 shows that within this import-substitution framework, consumer goods have tended to be subject to relatively higher rates of effective protection than intermediate goods or capital-goods industries. Given these countries' capital deficiencies and their balance-of-payments weaknesses, this is perhaps an unfortunate pattern of distortion since it encourages the use of capital-intensive and imported, input-expensive processes.

However, we must re-emphasise that even if effective rates give a reasonable indication of the direction of resource pulls, they do not tell us what distortions will actually occur; we need also to know the supply elasticities. In the extreme, for example, if the domestic elasticity of supply is zero then there will be no domestic resource movement, however high the effective rate. In any case the domestic price may remain less than the free-trade world price plus the tariff, i.e. there may be some tariff 'redundancy'. Although this apparent redundancy may be explained by quality differences (real or perceived) between the

Table 2.1 Nominal and effective rates of protection in the US and UK, by product groups, 1972

Year 1972*	Nominal tariffs		Effective rates: (including non-tariff measures)	
	US (%)	UK (%)	US (%)	UK (%)
Primary products	7	2	17	18
Intermediate and consumer goods	7	3	18	11
Capital goods	6	8	7	17

*Rates include reductions agreed in Kennedy Round of GATT negotiations
Source: adapted from Baldwin (1971b), Tables 5 and 7, pp. 165 and 168

Table 2.2 Average effective protective rates in manufacturing in selected countries

	Average effective protective rates		
	Consumer goods (%)	Intermediate goods (%)	Capital goods (%)
Argentina (1958)	164	167	133
Brazil (1966)	230	68	31
Mexico (1960)	22	34	55
Pakistan (1963/4)	883	88	155
Philippines (1965)	94	65	80

Source: Little, Scitovsky and Scott (1970), p. 174

domestic product and the import substitute, effective rates are calculated on the assumption that the domestic and imported product are perfect substitutes. In the presence of product differentiation therefore, we would need to know elasticities of substitution of domestic consumers in order to measure the impact of a tariff on domestic production.

2.6 Global interdependence and commercial policy

The implications of the effective-tariff concept have long been appreciated by the negotiators of trade policy, although the consequences were not rationalised. Nevertheless, negotiations of tariff liberalisation in the post-war period undertaken to restore multilateral trade have concentrated on nominal tariff reduction. As a result trade policy issues increasingly relate to the problems that this emphasis has created. On the one hand, the reduction of tariff barriers has tended to identify the importance and diversification of non-tariff barriers to trade. On the other, the effective discrimination produced by this pattern of liberalisation has biased global development towards the already industrialised nations.

Recent developments in the global economy have increased awareness of the growing interdependence between the developed countries and between developed and less developed countries, and of the need therefore to redress these problems. However, our discussion of the case for and against unrestricted trade has highlighted the difficulties facing the reconciliation of the case for global liberalisation with national self-interest and with electoral pressures for employment protection. The current round of multilateral trade negotiations (the 'Tokyo Round') has been faced with divergent pressures as a result. Further reduction of trade barriers (nominal and effective) is likely only if suitable safeguards can be guaranteed, especially for 'sensitive' goods threatened by 'market disruption' (Robertson, 1973).

Reciprocity and non-discrimination
The initial aim of post-war trade policy was to return to a multilateral trading system and to reconstruct the European economy. For example, the Organisation for European Economic Cooperation (OEEC) was established in 1948 to administer the financing of Western Europe's economic recovery and to eliminate payments and trade restrictions on intra-European trade.

At the global level the intention was to establish a trade equivalent to the IMF.[9] However the proposals laid down in the Havana Charter for an International Trade Organisation (ITO) failed to be ratified in 1949 by the US, (among other countries). By necessity therefore, the world fell back on the provisional arrangement made in 1947 in anticipation of the ITO – the General Agreement on Tariffs and Trade

(GATT). This agreement proscribed against the use of quotas, except for temporary balance-of-payments purposes, and provided a framework for the reduction or elimination of tariffs based on the principles of reciprocal action and non-discrimination. On the one hand, countries could not expect or be expected to undertake unilateral action; on the other, they could not selectively discriminate against countries. The exception to this latter requirement, that discrimination was acceptable where this was to be based on regional groupings within which trade was to be totally liberated, was in practice to significantly influence the pattern of tariff liberalisation.

The GATT philosophy of non-discrimination was achieved by the continuation of the well-established principle of the 'most-favoured nation' (mfn). The mfn clause required that any tariff preference offered by a country to another GATT signatory, had to be extended to all other GATT signatories. The outlet to the mfn principle offered by regional integration was an attractive option to groupings that already had strong trading links. In order to encourage Western European development for instance, European integration was also encouraged by the US.[10] With the recovery of Western Europe, however, during the 1950s, and the increasing importance of potential US trade diverted to within Europe, the US pressed for further reductions in tariff barriers.[11] These negotiations, which took place between 1962 and 1967, are usually known as the 'Kennedy Round' of GATT negotiations. Given the overwhelming dominance of world trade (in particular in manufactures) at this time of the US and EEC, agreement between these two parties was essential. The US pressed for common reciprocal reductions in tariff protection on manufactures, and for a reduction in Europe's agricultural protectionism. Prior disparities in average nominal tariff rates (the US rates were in general higher), prompted the EEC, however, to argue for a differential pattern of tariff reduction. From the US viewpoint an equal 50 per cent cut offered comparable potential trade-creating effects. From the viewpoint of the EEC a common reduction would leave US tariff rates absolutely higher, and more likely as a result to be prohibitive. (The factors influencing the actual effects of a given amount of nominal tariff reduction have been considered in Section 2.5.) In the event the tariff reductions agreed upon ranged from 35 to 40 per cent on industrial goods and were spread over a five-year period.

Problem of hidden barriers

Despite the lack of central authority over the 'contracting parties', the GATT framework has made a major contribution to tariff liberalisation. With the reduction of tariff barriers, however, the significance of non-tariff barriers to trade has been emphasised. Part II of the General Agreement does provide rules for controlling non-tariff distortions. Where such distortions have been identifiable and quantifiable, their removal has been negotiable. Quotas, for example, were successfully dismantled in the early post-war period. Direct export subsidies or para-tariffs (e.g. special charges or discriminatory customs procedures; see Robertson, 1972) have similarly been more successfully standardised and reduced through GATT negotiation.

Identification of non-tariff barriers remains, however, a serious problem. Governments can deliberately seek to circumvent GATT rules and operate 'hidden' barriers against trade (see G. and V. Curzon, 1971). Rather than providing direct export subsidies, for example, governments can provide the equivalent assistance to exports by providing export credit at subsidised rates, via government-sponsored agencies. The method is less overt and therefore less controllable. Even where the method of distortion is identifiable the motive and effects may be more difficult to ascertain. There may for instance, be legitimate social reasons (e.g. health and safety factors) for imposing technical regulations on certain imported goods. The existence of technical and administrative regulations provides the opportunity for abuse, however. Unjustifiable hindrances to trade may arise because it is virtually impossible to distinguish between the 'social' and 'protective' elements of the regulation. Where a prohibitive motive is identified, quantifying the protective effect for negotiation purposes may be a further constraint. Border adjustment of indirect taxes is for instance permissible under GATT rules, on the assumption that all indirect taxes are shifted on to final consumers and all direct taxes borne by the producer. If we reject this assumption, then international differences in the distribution of the tax burden between direct and indirect sources will have trade-distorting effects. The US for example feel that the EEC has taken undue advantage of GATT by shifting to indirect, value-added methods of taxation. The effects of such a shift are however extremely difficult to quantify.

Despite these enormous difficulties GATT has made some progress on the problem of non-tariff barriers. Experience and extension of the list of forbidden activities have brought progress through negotiation. Standardisation of methods of customs evaluation and licensing have been achieved, for example. Gaps in the list remain nevertheless, and these become more important as greater awareness of non-tariff barriers enables countries to adopt more hidden forms of protection.

Preferential trade and the LDCs
Post-war tariff liberalisation, as we have seen, has tended to bias growth and trade in favour of the developed countries. The global pattern of dependence and unequal exchange has tended to be perpetuated. The escalated pattern of effective protection, and the requirement of reciprocal trade liberalisation made against the LDCs have helped to maintain the LDCs concentration on primary exports, and to produce what the LDCs see as a secular deterioration in their terms of trade.

The evidence on the terms of trade has not in fact been unequivocal, since it depends crucially on the definition, and commodity and country coverage chosen. By the early 1960s, however, increasing political independence was accompanied by increasing pressure from the LDCs for reduced economic dependence. Development assistance based on aid rather than trade was seen as perpetuating the existing pattern of dependence and as retarding development. The LDCs had low absorptive capacities, a characteristic which was unlikely to disappear while aid was 'tied' to trade, i.e. to goods imported from the donor, developed nation. This pressure for a new approach to the development problem culminated in the first United Nation Conference on Trade and Development (UNCTAD), which was convened in Geneva in 1964. UNCTAD has become a permanent UN agency, a forum for the LDCs to confront the developed countries. (Subsequent UNCTADs have been held in New Delhi (1968), Santiago (1972) and Nairobi (1976).)

Since the initial attempts to identify problems in 1964, subsequent UNCTADs have set more realistic and specific aims. They have called for a greater say in international monetary affairs (an issue we will return to in Chapter 8), for an increase in financial aid, for the revision of commodity agreements, and for preferential (non-reciprocal) access to the markets of the industrial nations. Some progress has in fact been made with the last aim. The third UNCTAD in 1972 welcomed the institution of a 'generalised system of tariff preference' for the LDCs agreed upon in 1971. Failure to agree a common pattern of preferences, however, resulted in differing and temporary concessions being offered by different countries. A further major step towards preferential trade came though with the signing by the EEC and 44 African, Caribbean and Pacific States (APC) of the Lomé Agreement in 1975 (see Coffey, 1975). The broad result of the agreement was that the EEC and APC states had formed a large preferential trading area in which the EEC has relinquished the right of reciprocity.

The Lomé Agreement also guaranteed APC countries stable and equitable prices in EEC markets for their main export-earning commodities (the so-called 'Stabex' scheme). The LDCs had become increasingly dissatisfied with the functioning of primary-product markets, and with the deterioration in the barter terms of trade (see Chapter 4). Following recent experiences, however, the developed nations were quite anxious also to introduce commodity stabilisation schemes. Of more significance will be the developed nations' reactions to the demands of the fourth UNCTAD for a new international economic order which would replace old patterns of dependence and unequal exchange (see Kirkpatrick and Nixson, 1976).

If these demands are to be satisfied, then a substantial rise in the LDCs' share of trade in manufactures must take place. At present they account for only 10 per cent of this trade. As tariff preferences encourage multinational corporations to transfer more of the labour-intensive parts of production processes to cheaper labour LDCs, then the LDCs' demands are likely also to be matched by protectionist pressures within the developed countries. The problem of preferential and unrestricted market access for 'sensitive' goods, in particular on a general basis, is exaggerated by the fact that exports of manufactures by LDCs are dominated by a relatively small number of countries. These and a few other countries (including for instance South Korea and Singapore) will increasingly become strong competitors in world markets in the next decade. Escape clauses and safeguards will be essential therefore, if further effective trade liberalisation for the LDCs in particular is to be achieved.

Whatever the response of the industrialised nations, recent developments indicate that the countries of the Third World are beginning to appreciate the benefits of integration, the benefits from intra-union trade and from collective, political pressure. It is to a consideration of the rationale for, and significance of, regional trading blocks that we will turn to in Chapter 3.

Notes

1. The assumptions Samuelson explicitly makes are:
    (a) Two countries, two commodities, two factors of production.
    (b) Production functions exhibit constant returns to scale.
    (c) The law of diminishing marginal productivity holds.
    (d) Differing factor intensities in the production of the two commodities.
    (e) Production functions are the same in both countries.
    (f) No tariffs or transport costs.
    (g) International immobility of factors.
    (h) Incomplete specialisation.
                                        (see Samuelson, 1949, p. 181–2.)
2. Precisely the same conclusion is reached when we reason from the relative price of capital and grain. This is something the student should check for his/her self.
3. The Kaldor–Hicks compensation test is one of the basic principles of welfare economics. The 'pure' Paretian criterion for assessing the welfare effects of an economic policy states that society as a whole can be considered better off if the policy results in someone being made better off whilst no one else is made worse off. Clearly this is of very limited value since most economic policies result in some people being made better off, some worse off. In this situation Kaldor and Hicks (1939) suggested that if the beneficiaries of a change gain enough to compensate the losers, then everyone is better off. This compensation need not actually take place, the fact it **could** take place is sufficient.
4. Consumers' surplus is the difference between the price a consumer is charged for a particular good or service, and the amount he would be willing to pay. It is therefore approximated by the area below the demand curve, and above the price line.
5. The tariff rate is ascertained from the additional imports required, over the free trade imports. In our case this is GH/FG.
6. Criticisms of Haberler's pioneering work on externality problems are to be found in Bhagwati and Ramaswami (1963) and Johnson (1965a).
7. Anti-dumping duties are permitted under GATT rules, although identification and proof of dumping remains extrmely difficult.
8. A quota is usually seen as having the same effects as a tariff of comparable size,

except that redistribution effects may differ. Bhagwati (1969b) however argues that this equivalence is only achieved under restrictive assumptions.

9. The formation and functions of the International Monetary Fund are considered in Chapters 7 and 8.

10. For a consideration of the post-war movement towards European integration see Swann (1970), Ch. 1. The economic consequences of European integration are also investigated in Chapter 3.

11. Multilateral reductions in tariffs had been achieved by the earlier Dillon Round of negotiations.

Restricted free trade

3.1 Introduction

In Chapter 2 we examined the motives for and consequences of free and restricted trade. Throughout we implicitly assumed that trade policy was non-discriminatory in nature; that is, the same policy was applied to particular imports irrespective of their origin. That assumption is not altogether appropriate for a post-war period which has witnessed increasing economic integration, in both the developed and less-developed world. We will examine the varying forms of this integration in Section 3.2. However, the initial stage of integration has usually taken the form of a regional trading arrangement. Discriminatory commercial policies have been established, which restrict the freeing or liberalisation of trade to within the particular block of countries.

Examination of the economic effects of these geographically discriminatory changes in trade barriers has been rationalised in economics by the theory of the customs union. This relatively modern branch of tariff theory will be examined in Sections 3.3 and 3.4. Prior to the development of the modern theory the presumption was that since a customs union appeared to be a step towards free trade, it was necessarily desirable. However, the principles of the theory of second best have shown that movement towards fulfilment of some of the Pareto conditions for optimality does not necessarily guarantee welfare improvement. More detailed examination of the effects of customs union formation is required. Section 3.3 therefore seeks to distinguish between the trade-creating and trade-diverting effects of a customs union, and to identify the factors which determine the relative size of these effects. Section 3.4 will then seek to examine the costs and benefits which may be attached to these static trade effects, in partial and general terms, and to the possible dynamic effects of integration on production.

Simple and general policy prescriptions are difficult to make, however, on the basis of customs union theory. The final section (3.5) will provide a survey of some of the empirical evidence on specific examples of economic integration. This will enable us to contrast the impact of integration under differing conditions and patterns of membership.

3.2 Economic regionalism: forms and motives

Most of the basic theory of product-market integration is presented in terms of the customs union. There are, however, other forms of international economic integration, such as free-trade areas, common markets and full economic unions. Given the post-war emergence of such economic regionalism it is important that first we explain the difference between each form of integration, and second we begin to analyse why countries should consider joining a regional grouping, when they can reap the benefits of free or freer trade through non-preferential tariff reductions.

Forms of integration

In terms of political commitment there is a clear ordering in the degree of integration, from a free-trade area to a customs union and common market, and finally to a full economic union. The European Free Trade Association (EFTA) is an example of a free-trade area. This type of regional grouping involves the removal of tariffs and other restrictions on trade, in all or specific goods, between members of the grouping (in the case of EFTA the emphasis for liberalisation was placed on trade in industrial products). However, members of the trading area are able to retain and arrange their own commercial policies with countries outside the area. Membership by the UK of EFTA, prior to membership of the European Economic Community (EEC) for example, enabled the UK to maintain Commonwealth preference.[1]

The customs-union principle by contrast requires commitment on the part of members to act in concert in commercial relations with third countries. In addition to eliminating intra-union trade restrictions, all members of a customs union apply common external tariffs on imports from non-members. In practice of course, special preferential arrangements may exist between members and third parties during an adjustment period, or between the union and another grouping. However, the general principle is that the customs union acts as a single body in global tariff negotiations.

The EEC is more than a customs union. By title it is an economic union or community, but as yet in practice it corresponds more closely to a common market. A common market extends the rules relating to the movement of goods and services, to the movement of factors of production. Harmonisation of taxation, industrial, and social policies is sought in order to permit the free movement of labour and capital within the enlarged market. Such integration is likely to require geographical proximity. This is also the case for full economic union, not least because cultural differences are less likely to prevent political harmony. The economic union implies therefore a customs union, a common market, and the coordination of macroeconomic policies, including monetary and exchange-rate policies. (Monetary integration is considered in Chapter 6.)

Loss of national sovereignty over economic policy determination is only to be expected where a significant degree of political union has been achieved. The primary objective may indeed be political union, with economic union acting as the vehicle for that union. But as economists, our task must be to identify economic motives for removing trade restrictions on a regional basis or to examine the motives for what Pinder (1969) calls 'negative integration'. Positive integration or the active harmonisation of economic policies is more immediately a political issue. (See Tsoukalis, 1977, for the political consequences of integration.)

Second-best solutions?

What are the economic motives for countries considering customs-union membership, when they can achieve greater liberalisation of trade through non-preferential tariff reduction? Cooper and Massell (1965) show that from a 'free-trade viewpoint' a customs union is necessarily inferior to an appropriate policy of non-preferential protection. This is because the non-preferential restriction of trade at least maximises the **opportunities** for creating trade; and for obtaining goods therefore from the most efficient source of production globally.

Such reasoning assumes however that a non-preferential reduction of tariffs is necessarily viewed by policy-makers as an alternative to a customs union. We must remember why trade restrictions are in operation in the first place. We considered for instance in Chapter 2 the protective motive for the restriction of trade. If such motives remain relevant then the policy-maker may consider the impact of a customs union on the terms of trade, employment or industrial production[2] acceptable, but the impact of general tariff reduction on such variables as unacceptable.

By permitting customs-union participants to draw upon one another's markets, a customs union may make it possible for its members to maintain a protected domestic market at less sacrifice in income than is possible through non-preferential protection.
(Cooper and Massell (1965), reprinted in Robson (1972), p. 97)

If this is the case then it is legitimate to assess the desirability of a move from an initial position of non-preferential trade restriction to a 'restricted' free-trade situation. However, the theory of second best (Lipsey and Lancaster (1956–57)) demonstrates that preferential tariff reduction, for instance, is not necessarily superior to maintaining the existing level of non-preferential trade restriction. Liberalising some, but not all, trade can result in welfare gains and losses. To identify the net welfare effects of customs-union formation therefore, we must describe the possible effects of preferential tariff reduction on the level and pattern of trade.

3.3 Trade creation and trade diversion

Our analysis of the impact of the formation of a customs union on volumes of domestic production and consumption will draw upon many of the tools of analysis developed in Chapter 2. As with non-discriminatory tariffs, we are interested in identifying changes in demand for and sources of supply of goods, corresponding to changes in import prices. With discriminatory tariffs, however, we are interested not only in changes from domestic to foreign sources of supply, but also in shifts between foreign supply sources. Viner (1950) distinguished in his pioneering work between the *trade-creating* and *trade-diverting* effects of customs-union formation. The former effect relates to the additional trade which results from the lowering of the price of importables to domestic consumers, and from the replacement of domestic supplies by lower-cost foreign supplies. The latter effect by contrast directs attention to the extent to which the union shifts the source of foreign supply from lower- to higher-cost sources of production.

We can illustrate this distinction by referring to Figs 3.1 and 3.2. In contrast to earlier analysis of the impact of tariffs, we need now to adopt a three-country model in order to demonstrate the discriminatory nature of commercial policy. We may assume that America and Canada are the countries contemplating forming a union, and that Britain is the lowest-cost producer, who like Canada is able to produce the importable (pottery) at constant costs. S_c and S_b are the supply curves of Canada and Britain respectively, while the demand and supply curves for America are represented by D_a and S_a.

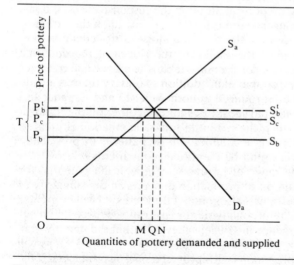

Fig. 3.1 A trade-creating customs union

In Fig. 3.1, the tariff imposed by America against imports from both Britain and Canada is initially totally prohibitive. It raises Britain's supply curve to S_b^t, such that at price P_b^t, OQ is consumed and produced domestically. (Pottery from Canada is also excluded from the American market since the price of such imports with a tariff applied would exceed P_b^t.) From a situation of zero imports, the liberalising of trade between America and Canada through the formation of a customs union can only have trade-creating effects. Provided that the common external tariff imposed by America and Canada against pottery imports from Britain is greater than the price difference between Canada and Britain (i.e. $P_c - P_b$), then trade between the customs-union members will be created. In the absence of tariff restrictions on imports from Canada, the price to the American consumer will fall to P_c. Domestic consumption will increase to ON; of which domestic producers can only supply OM at this lower price. The gap between domestic demand and supply will be filled by imports (MN) from Canada. Such trade created is composed therefore of two elements: the production effect, i.e. the fall in domestic production (MQ), and the consumption effect, i.e. the rise in domestic consumption (QN). Since Viner concentrated only on the production effects of customs-union formation, some commentators describe only the production effect (i.e. the replacement of less efficient production by imports) as pure trade creation. Cooper and Massell (1965) in fact describe the combined pure trade creation and consumption effects as the tariff-reduction effect (the distinction is one of definition alone).

What factors will influence the trade-creating effects of a customs union? From Fig. 3.1 it is clear that the size of the production and consumption effects are dependent upon the responsiveness of domestic suppliers and consumers to price change, and upon the extent of the price fall produced by the discriminatory tariff reduction (i.e. $P_b^t - P_c$). *Ceteris paribus*, the shallower the slopes of the domestic demand and supply *curves* for the importable, the more trade created.[3] Thus in terms of our example, if in addition to pottery there is a wide range of goods that are produced in both America and Canada, and that are therefore potential substitutes for each other on the removal of trade restriction, then the potential for trade creation is greater. Such rival or competitive economies, whose patterns of production overlap considerably, would be identified by high cross-elasticity of demand over a wide range of products. Although the potential for inter-country substitution of production depends on the similarity of industrial structures, the actual amount of trade created will be greater the more dissimilar are productivities or cost ratios between member countries. The divergence in efficiency levels within the union will in fact influence the extent of the price fall ($P_b^t - P_c$ in Fig. 3.1), as will the extent to which pre-union tariffs protect domestic producers. If the initial tariff (T) in Fig. 3.1 had been lower for instance, then some trade would have existed before union formation. The lower are pre-union tariffs, the smaller is the opportunity for trade creation. Similarly, the more that Canada's price (P_c) moves towards P_b (the lowest-cost supply), the more trade will be created by discriminatory tariff reduction. It follows therefore that the larger the union, the more likely it is to be a trade-creating union, because it is more likely that the lowest-cost producer in the world will be within the union.

What conclusions would we reach by contrast if the lowest-cost producer for a particular good was consistently outside the union? If we assume that with a non-discriminatory tariff a country satisfies some of its consumption needs with imports from the lowest-cost supply, then the application of discriminatory commercial policy is likely to bring about trade diversion. Such a situation is represented in Fig. 3.2. Again in this example America initially imposes a tariff on imports from both Britain and Canada. The tariff-distorted supply curve of Britain is S_b^t, and the lowest import price to American consumers is P_b^t. At P_b^t, however, domestic producers can only supply OM of pottery, and so pottery imports from Britain are MN. (Again the tariff excludes Canadian pottery from the American market.) If America and Canada now form a customs union, and exclude Britain from the American market by imposing a common external tariff in **excess** of $P_c - P_b$, i.e. the non-distorted cost difference between Canadian and British pottery exports, then all America's imports would be diverted from Britain to Canada. In these new circumstances Canada becomes the cheapest supply source, i.e. S_c. At price P_c domestic production and consumption remain unaltered, and no additional trade is generated by discriminatory tariff reduction. The source of the imports has shifted, however, from the lowest-cost producer in the world (Britain) to the lowest-cost producer within the union (Canada).

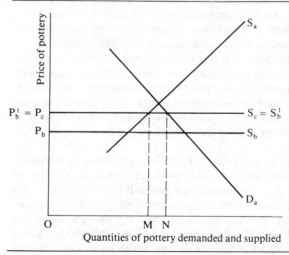

Fig. 3.2 A trade-diverting customs union

The degree of trade diversion generated by a customs union depends therefore upon the amount of trade with the non-union member (Britain) before union formation, and upon the size of the common external tariff applied by the union.[4] As we have already noted, the larger the union the greater the chance that the lowest-cost producer will be within the union, and therefore the less the likelihood of trade diversion. On the other hand, if the cheapest producer remains outside the union, the lower the common external tariff (CET) applied by the union, the smaller will be the trade diversion. In our example, if the CET had been less than the cost difference between British and Canadian pottery (i.e. less than $P_c - P_b$) then no trade would have been diverted from the lowest-cost producer (Britain). Indeed, a CET of less than $P_c - P_b$ would have generated additional trade.

3.4 The costs and benefits of customs-union formation

We have identified then, with the aid of partial equilibrium analysis, the possible immediate trade effects of customs-union formation. On the basis of this analysis we are in a position to make some assessment or evaluation of the desirability of discriminatory tariff policies, which in practice are likely to have both trade-creating and trade-diverting effects. We need now to attach costs and benefits to these trade effects, and ultimately to secondary terms of trade and dynamic effects.

Production and consumption effects
Viner (1950) concentrated on the production effects of customs-union formation. On the basis of economic criteria for allocative efficiency, trade creation was viewed as 'good', and trade diversion as 'bad'. Trade creation generated the opportunity cost benefits to be derived from obtaining imports at lower cost. Domestic resources could as a result be released to activities of relative cost advantage. By contrast, trade diversion reduced the efficiency with which resources were used, since it shifted production away from lower- to higher-cost producers. Viner's prescription was quite simple. If trade creation exceeded trade diversion there was a net welfare improvement. The production gains of trade creation exceeded the production losses of trade diversion, since the customs union moved the countries closer to the first-best solution, free trade.

This analysis is, however, subject to the important limitation that it abstracts from any consumption effects brought about by changes in the price of imported goods, in absolute and relative terms. The only way in fact in which we can abstract from consumption effects if prices change is to assume that the demand curve for the importable is perfectly inelastic. In Fig. 3.3 for example, the discriminatory removal of the tariff on imports of pottery from one of the equal-cost sources, say Canada, will result in all the domestic production being replaced by imports (OM) from Canada. The fall in price to American consumers from P_a to P_c does not have any effect on consumption. In other words there are no income and substitution effects to such a price change. Viner's conclusions are therefore incomplete since even in partial terms they ignore the fact that any fall in the price of an importable will usually result in a rise in consumption of that particular good. Indeed, we will demonstrate later that within a general equilibrium framework there is also likely to be a consumption effect from trade diversion, if the price of imports to consumers falls. Changes in relative prices are likely to bring about changes in consumption patterns, as imported goods are substituted for domestically produced goods. This total effect on consumption must be compared with the production effects.

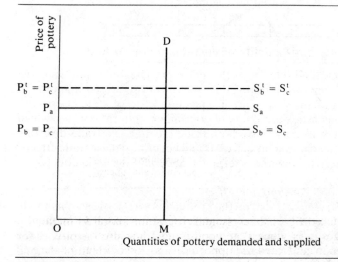

Fig. 3.3 The production effect of trade creation

Meade (1955) changed the emphasis of the assessment since he was concerned in particular with the impact of a customs union on consumption. He was aware that by changing relative prices, a customs union will change demand both within a country and between countries. Thus trade creation is brought about by the substitution of low-cost foreign supplies for domestic production, and by the increase in real income generated by a fall in import prices. Similarly, we have suggested that trade diversion may cause substitution in consumption. Such substitution effects cannot be identified within a partial equilibrium framework. We cannot show the impact of substitution on the overall pattern of consumption, only the effect on the importable good itself. In Fig. 3.4, with a tariff applied to imports from both Britain and Canada, America will import MN of pottery from Britain. (At price P_b^t domestic consumption will be ON and domestic production OM). As should now be apparent, the formation of a union between America and Canada, accompanied by a continuation of the existing tariff against imports from Britain, will result in both trade creation and trade diversion. The price of pottery will fall to P$_c$. The result will be a rise in consumption in America to OP and a fall in domestic production to OL. Imports rise therefore to LP, and MN is diverted from Britain to Canada. LM and NP represent the additional imports of pottery (also from Britain to Canada).

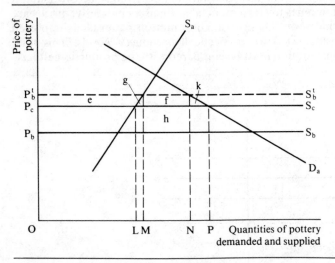

Fig. 3.4 A trade-creating and diverting customs union

We can make a partial assessment of customs-union formation by using changes in producers' and consumers' surpluses as proxies for the production and consumption gains and losses (Humphrey and Ferguson, 1960). The fall in price to consumers from P$_{bt}$ to P$_c$ increases consumers' surplus by the area (e + g + f + k). However, producers' surplus falls by the area (e), and tariff revenue by the area (f + h). The net welfare impact of union formation, using this method of measurement, is therefore (e + g + f + k) minus (e + f + h); in other words the area (g + k − h). The area (g) is the production benefit, and the area (k) the consumption benefit of trade creation,[5] whilst area (h) is the production loss from diverting imports to a higher-cost source. In other words (h) represents the additional resource cost of obtaining pottery imports from Canada rather than from Britain. Although prior to the union American consumers paid the full resource cost of Britain's pottery exports plus the tariff levy, we may assume that the tariff revenue collected by the government was returned to consumers in some way. (Any redistributional effects are ignored.)

If (h) is greater than (g + k) and trade diversion predominates, then this analysis proscribes that customs-union formation will reduce economic welfare.[6] It has been suggested, however, that the analysis is incomplete. We need to examine the general, rather than partial, effects of price changes on production and consumption.

General equilibrium models

Rather than using the term 'production and consumption effects', Lipsey (1960) prefers to identify substitution effects of customs-union formation; substitution, that is, between countries and between commodities. This inter-country and inter-commodity substitution is brought about by several different and interdependent types of consumption and production effects. Once in fact we consider the impact of substitutions produced by changes in relative prices, then we may wish to amend our initial assessment of the costs and benefits of customs-union formation.

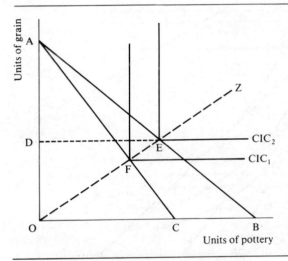

Fig. 3.5 Trade diversion with fixed consumption patterns

Lipsey (1960) has shown that Viner's presumption that trade diversion lowers welfare relies on the assumption that consumption patterns remain **unaltered** after the union is established. The argument is illustrated by Fig. 3.5. If we assume complete specialisation, then America produces OA of grain and imports pottery from the lowest-cost producer, Britain. The slope of AB represents the terms of trade offered by Britain to America. The application of a tariff by America on imports from Britain is assumed not to be protective, or to alter the terms of trade. (This latter assumption can be justified for example if the American authorities redistribute any revenue raised by the tariff in the form of lump-sum transfers.) If America's consumption pattern is depicted by point E, then America consumes OD of grain and DE of imported pottery. These imports are received in exchange for DA of grain exports to Britain. Should America now form a customs union with a higher-cost producer (Canada), the terms of trade would shift to AC. The common external tariff applied by America and Canada against British exports is now assumed to be protective. If the consumption pattern is to remain constant, that is to remain on the path OZ, then welfare must fall as a result of the diversion of trade from Britain and Canada. In Fig. 3.5 the reduced consumption of both grain and pottery by America at point F pushes the community's welfare down from CIC_2 to CIC_1.

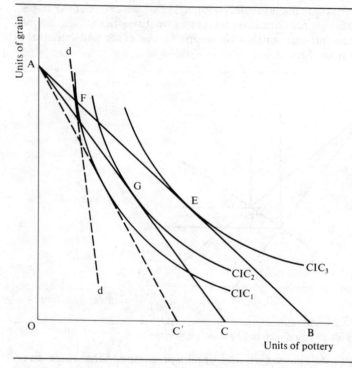

Fig. 3.6 Trade diversion with variable consumption patterns

Once we relax the assumption that consumption patterns remain unaltered and consider a **variable** consumption model, then the conclusions may well differ. Again using Lipsey's methodology we can show, with the aid of Fig. 3.6, that trade diversion can in fact raise rather than lower welfare. The tangency position E is the free-trade equilibrium. America again specialises completely in the production of grain, which it exchanges for pottery from Britain. The imposition of a tariff on pottery imports, which is now protective, affects also domestic prices in America. The domestic price ratio (dd) diverges from the international price ratio (AB). Increased domestic pottery prices reduce pottery consumption in America, and stimulate grain consumption. The tariff-distorted equilibrium is therefore at point F, where the domestic price line cuts the international price line, since domestic consumption is constrained by what America can obtain through trade with Britain. Understandably, the tariff-distorted equilibrium (F) is at a lower level of welfare than the free-trade equilibrium (E), i.e. on CIC_1 rather than CIC_3. The formation of a customs union, however, between America and Canada, a higher-cost producer of pottery, will move the international terms of trade from AB. If for example the intra-union terms of trade are represented by AC, then the source of pottery imports will shift to Canada. In these circumstances equilibrium is at G, which provides a higher level of welfare (CIC_2) than does tariff-distorted trade with Britain (point F on CIC_1). The reduction in import prices of pottery to consumers in America (the domestic price of imports from Canada is less than the tariff-inclusive price of imports from Britain) permits substitution of pottery for grain. Thus the favourable substitution effects of trade diversion on consumption can compensate for the unfavourable production effects. Of course, if the terms of trade (AC) between America and Canada were to move further away from AB, then it is possible that welfare would fall below the level CIC_1. In Fig. 3.6 a deterioration in the intra-union terms of trade beyond AC' would place America on a lower level of welfare, after the formation of the union, i.e. on a lower indifference curve than CIC_1.[7]

We have demonstrated therefore that the presumption that trade diversion lowers welfare is unjustified, once we are able to examine the effects of changes in the relative price of imported and domestically produced goods. If we look back to the partial analysis of Fig. 3.4 we can see that discriminatory tariff removal reduced the price of pottery imports from P_b^t to P_c. We had no means at that stage of assessing the income and substitution effects of that price change on the consumption of both pottery and grain. Our subsequent general equilibrium analysis has shown, however, that the net effect of such relative price changes may be to raise, lower, or leave unaltered the community's welfare.

Of course, if there is no change in import prices following customs-union formation then trade diversion will not produce any offsetting consumption gains through substitution. This rather unusual situation was depicted in Fig. 3.2. If discriminatory tariff removal leaves prices unaltered then there is no *a priori* reason why the source of imports should change, unless there is union preference, or as in Fig. 3.2 we assume that the tariff applied against non-members is raised after the union is formed. In terms of our general equilibrium analysis in Fig. 3.6, this rather exceptional situation would be produced when the intra-union price line (AC) was parallel to the pre-union domestic price line (dd). This would require the terms of trade offered by Canada to America to move further inwards from AC'. Customs-union formation clearly reduces welfare in these conditions because trade diversion involves only a production loss, produced by the shift from a lower- to a higher-cost supply source.

Terms-of-trade effects

So far the analysis has not been fully general equilibrium in its approach. We have varied consumption and production in isolation. In order to simultaneously vary production and consumption we need to apply our offer-curve techniques. If we can represent an equilibrium situation between three countries for two goods, then it will be possible to examine the total effect of the union on trade volumes and the terms of trade; the terms of trade, that is, between union members and between the union and the rest of the world.

Vanek (1965) has provided a means of analysing customs-union formation with offer-curve techniques. He overcame the problem of representing the union's offer relationship with the rest of the world by constructing an *excess offer curve* for the union. It is a net offer curve for the potential union, i.e. the quantities that America and Canada acting jointly in trade would be prepared to exchange for goods from Britain. Derivation of an excess offer curve is demonstrated in Fig. 3.7.

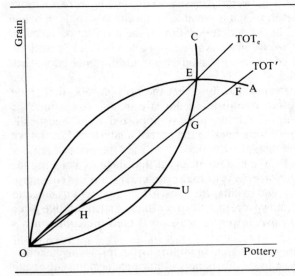

Fig. 3.7 Derivation of the excess offer curve

The offers between America and Canada are represented by the curves OA and OC respectively. For example, OA represents America's offer of its exportable grain to Canada. In equilibrium, the terms of trade TOT$_e$ between America and Canada are such that trade between the two countries is in balance. In other words there is no excess offer by either country, and the excess offer curve will pass through the origin when the equilibrium terms of trade are achieved. If, however, the terms of trade shift to TOT′, then trade between America and Canada is no longer in balance. When translated to the grain axis, the distance GF represents the excess offer of grain for pottery. In other words America's offer of grain exceeds Canada's demand for it. The line GF is equivalent to a point H on the excess offer curve (OU), where the distance OH equals the distance GF. The excess offer curve in fact identifies all America's, or rather the potential union's, excess offers of grain, for all terms-of-trade lines which are shallower than TOT$_e$. (Of course, we could also construct the union's excess offer curve for pottery, if terms-of-trade lines with steeper slopes than TOT$_e$ were considered).

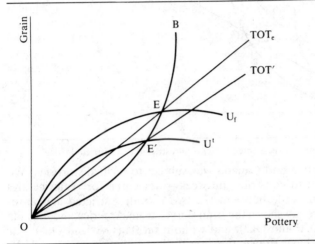

Fig. 3.8 The 'restricted' free-trade equilibrium

We can illustrate the effects of customs-union formation on the union's external trade with the help of Fig. 3.8. OU$_f$ is the excess offer curve of America and Canada acting jointly in trade, and with unrestricted trade between each other. OB represents Britain's offer of pottery to America and Canada. Thus we are able to identify the price ratio or terms of trade TOT$_e$ which clears the markets for both grain and pottery in all three countries, with unrestricted trade. Trade between the potential union and Britain is balanced at equilibrium point E. However, with the establishment of a customs union between America and Canada, a common external tariff will be applied against imports of pottery from non-union member Britain. Our earlier analysis of tariffs has shown that this will shift the union's excess offer curve from OU$_f$ to OU^t.[8] The restricted trade equilibrium will now shift to E'. The terms of trade shift as a result in the union's favour, i.e. from TOT$_e$ to TOT', whilst the volume of trade between the union and Britain is reduced. The extent of such trade diversion to within the union is, as we have seen earlier, dependent on the size of the union's external tariff.

To illustrate the effects of union formation more precisely, however, it would be more plausible to assume that prior to the union, trade

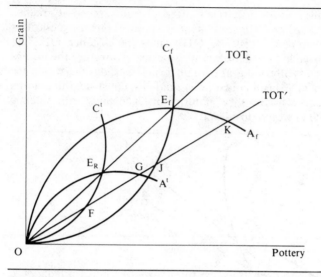

Fig. 3.9 Derivation of excess offer curves – unrestricted and restricted trade

between America and Canada was subject to tariff distortions. We need therefore to construct an excess offer curve for America and Canada, where trade between the two is both restricted and unrestricted. Figure 3.9 shows the offer curves from America and Canada with tariffs (OA^t and OC^t), and without tariffs (OA$_f$ and OC$_f$). For simplicity we have drawn the free-trade equilibrium (E$_f$) and the restricted-trade equilibrium (E$_R$) so that the terms of trade remain unaltered at TOT$_e$. Both excess offer curves, again for grain, can therefore be constructed by shifting the price line towards TOT$'$ and beyond. Hopefully the relative positions of the unrestricted and restricted excess offer curves (OU$_f$ and OU$_R$ respectively in Fig. 3.10) can be intuitively appreciated by considering the excess offers with the terms of trade at TOT$'$ in Fig. 3.9. At price line TOT$'$ the unrestricted excess offer of pottery is represented by the line JK, while the restricted excess offer is represented by the line FG. The distance JK is greater than FG, as are the corresponding distances on the grain axis. In other words, tariff restriction reduces the quantities of exportables offered for trade, and therefore it reduces also the net or excess offers at any particular terms of trade.[9] As a result the restricted excess offer curve (OU$_R$) of America and Canada is below the unrestricted excess offer curve (OU$_f$) in Fig. 3.10.

Figure 3.10 provides a summary of the possible terms-of-trade effects of customs-union formation. Since OU$_t$ is the union's excess offer curve with a common external tariff applied against imports of pottery from Britain, Fig. 3.10 represents a deterioration in Britain's terms of trade from TOT$''$ to TOT$'$ following union formation. If, however, the common external tariff were smaller and/or the pre-

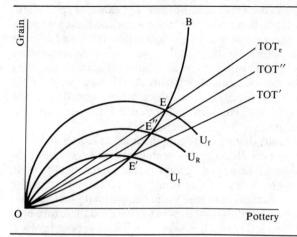

Fig. 3.10 Terms-of-trade effects of customs-union formation

union tariffs imposed on trade between America and Canada were larger, then the excess offer curve OU_t could be above OU_R.[10] In this instance Britain's terms of trade would improve as a result of union formation.

The freeing of trade between the union members has the effect of shifting the intra-union terms of trade against the country whose exportable is in excess offer, or alternatively in favour of that country whose exportable displaces within the union imports from outside the union. In Fig. 3.10 the intra-union terms of trade shift from TOT'' to TOT_e. Canada benefits from the movement in intra-union terms of trade since it is able to obtain more grain from America for a given quantity of pottery. From the American viewpoint this terms-of-trade deterioration is compensated for by the expansion of her grain exports to Canada. These conclusions are, however, only tentative, since we have examined a situation in which the rest of the world, or Britain, imported only America's exportable grain. We could for instance assume that Canada's exportable pottery is also in excess supply, and that Britain offered grain in exchange for this pottery. To complete our analysis, we would need to consider the impact of union formation on the simultaneous exchange of both grain and pottery between the union and the rest of the world.

The dynamic consequences
Thus far we have examined only the static trade effects of customs-union formation. We need also to consider the less easily quantifiable but equally important issues relating to the dynamic consequences of customs-union formation. If the growth of production was to increase as a result of changes in the underlying conditions, then it may be the case that these dynamic benefits to individual member countries, the

union and the rest of the world could offset, for example, any static costs produced by trade diversion. We are concerned therefore with identifying the impact of customs-union formation on scales of production and market concentration, and in turn with the impact of changes in these economic variables on investment, technical progress and therefore on the rate of economic growth. At this stage we can only seek to rehearse some of the arguments, since precise conclusions are too difficult to reach. We will turn in Section 3.5 to some specific case-study illustrations.

Balassa (1961) claims that by enlarging the market facing domestic producers, increased opportunities for economies of large-scale production will be created. The opposing view is that increasing the scale of production does not necessarily produce any economies. Existing domestic and export markets may mean that the optimal plant size has already been achieved. Further increases in scale would therefore only result in internal and external diseconomies. In any case, even if potential economies exist, language and institutional differences may place a constraint on the extent to which advantage is taken of this opportunity. If advantage is taken of this opportunity, however, then it is possible to identify potential positive effects on the rate of economic growth. Increasing the scale of production will of itself necessitate increased expenditure on plant and equipment; albeit a once-and-for-all increase in investment expenditure. Genuine ongoing dynamic benefits may however accrue if increased scale reduces uncertainty, increases expectations of market outlets and permanently raises as a result the rate of investment. Rationalisation may also permit and encourage larger expenditure by firms on research and development (R and D), and economies in research. Whether increased R and D expenditure produces more rapid innovation, and therefore growth, is less certain. The empirical evidence is far from conclusive.

Conflicting sentiments can similarly be expressed about the effect of a customs union on competitiveness and of competitiveness upon economic growth. Although enlarging the market facing domestic producers by removing tariff barriers on intra-union trade may encourage rationalisation and a reduction in the number of producers within the union, the end-product may be an intensification of competition. This will be the case when domestic or national monopolists effectively become oligopolists within the enlarged market, and face competition from other, previously national monopolies. Scitovsky (1958) argued that such increases in effective competition would bring about domestic reorganisation, and raise productive and allocative efficiency. Psychological changes brought about by the shift towards more impersonalised competition across national barriers would, for example, reduce domestic monopolies and national governments' tolerance of smaller, less efficient firms. Correspondingly, when faced with less secure domestic markets, domestic producers may be more aggressive in their search for new products and new market outlets.

The extent, of course, to which such competitive effects or increased rivalry are sustained after the initial period of intra-union trade liberalisation, would be dependent upon how firms reacted to these new oligopolistic market structures. Market conduct cannot simply be predicted from market structure. The student of industrial economics will be well aware that oligopoly is not always typified by rivalry.

A competitive effect is in any case only dynamically beneficial if it results in a permanently higher rate of investment and/or technical progress. Competition is traditionally seen as providing the optimal environment for stimulating the search for cost reduction through new investment and innovation. Alternatively, one may argue that increased competition erodes returns on investment and reduces the incentive to innovate therefore. Unequivocal theorising about market structure, conduct and performance is not in fact possible. (For a fuller discussion of these issues, see Scherer, 1970). A consideration of some of the empirical evidence may or may not help. The presumption remains nevertheless that both increased competition and rationalisation are desirable, and reconcilable, and achievable by customs-union formation. This presumption is based in turn, however, on the assumption that the customs union is trade-creating. If preferential tariff reduction was by contrast to divert trade consistently to single monopoly sources within the union, then domestic monopolies would become union monopolies! It is to a consideration of the practical evidence of trade creation and diversion that we now turn.

3.5 Some empirical evidence

Most of the empirical work on the effects of customs-union formation is of an *ex post* nature.[11] In other words, it attempts to measure the actual changes that have taken place since the customs union was established. But since *ceteris paribus* conditions are unlikely to apply, then the problem is one of isolating the specific trade effects of integration. As Waelbroeck argues:

Measuring the effect of integration necessitates the construction of such a fictitious anti-monde, which represents what the world economy would be like if obstacles to trade had not been removed.
(Waelbroeck (1976), in Machlup (ed.), p. 90)

The other things that are likely to influence trade flows, and which need therefore to be eliminated in our calculations, are the impact of global tariff reductions or changes in the growth and structure of the world economy. As we shall see, the alternative methods of measurement achieve this separation of 'non-union' effects to a greater or lesser extent.

Interpretation of the 'union effect' is not in itself without difficulties. On the one hand there is the problem of estimating what part of the additional intra-union trade generated (what Balassa, (1967b) describes as 'gross trade creation') is due to trade creation and trade diversion in the sense of these terms as used in customs-union theory. On the other, the establishment of a common external tariff by union members may well require some members to raise, and others to lower their existing tariffs against non-members. Where the CET is lower than the pre-union tariff there may be some additional trade generated between the union and the non-member countries. Balassa (1967b) describes this 'union effect' as 'external trade creation'.

Alternative methods of measurement
The methods of *ex post* measurement can be classified under the headings of residual imputation or of structural modelling. In the case of the former method, the effect of integration is seen as the residual or difference between the actual level of trade and the projected level in the absence of integration. The control to which the actual situation is usually compared is the pre-integration period, on the assumption that the market share of imports, or import elasticities, would have remained stable in the absence of integration. By contrast, structural models seek to directly specify the variables determining production and trade, and to directly measure the effects of integration.

For a fuller survey of the various methods of measurement based on the analysis of market shares, see Williamson and Bottrill (1971). In general the early attempts at share analysis (Major, 1962) merely compared changes in the proportions of intra- and extra-union imports in the total imports of the integrating bloc. The method identifies only gross trade creation; and it is also doubtful whether other possible influences on market shares will have been neutralised. A rise in the proportion of intra-union trade in the union's total trade could for example be accounted for by the increasing importance of the union in world markets, or by an improvement in the competitive position of the union.

To overcome this problem Lamfalussy (1963) suggests that we may assume that all non-members would have changed their share of the union market by the same proportion as they did in third markets. Alternatively, we may extrapolate the rate of change of the share of imports in domestic demand from the pre-integration period. This approach has been used by the EFTA Secretariat (1969) to estimate the effects of EFTA on its members' trade. Import shares were extrapolated from information on the 1954–58 period for the 1959–65 period. An excess of actual over projected *intra*-union imports was interpreted as evidence of trade creation, while an excess of projected over actual *extra*-union imports was interpreted as trade diversion.

Subsequently the EFTA Secretariat (1972) have applied the same technique to analyse the trade effects of both EFTA and the EEC over the period 1959–67. A summary of the results from EFTA for 1967 is presented in Table 3.1 with estimates of trade creation and diversion

Table 3.1 Estimates of trade creation and trade diversion in EFTA (1967)

	Trade creation (million $)	Trade diversion (million $)
(a) By country		
Austria	89	62
Denmark	259	178
Finland	32	96
Norway	202	108
Portugal	18	14
Sweden	233	265
Switzerland	147	47
UK	309	145
(b) By commodity		
Leather, footwear, rubber	68	20
Wood and paper products	264	121
Textiles and clothing	298	194
Chemicals and petroleum products	56	127
Non-metallic mineral manufactures	16	15
Metals and metal manufactures	209	96
Machinery	276	164
Land transport equipment	49	76
Watches, clocks and instruments	3	30
Miscellaneous	49	72
Total	1 289	915

Source: EFTA Secretariat (1972), from Tables 6 and 11, pp. 26 and 38

provided on a country and commodity basis. The total 'EFTA effect' on intra-area trade in 1967 was estimated to be $2 204 million, of which as in earlier years, about 60 per cent was estimated to be created trade. Over three-quarters of this additional trade was however concentrated on Denmark, Norway, Sweden and the UK, and in certain commodity groups. Rivalry between these countries in textiles, wood and paper products, metals and machinery, as predicted by the theory, appeared to have brought about greater intra-industry specialisation. Similarly, the evidence of trade diversion in excess of trade creation in chemicals and petroleum products and land transport equipment can be explained in terms of our earlier theoretical analysis. Production of chemicals was concentrated within EFTA in the UK and Switzerland, and of vehicles in the UK and Sweden. Given a lack of rivalry and of similarity of industrial structures, trade diversion was likely to be produced.

The dissimilarity of industrial structures within EFTA at that point in time is consistent with Williamson and Bottrill's conclusion, that the EFTA study had understated the trade-diverting 'EFTA effect'. They argue that the 1954–59 period witnessed exceptionally rapid trade expansion in Europe, and linear extrapolation from this period produces an overestimate of the import shares that would have occurred in the absence of EFTA formation. Williamson and Bottrill (1971) in fact claim that a preferable control for the hypothetical market shares is not the pre-integration period, but share performance in third markets. Their revised estimates for EFTA on this basis are $900 million of trade creation, and $1 100 million of trade diversion in 1967.

Williamson and Bottrill's results for the EEC, using the same method, are, however, more optimistic. Their results, using the more conservative assumptions, are summarised in Table 3.2 for the period 1961–69. The net trade-creating nature of the EEC is also substantiated by Balassa (1967b). Balassa reaches this conclusion, however, on the basis of an investigation of income elasticities for imports pre- and post-integration. He assumes that the income elasticity of import demand would remain unaltered in the absence of integration, and that changes in these income elasticity values are therefore induced by integration.[12] In his study he contrasts the income elasticity for imports

Table 3.2 Estimates of trade creation and trade diversion for the EEC, 1961–9

Year	Trade creation (million $)	Trade diversion (million $)
1961	100	100
1962	600	300
1963	1 400	700
1964	2 200	1 100
1965	2 900	1 400
1966	3 500	1 700
1967	3 500	1 700
1968	4 400	2 200
1969	6 400	3 200

Source: Williamson and Bottrill (1971), adapted from Table III, p. 338

Table 3.3 Changes* in income elasticities of import demand for the EEC

Income elasticities for:			
Commodity:	(A) Total imports	(B) Intra-area imports	(C) Extra-area imports
Non-tropical food, beverage and tobacco	−0.1	−0.1	−0.2
Raw materials	0.0	0.0	−0.1
Fuels	+0.7	+0.2	+0.7
Chemicals	+0.3	+1.0	−0.3
Machinery	+1.3	+1.0	+1.6
Transport equipment	+0.8	+0.9	+0.2
Other manufactured goods	−0.1	+0.1	−0.6
Total	+0.3	+0.4	+0.1

*In averages for the 1953–9 and 1959–65 periods
Source: from Balassa (1967b), Table 1

on intra- and extra-union trade for the pre-union period (1953–59) with that of the post-union period (1959–65). A summary of Balassa's results is set out in Table 3.3.

The aggregate evidence in Table 3.3 points to the trade-creating nature of the EEC for the period covered. The presumption is that the rise in income elasticity for intra-area imports is indicative of gross trade creation (i.e. trade creation and/or trade diversion). But since the income elasticity for imports from outside the EEC did not fall, then the EEC is seen in these terms as trade-creating. There are, however, several commodity groups which appear to have been influenced by trade diversion. This is indicated by the fall in income elasticity for food, raw materials, chemicals and other manufactures. In the case of certain categories of food it may be due to the Common Agricultural Policy, but the effect is small as it is for raw materials. In fact semi-manufactures and non-durable consumer goods (included in other manufactures) are the only area of manufacture in which establishment of the EEC appears to have produced trade diversion. This appears to have been offset, however, by other commodities for which there has been substantial 'external trade creation'. The income elasticity for fuel imports from outside the EEC rose substantially for example, due presumably to the policy shift in favour of oil imports from the LDCs in place of higher-cost domestic supplies of coal. The rise in machinery imports from outside the EEC is less easily explained. (The income elasticity for extra-area machinery imports rose by 1.6.) Balassa suggests that this may be explained by capacity deficiencies within the EEC in the face of the investment boom precipitated by EEC formation.

Balassa's results probably give an incomplete picture of the impact of the EEC, since they cover the adjustment period after formation of the customs union. Internal tariffs were reduced in stages during this period, and by 1965 they still stood at 30 per cent of pre-union levels. There have been further internal tariff reductions and additions to the community since, which are likely to have had further trade-creating and diverting effects. Table 3.2 confirmed this expectation for the years up to 1969. However, with all the methods of measurement based upon residual imputation, the uncertainty remains as to whether or not other factors besides integration have accounted for some of the divergence between expected and actual values. As a result we have witnessed in recent years the application of econometric techniques to the modelling of trade flows. A consideration of this methodology is beyond the scope of this book. Nevertheless, the more advanced student may wish to research further into some of the more advanced empirical work (for example, Balassa, 1974).

Measuring welfare gains
The varying estimates of the trade effects of integration are not usually insubstantial. However, when we attempt to translate these trade

effects into income or welfare terms, the impact of integration seems less significant. If we accept the validity of our basic model of trade determination, then it is possible to try to attach values to the welfare triangles generated by tariff reduction. These triangles are the changes in producers' and consumers' surplus generated by changes in domestic prices following trade liberalisation. Johnson (1958a) argues that the gain from trade creation will approximately equal the change in the value of imports multiplied by half of the tariff rate previously levied. If we take, for instance, the estimate of trade creation within the EEC in 1969 from Table 3.2 and multiply it by half of the average pre-EEC tariff of 12 per cent, then the estimated welfare effect of trade creation in that year is $(6 400 \times 0.12 \times 0.5)$ million, i.e. $380 million. From this value we would also need to subtract the cost of trade diversion. The quantitative welfare effects of integration would therefore appear relatively small. Even if we wish to revise the estimates to take account of more than the static trade-creating effects of integration, then the presumption is usually that the net effect of EEC formation is still equivalent to less than 1 per cent of the members' combined GNP. Balassa (Balassa *et al.*, 1974) confirms this valuation despite including various dynamic effects in his estimate, such as the return on increased scales, the impact of integration on investment, and the secondary effects of increased growth. (It must be remembered though that preferential tariff reduction may be sought for other than income reasons.)

Of course the dynamic effects could be greater than the empirical work suggests. The effects of integration on psychological barriers to productivity increase are difficult to ascertain. The subjective support from this viewpoint is not particularly strong, however; not, that is, in the case of Western Europe. Unfortunately the bulk of the empirical work is concerned with this one particular grouping. It may indeed be the case that the effects of integration are more substantial where the membership is different. The post-war performance of the 'COMECON'[13] countries may for instance be explained by the greater compatibility of integration with planned socialist systems. The similarity of members socio-political structures may for example produce a more rapid reduction in the psychological barriers to productivity growth. The very rapid growth of inter-COMECON trade and of members' national incomes during the post-war period, at least provides some justification for this type of conjecture. (For a fuller consideration see Kaser, 1967.)

The impact of commercial policy decisions may also be much more significant in the case of integration between less-developed countries. Our discussion of effective protection in Chapter 2 demonstrated the extent and consequences of the LDCs autarkic strategies. The LDCs are likely, however, to be more concerned with the impact of integration on the opportunities for industrial growth and diversification, than with the traditional welfare effects of trade creation and diversion. The debate in this area is in fact controversial, but the controversy in itself suggests that much larger costs and benefits (than appears to be the case in developed countries) rest on the adoption of correct trade strategies by developing countries.

It is to a consideration of trade, growth and development, or under-development that we now turn to in Chapter 4. We will therefore return to the issue of economic integration amongst less-developed countries again.

Notes

1. See Swann (1970) Ch. 1 for a consideration of post-war integration trends in Western Europe.
2. Johnson (1965b) develops a theory of protectionism and customs-union formation based on countries' preferences for industrial production rather than real income.
3. In this instance we are concerned with the slopes of the demand and supply curves, rather than with the price elasticities of demand and supply. Although slope and elasticity are **not** equivalent, for a given range of prices a shallower demand curve indicates, *ceteris paribus,* **greater** price elasticity of demand.
4. If our model was less partial, the amount of trade diversion would also depend upon the commercial policies applied by non-members against exports of the union.
5. In partial terms the area (k) is clearly a consumption gain, but the total effect on consumption would depend on the substitution effects of the price fall.
6. This assessment is in national, union and global terms, because we have assumed that the rest of the world is able to supply pottery at constant costs. Changes in the level and origin of America's imports have no effect therefore on prices in Britain and Canada. Relaxing the constant-costs assumption complicates the assessment. Although trade creation remains desirable and trade diversion undesirable in production terms, customs-union formation is now likely to have consumption effects in both Britain and Canada. The reader may wish to consider these effects in the event of both increasing and decreasing costs.
7. Our conclusions are based on the two-good case. Gehrels (1956) has shown, however, that in the three-good case consumption effects are not *a priori* favour-able.
8. This assumes of course that Britain's offer curve is not perfectly elastic.
9. This assumes of course that the goods offered for trade are not 'Giffen' goods.
10. The result depends upon Canada's offer curve being sufficiently inelastic over a certain range of price ratios.
11. Balassa (1967b) distinguishes between *ex post* measurement and *ex ante* testing of integration theory.
12. Income elasticity of import demand was measured by the ratio of the average annual rate of change of imports to that of GNP.
13. 'COMECON' is a term frequently used to describe the Council for Mutual Economic Assistance (CMEA) established in 1949 to provide a framework for cooperation between the Soviet Union, Bulgaria, Czechoslovakia, Hungary, Poland and Romania. Subsequently the German Democratic Republic, Mongolia and Cuba have joined, whilst Albania has joined and left again.

Chapter 4

International trade and economic expansion

4.1 Introduction

We have now extended our H–O model from a simple analysis of the effects of differing factor endowments to take account of tariff distortions and economic integration. Throughout our analysis we assumed that neither of the economies in our two-country world expanded over time.

To take account of this possibility we must relax two further assumptions which have underpinned our model, namely given factor endowments and given factor productivities. Once we relax the former assumption we can analyse the effects on trade of population growth, capital accumulation, or land reclamation. Such factor accumulation must affect production and consumption possibilities and trading equilibria. Even where factor endowments are unchanged, production possibilities might still be altered as a result of changes in factor productivity, due perhaps to technological development.

The impact of economic growth on international trade, whether it be due to factor accumulation or technical progress, will form the initial point of focus of this chapter. We will remain largely within the framework so far developed to consider the consequences of economic growth for domestic production and consumption, exports and imports, and the international terms of trade. As we have already noted, this simply involves an elaboration of the framework so far developed. As such, it will entail extensive use of the theoretical tools with which we should by now be familiar.

In contrast, the latter half of the chapter will be much more policy-oriented. Here we will consider not the effects of economic growth on international trade, but rather the implications of international trade for economic growth. This is a question which is of crucial importance to the future development of the poorer countries of the world, and some would maintain, the very stability of the international economy. As we will see, some authorities argue that international trade provides the foremost avenue for development of the LDCs. To others, however, participation in international trade merely serves to constrain the development prospects of the LDCs.

4.2 The effects of economic growth on international trade

The development of trade theory to incorporate an analysis of the effects of economic expansion on trade has been very much a post-war phenomenon. An integral part of this development has been the attempt to simplify what is after all a very complicated process. This has largely been done by classifying 'types' of growth in accordance with their impact on trade flows. Thus, in a pioneering work Hicks referred to growth as being 'export biased', 'import biased' or 'neutral', depending on whether growth resulted in increased production of exportables, import substitutes, or a proportionate growth in both (Hicks, 1953).

Although Hicks's analysis was incomplete in several respects (not least because it focused almost entirely on the production effects of growth), it nevertheless provided the very solid foundations on which later theorists built. Johnson (1955 and 1959), Corden (1956), Bhagwati (1958), and Findlay and Grubert (1959) all made important contributions. Of these, Johnson's 1959 work has come to be most widely regarded as the standard source of reference, and provides the classification of growth types most often adhered to.

In the absence of complete specialisation, growth will affect production, consumption and the international terms of trade. We will now consider these effects in one country. Initially we will assume that the growing country (Britain) is too small for expansion to have any effect on international prices. In other words, we will hold the international terms of trade constant whilst examining production and consumption effects.

As before, relative factor endowments ensure that Britain enjoys a comparative advantage in the production of pottery. Prior to any economic expansion she is therefore incompletely specialised in pottery production, exchanging her surplus requirements for imports of grain from America.

Production effects

By definition, economic growth expands a country's production possibilities. In terms of Fig. 4.1, growth will result in a shift of the PPC outwards beyond PR. If initially Britain produces at point A where her PPC is tangential to the international terms of trade (T_1T_1) once growth has occurred her production possibilities will widen, so that it is now possible to reach a point of tangency with T_2T_2. (T_2T_2 is of course parallel to T_1T_1 in line with our assumption that growth in Britain leaves the terms of trade unaffected.) We can identify different production effects of growth, according to where precisely the point of tangency between the new PPC and T_2T_2 is located.

Suppose for example the production frontier expanded so that Britain's post-growth equilibrium was established at B. This shift is consistent with an increase in the rate of growth in the production of exportables (pottery) and importables, or import substitutes (grain) in exact proportion to the growth of total output. In these circumstances, we would say that growth has had a *neutral* production effect, because it leaves the country's overall output mix unaffected.

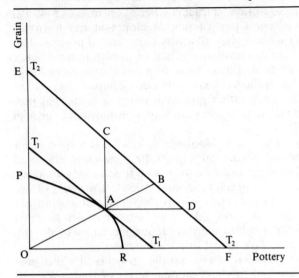

Fig. 4.1 Effects of growth on production

If, in contrast, growth facilitated the attainment of any point between B and C, although production of both commodities would increase, the increase in grain output would be proportionately greater than the increase in pottery production. If this were the case British dependence on imported grain would not expand in line with the rate of growth. In other words Britain would be becoming relatively more self-sufficient. For this reason this type of production effect is classified as *anti-trade biased* (ATB). Similarly, if the tangency between the PPC and the terms of trade line were in the range C–E, production of importables would not only increase faster than production of exportables, production of exportables would actually decline. Since such a production shift would not only reduce British dependence on imported grain (in absolute terms), but would also reduce the amount of pottery available for export, it is referred to as *ultra anti-trade biased* (UATB).

What about the opposite situation where increased pottery production outstripped any increased grain production, as for instance between points B and D? If anything, such a production shift would increase the amount of goods available to be traded, greater than in proportion to the rate of growth of output, and would therefore be referred to as a *pro-trade biased* effect (PTB). If growth were such that production of exportables increased whilst production of importables actually decreased, as at all points between D and F, the shift would be termed *ultra pro-trade biased* (UPTB). This is so because Britain has become absolutely less self-sufficient, and thereby more dependent on international trade.

Clearly the ultimate production bias depends on the rate of growth of the import substitute sector, relative to the rate of growth in real output. This responsiveness of the import substitute sector to growth of national output is gauged by the output elasticity of supply (i.e. the percentage change in the supply of import substitutes divided by the percentage change in output). As we will see presently the rate at which the import substitute sector expands relative to the rest of the economy is dependent primarily on the source(s) of growth.

Consumption effects
We can analyse consumption effects in analogous fashion to our consideration of production effects. Suppose initially Britain consumes the commodity bundle denoted by point G in Fig. 4.2; G being a point of tangency between an indifference curve (CIC₁) and the international price ratio (T₁T₁).

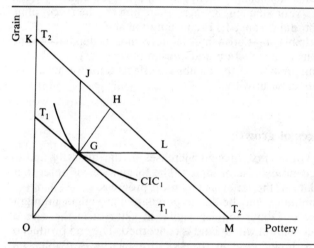

Fig. 4.2 Effects of growth on consumption

Now assume that economic growth facilitates the attainment of any commodity combination on the price line T_2T_2. Again we can classify our consumption shifts by reference to the eventual equilibrium established on T_2T_2. Thus, if point H were reached we would have a neutral consumption shift, since pottery and grain would be consumed in the same proportions after growth as before growth.

If, however, consumption settled somewhere between H and L, demand for pottery and grain would both be increasing but the demand for pottery would be increasing at a faster rate. Consequently, all equilibria in this range are ATB. Following on from this, we can readily see that consumption bundles between L and M represent UATB consumption shifts, because here growth results in an absolute decrease in the volume of importables (grain) demanded.

In the circumstances where increased consumption of grain exceeds any increased consumption of pottery (points H to J), we have a PTB consumption effect. To complete our classification, those points between J and K where demand for the exportable commodity actually decreases, whilst demand for importables increases, are consistent with an UPTB consumption effect.

The eventual equilibrium depends on the responsiveness of the demand for importables to changes in income. This, students will recognise as the income elasticity of demand for importables (i.e. the percentage change in the quantity of imports demanded, divided by the percentage change in income). Its value depends on the nature of the two commodities. If for example, grain is assumed to be an inferior good, then demand for grain will decrease as income increases (a negative income elasticity of demand), and we would have an UATB consumption shift in our above schema. If on the other hand we assumed that British consumers perceived grain to be a luxury good (income elasticity of demand greater than unity), then economic growth would stimulate an UPTB consumption shift.

The total trade bias that growth ultimately imparts depends on the relative strengths of production and consumption effects combined. We will defer an analysis of the combined effects until we have considered the sources of growth.

4.3 The sources of growth

Economic growth occurs through increases in the quantity and/or quality of the economy's factor inputs. The former we will refer to as factor accumulation, the latter as technical progress.

Factor accumulation may be due to population growth or immigration in the case of labour inputs; capital investment in the case of capital; and reclamation where land is concerned. The end product of any of these is an increase in the stock of factors available, and therefore in the potential for increased output.

Improvement in the quality of factors generally results in the same output being produced with fewer inputs, again resulting in the economy's potential capacity increasing. Improvement in the quality of factors, or 'technical progress' as it is generally termed, is often thought to apply to capital only. We must bear in mind, however, that labour can be 'improved' through education, and these improvements can make a significant contribution to the growth process. Indeed, one authority put the contribution of education to total growth at 23 per cent over a fairly lengthy period of time (Denison, 1962).

The question of the relative importance of factor accumulation and qualitative improvements is an interesting and important issue, both from a theoretical angle and a policy point of view. Unfortunately constraints on space do not permit us the luxury of such a digression.

Interested students are referred to Denison's momentous work (Denison, 1967), and Kennedy and Thirlwall's informative survey on technical progress (Kennedy and Thirlwall, 1972). Our main task at the moment is to ascertain what kind of trade bias different sources of growth impart.

Factor accumulation

The consequences of factor accumulation within the H–O framework are most easily analysed via the so-called Rybczinski theorem (Rybczinski, 1955). For illustrative purposes let us take the case of population growth in Britain. We will maintain our assumptions of zero growth in America, and unchanged terms of trade once expansion has taken place.

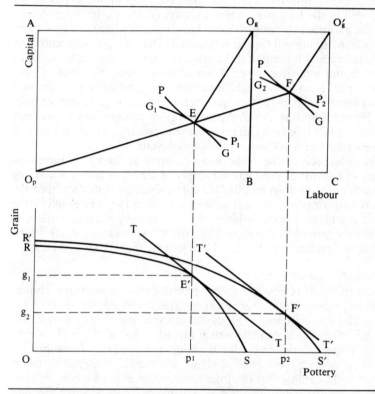

Fig. 4.3 The effect of population increase in Britain

The upper section of Fig. 4.3 delineates pre-growth British factor endowments as O_pAO_gB. Given relative factor intensities, Britain is in equilibrium at E. This output mix is represented by E' on the PPC in the lower section of Fig. 4.3. Population growth with an unchanged endowment of capital results in the Edgeworth Box extending from

O_pAO_gB to $O_pAO_g'C$, this extension being reflected in the outward shift of the PPC from RS to R'S'.

By assumption Britain faces unchanged terms of trade, therefore post-growth equilibrium must be established at F' on the new PPC (R'S'). As is obvious we have had an UPTB production effect, with pottery production increasing and grain production decreasing. We can explain the mechanics of this shift by reference to the Edgeworth Box, where post-growth equilibrium is at F (on a higher-pottery and lower-wheat isoquant). In order to ensure that factor intensities remain the same both before and after the population expansion, F must lie on the same ray from the pottery origin as E, whilst the grain factor intensity rays O_gE and $O_g'F$ must be parallel. Given these constraints the only possible point of intersection is at F.

On a more intuitive level, the increased labour force has to be employed in the labour-intensive industry (pottery). In order to employ the additional labour without changing factor intensity in pottery production, additional capital is required. The only possible source of increased capital is created if the grain industry contracts. Being relatively capital intensive, a run-down of grain production will release more capital than labour, which can then be used with the increased labour force to expand pottery production, at the original factor intensity. Equilibrium is re-established when grain production has declined sufficiently (GG_1 to GG_2), to provide the necessary capital such that all of the expanded workforce is fully employed.

The inference of the Rybczinski theorem is then that increased supply of a factor of production (supply of the other factor remaining constant) will result in an ultra-biased production shift. Whether the bias is anti- or pro-trade will depend on which industry employs the increasing factor relatively intensively. Thus the production effect of population growth in Britain will be UPTB, in America UATB; whilst capital accumulation will be UATB in Britain, and UPTB in America.

Technical progress

Conceptually, it is possible to distinguish between neutral technical progress, labour-saving technical progress, and capital-saving progress. The distinctions are self-explanatory; neutral progress refers to technological developments which are unbiased in the factors they save; labour-saving and capital-saving referring to developments which economise on the use of labour and capital respectively. Since any of these could occur in either industry, in either country, a complete taxonomy comprises twelve possible cases. It will suit our purposes to examine a few only in any depth.

Consider first what happens when neutral technical progress occurs in the pottery industry in Britain. Following the progress, the same labour and capital as formerly employed in producing pottery, produce an increased output. Unit costs of producing pottery are thereby lowered and if (by assumption) the product price ratio is to remain unchanged, factor prices and factor intensities must alter. How does this adjustment take place?

If as assumed, relative commodity prices must remain unchanged before and after the technical progress, then a lowering of unit costs in pottery production is tantamount to increased profit margins in that industry. Under our assumed conditions of perfect competition, this would provide a clear incentive for grain producers to switch their resources into pottery production. Because more capital than labour is released from the grain sector to be employed in the pottery sector, there is consequently an excess supply of capital, and an excess

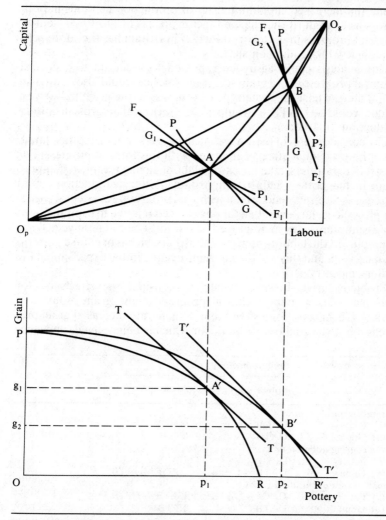

Fig. 4.4 The effect of neutral technical progress in the pottery industry in Britain

demand for labour. Factor prices must therefore alter in favour of labour and this provides the incentive for both industries to become relatively more capital intensive – the pottery industry operating at an increased level of output, the grain industry at a lower level.

These production changes are depicted in Fig. 4.4. Prior to the technical progress in the pottery industry, equilibrium output was at A in the Edgeworth Box, and A′ on the PPC. Following the technical progress, pottery production increases from PP_1 to PP_2, and grain production decreases from GG_1 to GG_2. These shifts correspond to the shift from A′ to B′ on the production frontier. The changed factor intensity rays (O_pA to O_pB for pottery, and O_gA to O_gB for grain) reflect the increased capital intensity of production methods in both sectors as a result of the changed factor prices (FF_1 to FF_2). Neutral technical progress in pottery production in Britain has therefore generated a UPTB production shift.

This analysis could easily be repeated to ascertain that neutral technical progress in the grain sector in America would also lead to an UPTB shift, whilst the same type of progress in the grain industry in Britain would be UATB, as would neutral technical progress in pottery production in America.

The consideration of biased technical progress is more complicated, since there are dual effects connected with this form of progress. For illustrative purposes, take the case of labour-saving technical progress, again in the pottery industry in Britain. Pottery production would increase as a consequence of the technical progress. An integral part of the progress is, however, that labour is saved relative to capital. Given our assumptions, any unemployed labour must be re-employed. To be re-employed the labour-intensive industry (which is of course pottery) must expand, and this will tend to reinforce the initial expansion of the pottery industry.

Problems arise, however, when we consider the effects of, for example, labour-saving technical progress in the grain industry in Britain. Technical progress will tend to generate increased grain production but since labour is the factor which is being saved, and since

Source of growth	Production effect	
	Britain	America
Neutral technical progress		
(a) Pottery	UPTB	UATB
(b) Grain	UATB	UPTB
Labour-saving technical progress		
(a) Pottery	UPTB	UATB
(b) Grain	UATB → UPTB	UPTB → UATB
Capital-saving technical progress		
(a) Pottery	UPTB → UATB	UATB → UPTB
(b) Grain	UATB	UPTB

grain production is relatively capital intensive, the extra labour may have to be employed in the pottery industry. Here we would obviously have conflicting tendencies and we could not say *a priori* what the eventual effect would be.

All the possibilities relating to biased technical progress are summarised in the table on page 102. In the light of our discussion so far, the reader should not face too many difficulties in working out the mechanics of each.

4.4 Production and consumption effects combined

Quite clearly, if consumption and production effects point in the same direction, the total effect of growth can be straightforwardly assessed. Thus, growth which resulted in British production of grain increasing whilst consumption decreased, would categorically point to some kind of anti-trade bias. (Whether the bias was an ultra one or not would depend on the relative production and consumption effects on pottery.) Furthermore, if one of the effects is neutral, whilst the other is biased, then the bias will tend to predominate, and again the total effect will be predictable. In the situation where the two effects are opposite, however, the total effect may be more difficult to assess. Figure 4.5 provides a shorthand method of approximating combined production and consumption effects.

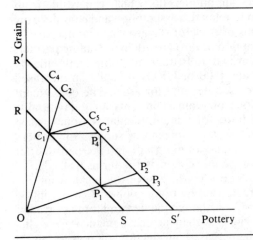

Fig. 4.5 Production and consumption effects of growth combined

RS and R'S' represent our given relative price lines before and after growth respectively. As with Figs 4.1 and 4.2 we exclude PPCs and CICs. In fact Fig. 4.5 is simply Figs 4.1 and 4.2 combined.

P_1 and C_1 represent pre-growth production and consumption respectively. If we had inserted the complete trade triangle, we would have found that the line P_1C_1 was its hypotenuse. The hypotenuse serves as a proxy for the volume of goods traded. Thus as its length increases (decreases), the trade triangle must be increasing (decreasing), and the volume of goods traded must also be increasing (decreasing). We can therefore ascertain the combined production and consumption effects of growth by reference to P_1C_1. If for instance the post-growth trade line were P_2C_2, we would have an overall unbiased or neutral impact, since there has been an equiproportionate growth in production and consumption of importables and exportables. If, however, production and consumption shifts resulted in the new equilibrium trade line being longer than P_2C_2, the total effect would be a pro-trade bias. More specifically, if it were greater than P_2C_2, but less than P_3C_4 we would have a PTB, whilst a trade line greater than P_3C_4 is consistent with an UPTB. Anything less than P_2C_5 ($= P_1C_1$) suggests a UATB since the volume of importables and exportables traded has declined absolutely. The only remaining possibility is where the post-growth trade line is greater than P_2C_5, but less than P_2C_2. This would imply ATB growth. Although the actual volume of trade has increased, the increase is less than in proportion to the increase in income.

Growth and the terms of trade
We have hitherto assumed that the growing country was too small for economic growth to affect its terms of trade. Having now analysed the various production and consumption shifts which can result from growth, we are in a position to relax this assumption and consider how growth may affect the terms of trade of the growing country.

If we maintain our assumption of zero growth in its trading partner, any form of pro-trade-bias growth in Britain must ultimately turn the terms of trade against Britain. PTB or UPTB generate an increased supply of pottery, and increased demand for grain. The consequent increase in the relative price of grain represents an unfavourable movement in the terms of trade for Britain. Similar reasoning must apply to neutral growth. Again, increased supply of pottery accompanied by increased demand for grain will shift the British offer curve, and generate an adverse movement in the terms of trade.

What about ATB and UATB growth? As we will recall from Fig. 4.5, ATB growth was characterised by production and consumption shifts in the range P_2C_2 to P_2C_5. Although the demand for importables is not increasing as much as the growth in income, demand is nevertheless increasing, along with increased production of pottery. ATB growth is therefore also likely to turn the terms of trade against the growing country. In fact the only form of growth which is likely to stimulate a favourable movement in the terms of trade is UATB growth. This is because UATB growth implies decreased production of pottery, as well as decreased consumption of grain. These effects are summarised in Fig. 4.6. America's offer curve remains unchanged at

OA, whilst Britain's shifts in accordance with the type of growth experienced. The student should be able to analyse the mechanics of the shifts him/herself, by extension of analysis used in Chapter 1. (See also Pryor, 1966.)

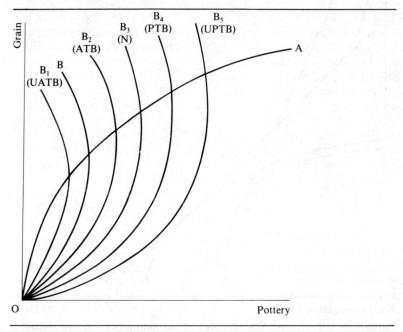

Fig. 4.6 Growth and the terms of trade

Growth and welfare

We have already stated that economic growth, by pushing out the production frontier, widens production and consumption possibilities and results in increased real income and welfare.[1] We now find that these effects may be mitigated somewhat by adverse shifts in the terms of trade. In general it is anticipated that the positive income-increasing effects associated with increased production and consumption will outweigh any negative effects from terms-of-trade shifts. Bhagwati, however, examined the possibility that adverse terms-of-trade shifts could more than offset beneficial production and consumption effects, so as to actually leave the growing country on a lower level of welfare than pre-growth. This extreme possibility is analysed in Fig. 4.7.

Prior to growth, production equilibrium is at A, consumption at B on CIC_1. Assume that economic growth is generated by population expansion and this results in UPTB growth. The subsequent increased supply of pottery, and increased demand for grain turns the terms of trade sharply against the growing country, from TT_1 to TT_2. Faced with these terms of trade, equilibrium is re-established at C and D. As is

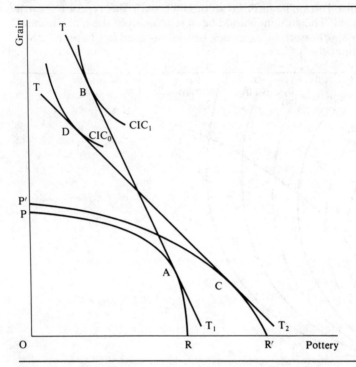

Fig. 4.7 Immiserizing growth

immediately apparent, the post-growth consumption equilibrium (at D) is on a lower indifference curve than pre-growth. In other words the terms of trade have deteriorated so sharply as to leave the country absolutely worse off than it was before the increase in factor inputs. This, Bhagwati termed *immiserizing growth* (Bhagwati, 1958 and 1973).

Is immiserizing growth a genuine possibility or is it merely a theoretical construct? Bhagwati himself suggested certain circumstances under which the possibility of immiserizing growth was enhanced: first, when the terms of trade deteriorate the relative price of importables increases, and there is a relatively low rate of substitution towards domestically produced import substitutes. This may be because the import substitute sector is small relative to the total import volume, or because it is slow to respond to price changes; second, when growth is UPTB, or when the exportable is in inelastic demand abroad.

The greatest likelihood of these conditions being fulfilled would perhaps be in the case of the LDCs. Many of the LDCs rely on primary products as their principal exportables, and these are products which tend to have a relatively low price, and income elasticity of demand. In addition they traditionally rely on imports of manufactured and semi-manufactured goods, and these often only have to compete with relatively small and underdeveloped import substitute sectors.

The question of the LDCs and the international terms of trade has been a controversial one for some years, and it is a subject which we will return to presently.

This then completes our analysis of the impact which economic growth has on international trade. The subject area is extensive and we have really only covered some of the more salient issues. We have investigated the impact which growth may have on a country's production and consumption patterns, and on the international terms of trade. In general we have only enquired into the effects of growth in one sector, in one country, at any point in time. The analysis can be further elaborated to take account of growth in more than one sector, and growth in more than one country. These issues necessitate more sophisticated mathematical formulations and as such, are beyond the scope of the present text. Interested students are referred to Södersten (1964 and 1970).

4.5 International trade and economic development

Until now we have concentrated on the extension of our H–O model in order to demonstrate the effects of growth on trade. We now turn our attention to the effects of trade on growth. In actual fact, what will occupy us for the remainder of this chapter is the perennial and controversial question of the developing countries, and the role which international trade has played in the past, and may play in their future development.

The LDCs generally tend to be categorised as including almost all of Asia (excluding Japan); Central and South America; all of Africa (excluding South Africa); 'Oceania' (excluding New Zealand and Australia); and often, some of the southern European countries such as Portugal, Spain and Greece.[2] Clearly, grouping such a vast number of nations together in one category and then referring to them as the LDCs is an extremely hazardous convention. We must bear in mind that such an oversimplified classification masks very wide differences. The LDCs exhibit a wide variety of socio-political systems; they differ markedly in their degree of underdevelopment (compare for instance Bangladesh with South Korea); very wide differences in wealth are apparent (e.g. the OPEC countries *vis-à-vis* South East Asia); there are wide differences in resource endowments (compare again the Middle East to South East Asia); and they face a wide-ranging number of developmental problems.

Despite such obvious differences the LDCs as a rule exhibit one significant unifying characteristic: poverty. Poverty which is itself a function of underdevelopment. We must be careful to qualify this statement. Poverty is after all relative, rather than being any absolute state. Within the LDCs some countries are very much poorer than others. In general, however, the LDCs are regarded as being poor relative to the affluence of the rich 'Western' industrialised economies.

Table 4.1 Selected Developed and Less Developed Countries compared, 1965–74

Country	Population (millions)	Per capita GNP (US $)	Growth of per capita GNP (%)
	1974*	1974*	1960–74*
Switzerland	6.44	7 870	2.9
United States	211.89	6 670	2.9
West Germany	62.04	6 260	3.7
Japan	109.67	4 070	4.0
United Kingdom	55.97	3 590	2.3
Italy	55.41	2 820	4.2
Libyan Arab Republic	2.35	4 440	12.5
Saudi Arabia	8.01	2 830	8.4
Spain	35.10	2 490	5.8
Hong Kong	4.25	1 510	6.6
Argentina	24.64	1 520	2.8
Brazil	103.98	920	4.0
Zambia	4.78	520	2.3
Ghana	9.61	430	−0.2
Honduras	2.80	340	1.6
Nigeria	73.04	280	2.9
Uganda	11.18	240	1.8
Kenya	12.91	200	3.2
Zaire	24.07	150	2.6
India	595.58	140	1.1
Bangladesh	76.20	100	−0.5
Somalia	3.10	90	−0.3

This poverty is apparent from several key indicators. For example, income per head tends to be relatively low. This need not always be the case. The prime exception would be the OPEC countries, some of whom have a higher income *per capita* than many of the 'developed' or 'industrialised' countries. Despite this they may yet be construed as being underdeveloped (to some degree or other). Manifestations of poverty and underdevelopment, apart from income per head, are multifarious and multidimensional. High levels of illiteracy, malnutrition, poor health services, highly skewed income distributions, a relatively high proportion of the workforce engaged in low-productivity (often subsistence) agriculture, structural rigidities (social and economic), and a dependence on the West for trade, aid and technology, all tend to be aspects of poverty and underdevelopment. Table 4.1 gives some indication of the position of some of the LDCs *vis-à-vis* the developed world, employing a wide range of 'indicators'.

The role of trade in development
The subject of development economics is a discipline of its own. Any reader interested in the wider policy issues (both internal and external)

Annual energy consumption (kilos per capita, coal equivalent) 1973†	Share of world reserves (%) 1974‡	Expectation of life at birth (Males) 1965–70§
3 951	3.99	70.1
11 897	7.28	67.4
5 993	14.69	67.6
3 932	6.13	70.5
5 588	3.14	67.8
3 103	3.14	68.9
5 057	1.64	52.1
1 218	6.47	42.3
2 021	2.93	69.7
1 040	n.a.	67.4
1 913	0.59	65.2
625	2.39	57.6
506	0.07	43.5
175	0.04	46.0
n.a.	n.a.	49.0
63	2.55	37.2
n.a.	n.a.	47.5
167	0.08	46.9
92	0.06	37.6
192	0.60	41.9
32	n.a.	n.a.
n.a.	n.a.	38.5

Sources: *World Bank, *Atlas,* 1976
†United Nations, *World Economic Survey,* 1975
‡*International Financial Statistics,* December, 1976
§United Nations, *Statistical Yearbook,* 1975

associated with economic development is referred to the rapidly grow-ing literature on the subject (see for example, Dasgupta, 1974; Elkan, 1974). Interesting and important as these wider issues may be, our main concern is to concentrate on the role which international trade could play, has played, and can play in the development process.

Considerable controversy exists over whether international trade is beneficial or detrimental to economic development. Those who argue the favourable effects of trade base their case heavily on the classical arguments for free trade. Their reasoning would be similar to that employed in explaining Fig. 2.1 on p. 37. As a direct result of free international trade, a country benefits by reaping gains from exchange and specialisation. It will be recalled that the former derives from the ability of the country to participate in international exchange; the latter from specialisation at the going international terms of trade. The combination of the two eventually takes the country on to a higher

CIC, thereby raising community welfare. These are simply the classic static benefits from free trade. In addition however, it is argued that a number of more dynamic forces are set in motion which ultimately yield long-run benefits, and confer on trade the principal role as 'engine of growth'.

It is argued that although trade has its primary impact on the export sector, unless this sector becomes an enclave isolated from the rest of the economy, its growth must generate *linkages*. In other words, increased demand for domestically produced inputs might create backward linkages which will stimulate growth. For instance, jute manufacture for export might provide a demand for domestically produced spinning and weaving machinery, and thereby provide the impetus for further development. Analogously, since not all of a country's produce will necessarily be exported, some outputs may be used as inputs for other activities, thereby generating forward linkages. Thus, jute manufacture might provide the basis for a forward linkage by stimulating development of a domestic sack-making industry.

It is further argued that expansion of the export sector (and any associated linkages) results in a fuller and more efficient use of resources. Labour which would have been formerly unemployed (or as is equally likely where the LDCs are concerned, underemployed in low-productivity agriculture) is brought into use. As a result of this, real income will increase and the level of savings will tend to increase also. Since increased savings facilitate further capital formation there will be a further impetus to growth and development.

In addition the opening of trade will provide the avenue for importation of technology. Countless empirical studies point to a strong positive association between research and technological development, and economic expansion. In general the LDCs lack the necessary facilities and expertise to engage in large-scale R and D. It is argued therefore, that in trading with the developed world the LDCs can import the fruits of their R and D efforts via the employment of specialised manpower, the import of machinery employing best-practice technology, and the general diffusion of ideas from abroad. This is especially beneficial one could argue, because the opportunity costs of technological advancement are greatest at the early stages, i.e. basic and applied research and innovation. By trading with the developed countries the LDCs can by-pass these early stages.

Thus as a result of these effects, trade permits the LDCs to exploit their factor endowments fully, and reap any comparative cost advantages they may have. This in turn generates growth and linkages which push out their PPCs, thereby widening both production and consumption possibilities.

The role of trade in underdevelopment

Against this, however, a number of commentators have argued very persuasively that trade has, on balance, been detrimental to the development efforts of the LDCs.

It is commonly argued that the domestic economy does not benefit from any lasting linkage effects. Rather, the export sector becomes an enclave, and a 'dual economy' is often created. On the one hand, there is a relatively advanced export sector which tends to be dominated by foreign expertise and capital. A pronounced symptom of this would be where GNP is substantially less than GDP, because much of the income earned within the export sector goes abroad. Juxtaposed with this is the still largely underdeveloped subsistence economy, gaining little or no material benefit from the developing export sector.

Moreover as Singer (1950), Prebisch (1964) and others have co-gently argued, the developmental contribution of the export sector itself is questionable, since very often this proves to be a source of instability. Traditionally, exports from the LDCs are primary products and agricultural goods. As late as 1969 manufactured products still only accounted for around 25 per cent of their total export earnings. Although it can be difficult to generalise, primary products tend to be in relatively inelastic demand. For example, Maizels (1968) estimated the price elasticity of demand for coffee, cocoa and sugar at less than 0.5 (ignoring signs) and those for tea, natural rubber and bananas at between 0.5 and 1.0. Many of such products are susceptible to random or cyclical fluctuations. Given relatively low price elasticities, small changes in supply are transmitted into relatively large fluctuations in price. This in turn can mean unpredictable and unstable export earnings.

Where agricultural commodities are concerned, random shocks to supply, due perhaps to aberrations in weather conditions, can take years to work themselves out (even where adjustment is stable and not in 'cobweb' fashion). This point has been well illustrated by the behaviour of coffee prices recently. Late frosts in Brazil in spring 1975 caused extensive damage to the current year's crop, and to the coffee trees themselves. Price increases in 1975 were relatively modest, but the full impact of damage to the trees was only felt in 1976 and 1977, when coffee prices rocketed.

In addition, income elasticity of demand for the LDCs' agricultural produce also tends to be relatively low. Thus demand for their produce does not grow in proportion to increases in income in the West. When coupled with the fact that population growth in the developed countries is relatively modest, it is clear that the Western world does not constitute a very rapidly growing market for agricultural commodities.

To exacerbate this situation, some of the trade policies of the Western world have been positively harmful to the LDCs' trading prospects. Many developed countries promote domestic import-substitute industries behind high tariff walls in order to reduce dependence on imported foodstuffs. Sugar beet, grain, vegetable oils and meat production all enjoy protection in North America and Western Europe. (Allied to this, technological progress has seen the development of synthetic substitutes for many primary products. Synthetic rubber and plastics have narrowed the market for natural rubber; man-made fibres have gradually been substituted for jute, and hides and skins; chemical fertilisers have largely replaced phosphates; and so on.)

Again we must take care not to over-generalise. These problems we have been discussing are not nearly so intractable for mineral producers. Although demand tends to be price-inelastic, mineral production is not subject to the same type of random fluctuations on the supply side as agricultural commodities. Furthermore, mineral producers face a higher income elasticity of demand. The West has therefore tended to provide a growing rather than declining market for these commodities. Export earnings may still, however, be relatively unstable. Because demand tends to be income-elastic, demand for these commodities may fluctuate markedly over the business cycle in the West.

Export instability (whether it be due to demand-based or supply-based factors) has long been recognised as one of the principal challenges facing the LDCs. Clearly, if the export sector is a 'leading sector', instability is not in any way conducive to stable growth. Furthermore, export instability usually has its concomitant in unstable foreign exchange earnings. This in turn serves merely to exacerbate balance-of-payments difficulties. (The relationship between export instability and economic growth is not easy to analyse empirically. As Stein (1977) demonstrates, the available empirical evidence is ambiguous.)

A further area of debate is the question of the long-run terms of trade of the LDCs as a whole. It has been argued that there has been a secular adverse movement in the commodity terms of trade (i.e. the price of exports relative to imports) against the LDCs. It is claimed that this trend has partially offset some of the welfare gains from trade and economic expansion. We have already noted that the income elasticity of demand for many of the LDCs' exports is relatively low, and that many of their Western markets have been gradually contracting. In addition to this much of their produce is sold in competitive world markets. This often means that technical progress which results in productivity gains and increases in output, eventually also results in relatively lower prices (as in Bhagwati's immiserizing growth). Simultaneously, opposing forces tend to be at work in the developed countries. Their manufactured and semi-manufactured exports (which usually constitute imports into the LDCs), tend to have a relatively higher income elasticity of demand. Also, because of Western industrial structures and industrial relations, productivity gains often find their way into higher factor rewards rather than lower prices. When these tendencies are combined, the result could be a long-run movement in the terms of trade against the LDCs.

According to the 'Singer–Prebisch' thesis, this deterioration means that the LDCs are not reaping their fair share of the gains from trade. This assertion is, however, seriously open to question and has been debated and contested at length. Because of the statistical pitfalls inherent in any attempt to compute representative indices of export and import prices, and because of the hazards involved in generalising from any indices, both the actual fact of deterioration itself and the significance of any perceived deterioration must be questioned.

For instance, although deterioration in the commodity terms of trade for the LDCs as a whole can be shown, so too can improvement. It depends quite simply on the base-year selected. Even where deterioration is observed its significance can be challenged. The commodity terms of trade are so broad a concept as to be of questionable analytical usefulness. Anyway, deterioration of such a composite price index need not be consistent with net welfare losses. Productivity gains, we have noted, may lead to price decreases. The latter would be reflected in the terms-of-trade index, but the positive gains of the former would not. Nor would quality changes be taken into account. The same applies to quality improvements in manufactured exports from the developed countries which would not register in the index.

Wider definitions of the terms of trade have been devised which attempt to take some account of these deficiencies. The so-called 'factoral terms of trade' attempts to make allowance for productivity changes, whilst the 'income terms of trade' focuses on the purchasing power of exports, thereby taking account of changes in export prices, and volumes.[3]

4.6 Policies for trade and development

Irrespective of whether trade is broadly speaking beneficial or detrimental, if the LDCs are to continue participating in international trade they would appear to face two very broad, but interrelated problems. On the one hand, undue dependence on one or a few exportables has tended to result in susceptibility to export instability. This, coupled with a relatively inelastic demand for imports, has helped cause payments variability, and imposed severe constraints on development. A number of possible policy options to alleviate or eliminate these problems can be suggested (see Johnson, 1967a).

Commodity stabilisation schemes
Export instability occurs because of fluctuations in demand and/or supply. Some commodities, for example foodstuffs like coffee, tea, cocoa and bananas, face a relatively stable and predictable demand, but because of their susceptibility to random variations in weather conditions, supply can be unstable. Other commodities like natural rubber and jute may face similar supply conditions, and may also be vulnerable to demand variations due to the fact that they are inputs into other industries. Another possibility is that some commodities, especially minerals, might find that although supply conditions are relatively stable, demand can be unstable.

Irrespective of whether demand- and/or supply-based factors are responsible the end product is the same, instability in prices and producers' earnings. Table 4.2 illustrates this point by comparing average fluctuations, and dispersion around the average for exports from industrial and developing countries. (See also MacBean, 1966; Erb and Schiavo-Campo, 1969; Stern, 1976.)

In an attempt to stabilise their prices and earnings, groups of producers have in the past cooperated to experiment with different forms of commodity stabilisation schemes, most commonly through a buffer-stock type mechanism or through the allocation of quotas. Buffer-stock schemes are frequently employed as instruments of price stabilisation, or price maintenance, by some of the Western economies. An outstanding example here is the extensive use of buffer stocks by the EEC as part of the Common Agricultural Policy. The two most notable attempts at price stabilisation via a buffer stock among primary producers have been the International Tin Agreements (1956–present), and the International Cocoa Agreements (1973–present). More in evidence, however, have been various types of quota schemes. Here the mechanism of control is the allocation of export quotas to individual producers, which they must adhere to strictly unless prices fluctuate beyond certain predetermined 'floors' and 'ceilings'.

Table 4.2 Exports from industrial and Developing Countries: average fluctuation indices and dispersion around the average 1950–65 and 1953–65

	Average fluctuation indices*		Dispersion around the average†	
	1950–65	1953–65‡	1950–65	1953–65‡
Industrial countries	%	%	%	%
Prices	3.7	2.1	1.1	0.6
Quantities	5.6	4.5	2.7	3.3
Earnings	6.2	4.2	2.1	1.6
Developing countries				
Prices	8.8	6.8	3.1	2.8
Quantities	9.5	8.0	8.4	4.5
Earnings	11.8	9.6	7.1	6.1

*Average annual percentage deviation from the trend
†Standard deviation from the mean. (A review of the different measures of export instability can be found in Stein, 1977)
‡Years 1950–65 and 1953–65 taken to allow for the effect of the Korean War boom
Source: Helleiner (1972), p. 79

Commodity stabilisation schemes cannot be used to stabilise any commodity. To stand any chance of operating successfully, certain preconditions must be fulfilled. First, the commodity in question ought to have a relatively low price elasticity of demand. There would be little point in attempting to regulate supply when demand is price-elastic and substitutes are readily available. Second, any agreement ought to aim to encompass as many producers (and perhaps consumers) as possible. If all producers are not party to the agreement, it could prove difficult to stabilise prices. The importance of this problem is dependent on the market share of any non-participant. If for example, Brazil refused to cooperate in any agreement to stabilise coffee prices, the agreement would probably prove unworkable since Brazil is responsible for over 30 per cent of total coffee exports. Non-participation on the part of exporters like Haiti or Honduras would probably be of little significance, since they only control 0.7 and 0.9 per cent (by value) of total coffee exports (1971–73). Cooperation on the part of consuming nations can be very useful as a policing device. Stabilisation schemes will only operate successfully if parties to the agreement abide by its rules and do not vary from agreed prices and quotas. This is a common problem faced by any group of producers (intranational or international), which attempts to regulate supply. Where consumers are cooperating, it is at least possible to keep some kind of record of export volumes and revenues of particular countries. The third precondition is that the commodity ought not to have excessively high storage and depreciation costs, otherwise problems arise in years of surplus. (A much more comprehensive coverage of these issues can be found in Barker, 1977.)

The International Coffee Agreement fulfilled most of these preconditions and operated reasonably successfully between 1959 and 1972. The price elasticity of demand for coffee is relatively low (less than 0.5), and the agreement was adhered to by most producers and consumers. The mechanism of stabilisation was not a formal buffer stock, but a system of export quotas. A world annual export quota would be set and each signatory allocated an individual quota. If the world price fell below a pre-arranged 'floor', export quotas would be reduced to support the price, and conversely if the price exceeded an agreed 'ceiling', quotas would be increased. One complicating factor was that coffee does tend to have relatively high storage costs, and as part of the agreement members had to make their own storage arrangements. Clearly, in years of surplus there were incentives to 'cheat' in order to avoid storage costs. A loophole for this was provided inasmuch as exports to the COMECON countries, and other LDCs, did not count in the export quota.

Other agreements of a similar type which have operated with lesser degrees of success have been the International Sugar Agreements (1954–73) and the International Wheat Agreements (1949–present). Other less formal arrangements have operated for the stabilisation of tea, jute and sisal prices.

Since international commodity agreements can be difficult to negotiate[4] and costly to operate, a much more direct approach is for the main producers to cartelise and administer prices upwards without the approval or cooperation of the consuming countries. The most

Table 4.3   Major LDC exporters of manufactures, 1967 and 1972 (Source: *Review of International Trade and Development 1975:* report by the UNCTAD secretariat (TD/B/530/Add. 1/Rev. 1), United Nations publication)

Country	Share of manufactures in total exports	
	1967	1972
Hong Kong	95.1	93.3
Malta	74.0	89.6
Korea (Republic of)	66.7	83.7
Israel	69.2	74.9
Lebanon	43.0	67.0
Bangladesh	59.5	57.4
Pakistan	50.2	55.6
India	45.8	50.5
Jordan	15.0	43.1
Singapore	26.1	42.2
Mexico	18.9	35.5
Barbados	11.8	34.7
Egypt	22.1	31.0
El Salvador	28.2	29.9
Congo	8.0	27.6
Guatemala	20.5	26.3
Argentina	8.5	20.9
Costa Rica	17.8	19.8
Senegal	4.8	19.5
Brazil	9.7	18.6
Togo	7.4	16.5
Tunisia	21.3	15.1

Source: adapted from UNCTAD (1976), Table 18, pp. 35–6

strikingly successful example of this strategy has been the post-1973 action of the Organisation of Petroleum Exporting Countries (OPEC). OPEC has been operative since 1960. It has, however, only been since 1973 that they have taken action to 'exploit' their combined monopoly power to the fullest. From $2.47 a barrel on 31 December 1972, the posted price was administered upwards to $11.65 by 1 January 1974. The preconditions for such a resounding success were almost ideal. Petroleum had been relatively cheap throughout the post-war period, and most Western economies were heavily dependent on oil. OPEC therefore faced a relatively inelastic demand curve. In addition, supply could be easily controlled, storage causes few problems, and the action had full support from all OPEC members. One aspect of this price increase can be seen in Table 7.4, which shows the very rapid increase in the reserves of the oil exporters after 1973.

   Other exporters' organisations, such as CIPEC (copper), IBA (bauxite), and Café Mondial (coffee), have attempted to emulate OPEC's actions but without anything like the same degree of success.

Import substitution
The pursuit of import substitution policies has obvious appeal. If

successful, dependence on foreign trade is lessened and a source of balance-of-payments pressure may be relieved. Since import substitution will usually involve the development of manufacturing industry, the strategy has the additional attraction that it may provide the vehicle for industrialisation.

Typically, most import substitution policies have concentrated on manufactured consumer goods, for which a domestic market already exists. Often these are produced on a relatively labour-intensive basis behind tariff barriers (the rationale for protection would of course be provided by the infant-industry argument confronted in Chapter 2). Quite a number of the LDCs have enjoyed a considerable measure of success, not only in replacing imports with domestically produced substitutes but eventually exporting manufactured goods themselves. Tables 4.3 and 4.4 give an indication of how successful some of the LDCs have been in replacing imports, and exporting manufacturers.

Because, however, import substitution has generated a number of unanticipated problems, the process has been far less successful for many LDCs. Lessened dependence on foreign trade is not always a corollary of import substitution. Industrialisation generally stimulates increased demand for intermediate and capital goods. Thus although

Table 4.4 Imports as a percentage of total supplies for selected LDCs 1948–65

Country and year	Consumer goods	Intermediate goods	Capital goods
Brazil			
1949	9.0	25.9	63.7
1955	2.9	17.9	43.2
1959	1.9	11.7	32.9
1964	1.3	6.6	9.8
Mexico			
1950	2.4	13.2	66.5
1955	2.3	n.a.	63.4
1960	1.3	10.4	54.9
1965	n.a.	9.9	59.8
India			
1951	4.2	17.4	56.5
1957	2.5	25.9	58.6
1961	1.4	18.7	42.4
Pakistan			
1951–2	77.5	73.2	76.3
1954–5	23.1	52.4	71.8
1959–60	8.3	40.9	64.7
1964–5	11.4	15.0	62.3
Philippines			
1948	30.9	90.3	79.7
1956	10.0	68.3	60.2
1960	4.2	40.7	55.9
1965	4.7	36.3	62.9

Source: Little, Scitovsky and Scott (1970), p. 60

imports of consumer goods might decrease, imports of intermediate and capital goods very often increase. Table 4.4 illustrates how even some of those countries which appear to have accomplished the initial objectives of replacing imports of consumer goods, still find themselves heavily dependent on imports for intermediate and capital goods.

With their low *per capita* incomes, many LDCs have been unable to generate sufficient investment funds domestically to finance substitution. These countries have therefore tended to rely heavily on foreign investment, and this in turn has generated a fixed and continuous claim on the balance of payments in the form of remittances of interest and profit income.

The general concensus seems to take the view that import-substitution policies, although exhibiting some measure of success, have not entirely lived up to expectations. The principal reason for this seems to be a failure to attune development sufficiently to local conditions and needs, thereby often failing completely to create the all-important linkages. Furthermore, an over-zealous commitment to import substitution at the expense of export industries has often resulted in uneconomic import-substitute activities replacing, or, squeezing formerly viable primary-producing export sectors.

Economic integration among the LDCs

Chapter 3 focused at length on the theory and practice of customs-union formation, and the costs and benefits likely to accompany economic integration. It is felt by many that greater economic cooperation, possibly with an eye to ultimate integration, offers fruitful prospects for development of the LDCs. This belief is based on the prospect that integration may reduce or eliminate many of the bottlenecks which stand in the way of development, facilitate successful import substitution, and ultimately improve their export prospects.

One could argue first and foremost that one of the main constraints on successful industrial development for many LDCs is the absence of a wide enough home market. Cooperation (be it via the formation of a free-trade area, a common market, or a customs union) will widen the market and should facilitate successful exploitation of economies of scale. Eventually as unit costs decline, the industry will become competitive without the support of trade restrictions. With a number of industries the potential benefits to be reaped are substantial (as for instance with metal processing and manufacture, chemical production, and such like). We must keep this argument in perspective, however, by remembering that much industrial development in the LDCs has a relatively high labour component in value added, and economies of scale are largely exhausted at relatively low levels of output. This would seem to be the case for instance with textile manufacture, and assembly of imported components for re-export (so-called 'sourcing'; see Helleiner, 1973).

Related to the exploitation of scale economies is the notion that within a free-trade bloc there may be scope for intra-regional specialisation in order to ensure the best possible use of members' factor endowments. Some progress seems to have been made in this direction by the Caribbean Community (CARICOM),[5] which has encouraged and developed a degree of agricultural specialisation between members. The classic problem here is that certain areas may be especially suited to development and become growth poles, whilst other areas stagnate or grow at a very much slower rate. Within the East African Community (EAC) of Kenya, Uganda and Tanzania, Kenya provided by far the most conducive conditions for development. Similarly, within the Latin American Free Trade Area (LAFTA)[6] there is a wide difference in growth prospects between the more advanced countries (Brazil, Argentina and Mexico), and their more backward compatriots (Bolivia, Ecuador, and Paraguay).

Given the wide diversity of LDCs, any grouping will inevitably combine 'richer' and 'poorer' members. To overcome some of the economic and political problems this creates, the general freeing of trade within the bloc must be accompanied by some form of regional policy to attempt to keep some sort of 'balance' between the constituent parts. Where LDC integration is concerned, the most common approach to the problem is a phased programme of integration, with the weaker members of the group being allowed a steadier and slower entry, rather than having to face immediate unrestricted free trade. The EAC modified completely free trade flows by the use of 'transfer taxes' (effectively internal import duties), which deficit members (usually Uganda and Tanzania) levied on surplus members (usually Kenya). Such programmes are absolutely essential. For economic cooperation to have any realistic chance of success, effective political cooperation is a prerequisite. The prospects for political cooperation are lessened where regional imbalance persists (as for instance in the EAC).

One of the primary reasons for the relatively slow trend towards integration among LDCs has been the historical gearing of transport facilities, communication networks, and financial facilities, towards the old colonial connections. A significant potential benefit of integration should be the loosening of such structural and political bottlenecks, as transport and communications networks and financial services are developed in line with local requirements. Indeed the very survival of regional integration will largely rest on infrastructural developments. Prospects for the CARICOM and ASEAN[7] groups would be extremely limited without efficient shipping links and adequate port facilities, since both comprise mainly islands. Given the vast geographical area covered by LAFTA, again suitable infrastructural developments would seem to be a prerequisite to eventual integration.

There are a number of regional trading blocs comprising LDCs only, and they have enjoyed a variety of fortunes. Clearly any move towards integration is a long-term strategy, and most of the potential benefits of customs-union formation are long-term. In this sense it is early days yet to comment on the part they have played in economic development. One concrete benefit which does seem to have emerged, however, is the improved bargaining power of the various blocs. The increased confidence which concerted action has conferred on many of the LDCs is unquestionably beneficial, and has already yielded some tangible results, e.g. via the Lomé Agreement. Although the forty-six LDCs involved were not themselves one trading bloc, it does not seem unreasonable to suggest that their remarkable unity of purpose in the negotiations was at the absolute minimum assisted by their experience in trading groups like CARICOM, EAC, ECOWAS (the Economic Community of West African States)[8], UDEAC (Union Douaniere et Economique de L'Afrique Centrale)[9] and CEAO (Communauté Economique de L'Afrique de L'Ouest).[10] (For a more detailed empirical assessment see Robson, 1972 and United Nations, 1971.)

Trade policies of the developed world

We have already considered commercial policies of developed and less-developed countries at some length in Section 2.5. A few further comments are, however, required. To many commentators the policy variable which holds the key to future development of the LDCs is not in their own hands but in the hands of the developed world, inasmuch as more liberal policies could be pursued which would facilitate a greater impact of trade on economic development. Awareness of this is embodied in UNCTAD's general objective of reducing, or removing, the tariff and non-tariff barriers which the LDCs face on their exports to the developed world.

Much can yet be accomplished in this direction since relatively high tariff barriers face the export of primary commodities (which still account for close on 60 per cent of LDC exports). For instance, the Common Agricultural Policy of the EEC imposed a variable levy on all agricultural produce entering the Community in order to bring prices up to a specified level. The US and other European countries have used similar methods to increase agricultural incomes, encourage domestic production of foodstuffs, and therefore lessen dependence on imported food.

Furthermore, the LDCs commonly face trade restrictions on their exports of manufactured goods. Industries in the West such as textiles, clothing and footwear, which are at a competitive disadvantage to those of the LDCs, are often kept in operation behind tariff walls. The effect of this is twofold. Structural change is mitigated in the developed countries, whilst at the same time these industries do not expand to their full potential in the developing countries.

In addition, most LDCs tend to be confronted by a whole battery of non-tariff barriers relating to product specification, health and sanitary standards, government procurement rules, and occasionally quotas.

The GATT charter was extended in 1964 to accommodate non-reciprocal removal of tariff barriers on the part of the developed countries. It has only been since 1970, however, that any significant steps have been taken in this direction, with a move towards UNCTAD's proposed 'generalised system of preferences'. Some progress has been made, and again one could point to the Lomé Agreement, whereby the EEC agreed to permit over 94 per cent of the imports from the LDCs which were party to the agreement to enter duty-free.

Aid, trade, and development

The role of foreign aid is not entirely separable from the previous issue of the developed world's commercial policies. Aid and tariff reduction are often seen as alternatives, with the balance slightly more in favour of the former because of political expediency.

As with so many other important issues our discussion must be brief, and must of necessity confine itself to the overall perspective we have taken. (For a fuller analysis, see Mikesell, 1968; Hawkins, 1970.)

Broadly speaking we can conceive of aid taking the form of outright grants, or loans which may have a 'grant element' by virtue of the terms on which they are awarded (e.g. a loan at below market interest rate).[11] Other things being equal, grants are preferable to loans (concessionary or otherwise), since they involve no commitment to repay and therefore will involve no debt-servicing difficulties. Other things are rarely equal, however. The major portion of foreign aid is traditionally furnished on a bilateral basis and is frequently of a 'tied' nature, i.e. a condition of the aid being granted is that it be used for a specific project or programme, or more usually that it be 'spent' on the exports of the donor country. It is possible to contend that the tying of aid in such fashion is necessary since it facilitates a check on the use to which resources are being put, and thereby prevents aid being frittered away on unproductive political or military programmes. Unfortunately however (although arguably any aid is better than none), such aid has several inherent defects. First, although an immediate and readily available command over foreign resources is granted, the use to which these resources is put is limited. In consequence, tied aid may do little towards reducing dependence on exports of commodities which exhibit instability, because it fails to encourage industrial development. This will not of course always be the case. Assistance may be tied to specific development programmes where the particular needs of the recipient are identified, and the use of resources tailored to suit those needs.

A second general problem with bilateral developmental assistance is that aid (tied or untied) may not be granted in accordance with need, but rather on the basis of colonial preference (as has been the case for example with much British and French aid) or ideological preference (as with Soviet or American aid). Although by definition all LDCs require aid, some are quite obviously more needy than others. More emphasis ought therefore perhaps to be placed on multilateral aid, administered through international agencies. A number of international organisations exist to perform such a function. The World Bank Group (comprising the International Bank for Reconstruction and Development, the International Development Association, and the International Finance Corporation) is the most influential of the numerous multinational agencies and its role could easily be extended.

Such considerations strongly influenced the conclusions and recommendations of Pearson Commission (Pearson, 1969). Although the commission reported in 1969 its recommendations are still relevant, if for no other reason than to demonstrate how far the developed world remains from meeting what many regarded as minimum standards. According to the report, the overall objective of aid ought to be a raising of the growth rate of the LDCs to 6 per cent per annum by the year 2000. In order to meet this commitment it was felt that the total flow of aid should, by 1975, have been equivalent to at least 1 per cent of the GNP of the developed world. It was felt that this aid in general should be untied and should become more multilaterally oriented, with an initial commitment to raise multilateral aid to a minimum of 20 per cent of total assistance by 1975. With the greater responsibility passed on to international associations that this would entail, it would be possible to periodically review the use to which LDCs were putting any aid received. Future allocations could then be contingent on the satisfactory use of previous assistance. The Pearson Report felt that if these proposals were followed through, most of the developing world would be able to compete in world markets by 2000, and earnings from trade would by that date largely replace aid.

In the light of an inevitable widening of the gap between LDCs and the industrialised West in the latter quarter of the twentieth century, the Pearson Report was regarded by many as at best optimistic, at worse hopelessly inadequate. Despite this, close examination of recent trends in overseas development assistance (ODA) reveals a declining rather than increasing commitment towards aid on the part of the developed world. Although their combined GNP increased by 80 per cent in real terms over the period 1961–75, aid from the developed world barely increased (again in real terms). Whereas ODA stood at an average 0.53 per cent of GNP of the industrialised market economies in 1961, this proportion had fallen to 0.36 per cent by 1975. Not only was this a good deal short of the Pearson objectives, it also fell well short of the UN's objectives for its 'Second Development Decade' (1971–80), where the target was an average of 0.7 per cent of the developed countries' GNP.

Table 4.5 illustrates how, for the years 1974–75, ODA as a proportion of GNP only exceeded 0.70 per cent in two industrialised market economies (the Netherlands and Sweden), falling short in most others. In actual fact, of the developed market economies it is only really the

Table 4.5   Aid donors ranked by ODA as a proportion of GNP

Country	ODA as a % of GNP
Qatar	5.43
United Arab Emirates	4.29
Saudi Arabia	2.55
Kuwait	2.49
Iraq	2.24
Libyan Arab Republic	1.31
Iran	0.80
Sweden	0.78
Netherlands	0.70
Norway	0.62
France	0.60
Australia	0.58
Denmark	0.57
Belgium	0.55
Canada	0.54
New Zealand	0.42
Germany	0.39
United Kingdom	0.38
Algeria	0.25
United States	0.25
Japan	0.24
Austria	0.18
Finland	0.18
Switzerland	0.17
China, Peoples Republic	0.15
Venezuela	0.14
Italy	0.12
Nigeria	0.11
USSR	0.08
Eastern European Countries	0.02

Source: Finance and Development, Vol. 14, No. 2, June 1977

Scandinavian countries which have been increasing their contribution in recent years. The more traditional sources like the US, UK and France have reduced their commitment, probably due to the relaxation of East–West tensions on the part of the US, and the loosening of old colonial ties on the part of the UK and France.

A most striking aspect of Table 4.5 is the increased importance of the OPEC countries as sources of ODA. This is of course one further 'spin-off' of the huge increase in oil revenues since 1973. It is important to note that the bulk of this assistance does go to 'non-oil' Muslim states of the Middle East.

The total amount of ODA received by the Third World is a relatively small magnitude (for instance, total ODA in 1975 was equivalent to only 18 days' defence expenditure on the part of the East, West and OPEC nations), and its potency can be negated either because it is tied, or because of the restrictive trade policies of the developed world.

Despite the apparent lack of any significant statistical correlation between aid and economic growth (albeit on a cross-sectional basis), there can be little doubt that aid provides an important instrument for some limited amount of redistribution in the world economy and has an important role to play in development. How then can the quality and quantity of aid be improved?

Presumably the principal aim of the UN's 'Third Development Decade' (1981–90) will be to increase substantially the flow of resources from the developed world. To this end the UN's strongest weapon is exhortation, and this is likely to be insufficient. Perhaps therefore the main hope for increased aid will be via increased use of the Special Drawing Right, detailed consideration of which will be deferred until Chapters 7 and 8.

Conclusions

This then completes our survey of the salient issues relating to the problems faced by the LDCs in integrating fully into the world economy. By way of a temporary conclusion (until we consider international monetary reform), we can say that the LDCs can go some way towards solving their own problems. Undoubtedly, however, little lasting progress can be made unless the developed world plays its part. Precisely what that part is remains a perennial subject of debate in international fora. Permanent machinery does exist, the sole purpose of which is to coordinate 'north and south'. Perhaps the most important body is UNCTAD, the four sessions of which have, if nothing else, at least served to bring together the developing countries. This in itself is a considerable achievement. Although we have discussed at length the economics of trade and development, we must be aware of the political problems of gaining effective cooperation among the developing countries.

To argue that this has been the sole achievement would, however, considerably undervalue the work of UNCTAD, the UN in the wider sense, the World Bank Group, the IMF, and so on. Several tangible benefits have recently been seen, e.g. the progress made in developing the generalised system of tariff preferences, and widespread debt cancellation on the part of many developed countries. World recession has, however, only served to slow progress even further, and it remains no more than pure speculation as to what can be expected from the fifth UNCTAD, and the UN 'Third Development Decade' of 1981–90. One thing which would seem reasonably certain is that more positive action will have to be taken soon. The gravity and potential consequences of inaction were probably not overstated when the authors of a recent work asserted:

In the long run the world economy cannot expand rapidly if over two-thirds of the world's population live in abject poverty and misery. . . . The long term prosperity of the rich 'north' depends to a great extent on its own ability and willingness to share its advantages with the deprived 'south'. If this does not happen, the economic, political and social tensions that are building up in the poorer parts of the world threaten the stability, indeed the very existence, of the world order which has made the progress and prosperity of the richer countries possible.

Singer and Ansari (1977) pp. 30–31

Notes

1. This of course assumes that economic growth is equivalent to increased economic welfare. Some would contend that beyond a certain point the increased social costs associated with growth (associated with environmental destruction, pollution, etc.) outweigh the positive income increasing effects. For a summary of the issues involved see Mishan (1977).
2. The categorisation of LDCs can vary according to the organisation defining them.
3. The income terms of trade can be defined as

   $Qx \quad Px/Pm$

   where Px and Pm are price indices for exports and imports respectively, and Qx is an index of export volume.
   The single factoral terms of trade would be expressed as

   $Ex \cdot Px/Pm$

   where Px and Pm are as above, and Ex is a productivity index.
4. The ongoing debate (on commodity stabilisation schemes, among other things) between the developed nations and the LDCs has recently been dubbed the 'North–South axis' in contrast to the more overtly political 'East–West axis'.
5. The members of CARICOM are: Antigua, Barbados, Belize, Dominica, Granada, Guyana, Jamaica, Montserrat, St Kitts–Nevis–Anguilla, St Lucia, St Vincent, Trinidad and Tobago.
6. Members of LAFTA are: Argentina, Bolivia, Brazil, Chile, Columbia, Ecuador, Mexico, Paraguay, Peru, Uruguay, Venezuela.
7. The ASEAN (Association of South East Asian Nations), comprises: Indonesia, Malaysia, Philippines, Singapore, Thailand.
8. Members of ECOWAS are: Dahomey, Gambia, Ghana, Guinea, Guinea-Bissau, Ivory Coast, Liberia, Mali, Mauritania, Niger, Nigeria, Senegal, Sierra Leone, Togo, Upper Volta.
9. Members of UDEAC are: Cameroon, Central African Republic, Congo, Gabon.
10. Members of CEAO are: Ivory Coast, Mali, Mauritania, Niger, Senegal, Upper Volta.
11. Grants and loans are not of course the only forms which aid takes. Technical assistance, and aid in kind are not uncommon.

Chapter 5

International payments imbalance

5.1 Introduction

Our discussion so far has concentrated upon the nature and consequences of the international movement of goods, services and factor services. For these purposes we implicitly assumed that such real flows took place within the framework of an international barter economy. In all but the case of barter exchange, however, there will exist a corresponding system of monetary movements alongside the system of real (trade and investment) flows. Thus, as with development of any national or regional economy, so with the international economy we can trace the emergence of a money economy or monetary system.

One of the major aims of this second half of the text will be to examine how the purchase and sale of real assets across national frontiers is facilitated by the use of monetary assets. The existence of a money economy provides the advantages of convenience, and of increased opportunities for international specialisation. It is clearly more convenient and less costly in terms of resources to purchase a product from another country by paying with money rather than in kind. Similarly, the absence of the need to balance trade through barter between each country in the trading system widens the scope for the international division of labour. Rather than a flow of real assets from America to Britain having to be matched by an equal and opposite flow of real goods from Britain to America, the existence of a monetary framework means that real flows will be matched only by reverse flows of monetary assets. The efficiency with which the system of monetary flows operates will of course have important consequences for the level and distribution of benefits to be gained from the international movement of goods, services and capital. It is important, however, to emphasise from the beginning that although the monetary system is fashioned by the needs of the trading system, flows of funds may occur which are quite independent of any real flows. This and subsequent chapters will therefore examine the factors influencing these independent movements of monetary assets between financial centres in different countries.

If initially, however, we concentrate on flows of funds which are generated by the need to finance commercial trading transactions, then we must ask the question: In what way does the financing of trade across national frontiers pose special problems? With international transactions, whether it be between individuals, corporate bodies or national governments, we confront the difficulty of making or receiving payment in the appropriate currency. Given the existence of separate monetary denominations, a resident of one country may well be unwilling to accept payment in anything other than the currency that is domestically accepted as the medium of exchange. Unless for instance a US exporter to the UK is willing to have sterling accredited to his balance at a London bank (perhaps for the purchase of a UK product at some future date), then he is likely to require payment in dollars. The UK importer of the US goods will therefore need to exchange sterling for dollars in order to make the purchase.

The aim of this first chapter within the monetary section will in fact be to analyse the process of currency exchange under varying foreign-exchange market conditions. It will also examine the nature, causes and policy implications of imbalance in the flow of payments between one country and the rest of the world. This will permit us to examine in Chapter 6 the processes by which imbalance may be eliminated under alternative currency arrangements. Chapter 7 will consider the ways in which payments imbalance may be financed by different forms of international money. And finally Chapter 8 will seek in the light of the three preceding chapters to analyse the recent history of international monetary relations and to critically assess the relative merits of a range of reform proposals.

5.2 International payments and exchange rates

We have already suggested that the financing of commercial activities may well generate the need to convert domestic into foreign currency. The UK importer of US goods may need to convert sterling into dollars, and the US importer buying UK exports to convert dollars into sterling. The purchasing of goods and services in foreign markets generates the need for a foreign-exchange market for the conversion or exchange of currencies. A market in its analytical sense refers to a group of economic agents who wish to buy or sell a particular commodity. The foreign-exchange market is no different. It is a market where national monies are bought and sold. This buying and selling activity will therefore produce a market price, in this case an *exchange rate* for each currency with respect to each other currency for which it is exchanged. There is for instance a rate of exchange for sterling in terms of dollars, i.e. the number of dollars exchangeable for one pound sterling. But in addition to this exchange rate there will also be one between the German mark and the dollar, for example, and the German mark and sterling. These *cross rates* of exchange, and the rates in different financial centres at the same moment in time, are kept in line by *exchange arbitrage*. If, for example, the price of sterling is higher in terms of dollars in London than in New York, the arbitrageur can gain by buying sterling in New York to sell immediately in London. The increased buying activity in New York will tend to raise the price of sterling there, and the selling activity in London to depress the price there until such time as there is a common rate in both markets. (To reinforce this idea the student may wish to consider the impact of arbitrage activity when cross rates become unequal.)

In addition to these *spot market* transactions for the immediate conversion and transfer of funds (and the resulting spot rate of exchange), for many currencies heavily involved in trade and other commercial activities *forward markets* have developed. In this case the agreement is to buy and sell a currency at some future date at a price (the forward rate) fixed when the contract is made. The forward rate is often expressed in relation to the spot rate. We shall consider shortly the reasons why the forward rate may be quoted as a premium on or discount from the spot rate.

The decision to buy or sell in the forward market may be motivated by more than consideration of the current financing of a trading transaction. In addition to the transactions motive for exchanging currencies, i.e. demanding foreign exchange to finance the purchase of goods from abroad, individuals and institutions may wish to hold (frequently interest-bearing) foreign exchange in their portfolios for speculative and precautionary purposes. The inclusion of these motives for buying and selling currencies tends to complicate the analysis of exchange-rate determination, and initially we shall concentrate on the relationship between the commercial trading motive and the immediate price of foreign exchange. To explain for instance why it may cost two dollars to buy one pound, or why that rate of exchange may alter, we must examine the prevailing market conditions. In other words we must examine the factors influencing the spot demand for and supply of domestic (or foreign) currency.

The spot rate
In the construction of Fig. 5.1 we have made several simplifying assumptions. Firstly we have adopted a bilateral model of global trade, where the USA and the UK are assumed to be competing under unrestricted conditions. In addition we have assumed that each country is capable of meeting changes in demand for each other's production. Thirdly we have assumed that the foreign exchange market itself operates under freely competitive conditions, and that therefore it is not subject to large-scale buying and selling. There is for instance no intervention activity on the market by the Central Bank. Finally, we have ignored the possibility that there may be forward currency transactions, but have rather assumed that all transactions are for immediate payment and receipt.

The demand and supply schedules for sterling are drawn therefore under the usual *ceteris paribus* assumptions, i.e. that (real and money)

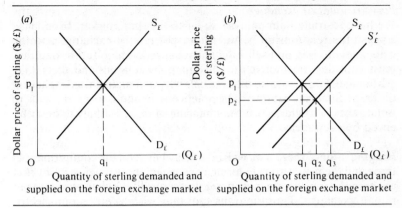

Fig. 5.1 Exchange rates under free market conditions

incomes, the state of technology and preferences remain unchanged. In Fig. 5.1(b) for example, the outward shift of the supply curve for sterling, which represents an increase in the quantity of sterling supplied at each rate of exchange, may arise out of an increase in incomes in the UK. (At the initial market exchange rate p_1, the excess supply of sterling ($q_3 - q_1$) will force down the rate of exchange to its new level, p_2.) In terms of this model therefore, the supply of domestic currency (sterling) on to the foreign exchange market arises out of the need for UK residents to purchase goods imported from the US in foreign currency (dollars). (The supply of sterling is therefore equivalent to the demand for dollars.) The supply curve is upward sloping and the demand curve downward sloping on the assumption that the foreign and domestic demand for a country's products is price-elastic.[1] In other words, it is assumed that other things being equal, the demand for importables will increase and therefore the supply of sterling increase, as the foreign-currency purchasing power of sterling increases. (On supply schedule $S_£$ in Fig. 5.1(b) a rise in the exchange rate from p_2 to p_1 would increase the quantity of sterling that UK residents were willing to supply from q_2 to q_3.) Conversely, the demand for sterling is generated in our model by US importers of British goods and services (UK exports). The shape of the demand curve indicates that a rise in the dollar price of sterling (or in other words a fall in the purchasing power of the dollar) results in a reduction in the quantity of sterling demanded by US residents. (In Fig. 5.1(b) again a rise in the dollar price of sterling from p_2 to p_1 results in a fall in the quantity of sterling demanded from q_2 to q_1.) Given these elasticity assumptions for importables and exportables therefore, there will be a market clearing rate of exchange. (Our present analysis has been framed in terms of the dollar price of sterling, but to reinforce his/her understanding of these basic relationships the reader may wish to construct a similar model from the alternative viewpoint of the sterling price of the dollar.)

Forward rates of exchange

We have restricted our analysis so far to the spot market. In order to analyse the relationship between the spot rate of exchange and the willingness to buy and sell foreign exchange at some future date, we must consider the motives for hedging, speculating and for taking advantage of interest-rate differentials between financial assets held in different financial centres.[2] (In practice it is likely to be difficult to isolate these motives, since the financing of trade is likely to be influenced by each factor.)

Hedging   Since there may well be a delay between the commitment to trade and the need to pay in foreign exchange, there is a possibility that the cost of a transaction may increase as a result of a change in the spot rate of exchange. Thus the transactor may wish to protect himself or 'hedge' against the possibility of exchange-rate changes. An individual or institution receiving a fixed foreign-exchange payment at some future date and after an anticipated appreciation of the domestic currency may therefore avoid the risk of loss by selling the foreign exchange at the forward rate. Conversely, an importer anticipating a depreciation of the domestic currency can pay immediately or buy the required foreign currency at the prevailing forward rate. To illustrate these possibilities we can consider a situation in which sterling is expected firstly to appreciate from £1 = $1.50 to £1 = $1.65 and secondly to depreciate from £1 = $1.65 to £1 = $1.50. In the first instance the receipt of $1.50 after the appreciation of sterling would no longer be worth one pound to the UK recipient. Similarly, in the second example the UK importer would require more than one pound to purchase $1.65 after the sterling depreciation. In the first instance forward selling of dollars at less than the expected post-appreciation value of sterling, e.g. £1 = $1.55, will reduce the loss in value of the receipt in domestic currency terms. Forward selling of dollars (i.e. buying of sterling) will in fact tend to push up the forward rate of sterling in excess of the spot rate of £1 = $1.50, so that there is a forward premium on sterling. (The reader may like to consider the impact of hedging activity on the forward rate, where sterling is expected to depreciate.)

Interest arbitrage   The arbitrage decision, or method of payment adopted, will depend however not only on expected changes in the spot rate and the cost of forward covering but also on domestic and foreign interest rates. If we ignore risk and liquidity considerations, under free market conditions the aim of interest arbitrage is to allocate short-term financial assets in such a manner as to maximise effective yields. By financial assets we mean short-term government bonds or commercial bank deposits which can be used to purchase goods or other currencies, but which for the convenience of our present analysis we must assume are held for interest arbitrage purposes. Nominally interest rates on

Treasury Bills for example of the same maturity set at 10 per cent in the UK and at 6 per cent in the US (i.e. a 4 per cent uncovered interest margin in favour of sterling) provide an incentive for switching funds from New York to London, i.e. out of dollars into sterling. Where, however, the exchange rate is free to fluctuate, the actual return or yield on the UK Treasury Bill to the foreign holder will also be influenced by what happens to the spot rate of sterling between the date of purchase and maturity of the bond. The investor in UK bonds may still receive a lower yield than if he had left his funds in the US, if a depreciation of sterling (i.e. a reduction in the number of dollars received from each pound) offsets the interest premium in the UK. (The reader may wish to examine this relationship more carefully by comparing the effective yields on funds held in the UK and US, when there is 5 per cent interest premium in the UK which is accompanied by a 5 per cent pre-maturity depreciation of sterling in terms of dollars.) To guarantee a profitable investment, however, the US investor may be able to engage in effective 'forward covering', i.e. to contract to sell sterling at the currently quoted forward rate for the time of maturity, such that the cost of this forward covering (the forward discount on sterling) is less than the interest differential between the two countries. If the forward rate of sterling is 2 per cent at discount against the spot rate, then there is a 3 per cent 'covered' interest rate or yield premium on sterling.

A covered interest-rate margin between the two countries will increase the spot demand for and the forward supply of the currency with the interest premium. The pushing up of the spot rate and depressing of the forward rate generates a forward discount on this currency which would (given a perfectly elastic supply of arbitrage funds) increase until there was an effective yield parity between short-term financial assets held in the different financial centres. The 'interest parity theorem' suggests that the flow of funds between the two centres should cease at this point. (Readers in fact may wish to reinforce their understanding of these relationships by considering the case where the rate of interest is higher in the US than in the UK and there is a forward premium on sterling in terms of dollars.) In practice, forward currency discounts or premiums do not necessarily equal nominal interest rate differentials, because risk and liquidity considerations also influence portfolio decisions.

Speculation   In any case the arbitrageur may also be the speculator. In practice the separation of motives is difficult. In principle the motives are distinct. The 'pure speculator' takes a risk in the expectation of profits; a risk about the future movement of the spot rate in relation to the forward rate. If for instance the spot rate at some given date in the future is expected to be higher than the forward rate for that time period, then the speculator may profit by buying forward exchange now with the intention of selling at the spot rate at this future date.

Alternatively, if the future spot rate is expected to fall below the current forward rate, there is a given probability of gain from selling forward exchange now to buy back at a lower spot rate in the future. Forward buying (selling) will of course tend to reduce the opportunity for capital gain from a given, expected appreciation (depreciation) of the spot rate, since it will increase the forward premium (discount).

Under free market conditions the speculator runs the risk of making a loss on a transaction if his expectations are not fulfilled. However, where the exchange rate is pegged or managed by some intervention authority on the foreign-exchange market at a level above or below the free market-clearing rate (as in Fig. 5.2) then the minimal risk of administrative adjustment of the peg or managed rate away from the equilibrium reduces the probability of loss considerably (other than from the costs of the actual transactions). It is to the management of exchange rates by the authorities that we turn our attention. We need therefore to relax our earlier assumption that the foreign-exchange market operates under freely competitive conditions.

Managed exchange rates
Figure 5.2 illustrates the 'buffer-stock' principle of exchange-rate management. The central monetary authority[3] seeks to maintain the spot[4] exchange rate at a certain level (p_m in Fig. 5.2(a)) or at least within a certain range of values or 'band' (between p_u and p_L in Fig. 5.2(b)) by intervention buying or selling of foreign exchange.

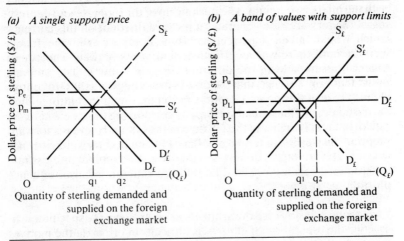

Fig. 5.2 Managed exchange rates: (a) A single support price; (b) A band of values with support limits

In Fig. 5.2(a) if the managed, target or pegged level (the appropriateness of each term depending on exactly what type of exchange-rate policy is being pursued) of the exchange rate (p_m) is consistent with the unconstrained market clearing equilibrium, there is no need for intervention activity. If, however, there are market pressures for the equilibrium rate to rise above the pegged level then the authorities must seek to resist these forces by supplying additional sterling on to the market to buy up foreign exchange. In terms of our simple bilateral model developed earlier in this chapter, a rise in the demand for sterling (perhaps resulting from a rise in real or money incomes in the US) will tend to push up the price of sterling in terms of dollars unless the UK authorities are obliged or willing to add dollars to their buffer stocks of reserves (possibly for future occasions when the need may arise to resist a depreciation of the currency). In Fig. 5.2(a) an upward shift in the demand schedule for sterling would, in the absence of intervention, push the price of sterling up to p_e. However, the provision of the necessary additional sterling ($q_2 - q_1$) by the authorities to buy up the excess dollars at p_m, thereby satisfying the demand for sterling, will prevent any alteration in the exchange rate. In this example the length of time that the authorities will seek to resist exchange-rate adjustment will depend upon their ability/willingness to alter the underlying demand and supply conditions for their currency through domestic policies, or to accumulate reserves of foreign currency.

Adjustment in the form of domestic deflationary or inflationary policies would shift the demand and supply curves in Fig. 5.2. In Fig. 5.2(a) for example, the pursuit of more inflationary policies in the UK would reduce the competitiveness of UK goods in the US market at each rate of exchange. The fall in the demand for UK goods and in turn for sterling at each exchange rate would tend to shift the demand curve $D_£$ back towards $D_£$. This reduction in the demand for sterling would therefore reduce the need for the authorities to pursue a policy of intervention buying. (In this example domestic inflationary policies would however also influence the UK's import demand and therefore the supply of sterling at each exchange rate.) Similarly, in Fig. 5.2(b) the reduction of domestic purchasing power through income deflation would reduce the demand for imports from the US and in turn the supply of sterling on to the foreign exchange market at each exchange rate. This would have the effect of pushing the supply curve $S_£$ back towards its original position ($S_£$), such that the unmanaged demand and supply curves intersect at an exchange rate within the permitted range of values (p_u to p_L).

In the absence of domestic adjustment and where there is pressure for a devaluation or depreciation of the currency, the limit on resistance is set by the size of a country's reserves of foreign currency (i.e. the amount of foreign currency available to buy up the surplus of the domestic currency at the present exchange rate) or by the country's ability to supplement those reserves by borrowing. In Fig. 5.2(b) (which represents more accurately the 'band'[5] features of the post-war adjustable peg system), the intervention authority uses stocks of dollars to purchase excess pounds ($q_2 - q_1$) when the exchange rate falls towards its lowest permitted level (p_L). (In reality, intervention buying of a currency is likely to occur before the exchange rate reaches the lower support value, and similarly selling by the authorities is likely to occur before the upper limit is reached.)

The pressures that the maintenance of managed rates generated and the reasons why the pegs were rarely adjusted under the Bretton Woods system will be considered in Chapter 8. At that stage also we will consider the collapse of the 'pegged' exchange rate system in the early 1970s into a system of 'managed' floating, which combines a mixture of the principles demonstrated in Figs 5.1 and 5.2. Freely floating exchange rates in principle remove the need for any official accommodating transactions. By contrast with anything less than a freely floating system, accommodating transactions may be necessary to support the exchange rate given a prevailing imbalance of international payments.

Autonomous and accommodating payments

So far our model of international payments and of the exchange rate has concentrated on the commercial trading motive for buying and selling foreign currency. In reality clearly the need to convert domestic into foreign currency arises not only when goods and services are traded internationally, but also when international capital (borrowing

Table 5.1   A stylised representation of the balance of payments

(*a*) *Current transactions*	
Items: *Credits*	*Debits*
1. Visible Exports	Visible Imports
2. Invisible Exports	Invisible Imports
3. Unilateral receipts	Unilateral payments
(government and private)	
(*b*) *Capital flows*	
4. Official long-term inflow	Official long-term outflow
5. Private long-term inflow	Private long-term outflow
(i) direct investment	(i) direct investment
(ii) portfolio investment	(ii) portfolio investment
6. Private short-term inflow	Private short-term outflow
(i) increase in foreign held	(i) reduction in foreign held
domestic liquid assets	liquid domestic assets
(ii) reduction in domestically	(ii) increase in domestically
owned foreign assets	owned foreign assets
7. (Errors and omissions, statistical	
discrepancy)	
8. Official short-term inflow	Official short-term outflow
– increase in officially held	
liquid liabilities	
9. (Allocation of SDRs)	
10. Fall in official reserves	Increase in official reserves
11. Official foreign currency	Official foreign currency
borrowing	lending

and lending) transactions of all kinds occur. The balance of payments as an accounting concept is therefore the summary record of all such transactions. In Table 5.1 there is a simplified schema of the balance-of-payments accounts. In an accounting sense, because for every credit there is a corresponding debit transaction, the balance of payments must balance. (A debit entry refers to the acquisition of a real or financial asset and a credit entry to the provision of either type of asset.) Why then may the balance of payments be a policy problem?

In just the same way that we consider sterling to be *ex ante* under-valued in terms of the dollar in Fig. 5.2(a), i.e. the *ex ante* equilibrium or market clearing rate (p_e) is in excess of the managed or *ex post* equilibrium rate (p_m), at which q_2 of sterling is demanded and supplied, then in similar fashion we may consider *ex ante* the balance of payments to be in surplus although the accounts technically balance.

In terms of the principles of exchange-rate determination already outlined, an excess demand for sterling on the foreign exchange market is equivalent to a surplus of credits over debits in the accounts, or rather in that set of transactions in the accounts that we can view as being autonomous or independent of balance-of-payments policy considerations. The removal of excess demand for sterling by exchange-rate adjustment has the effect, therefore, of restoring equality between these credits and debits. This can be illustrated by reference back to Fig. 5.1(b). The increase in the supply of sterling at each exchange rate generates an excess supply of sterling at exchange rate p_1. As long as the exchange rate remains at this level then the UK will tend *ex ante* to run a payments deficit (an excess of autonomous debits over credits), which would however be removed by allowing the excess supply to depress sterling's rate of exchange. Under the appropriate conditions the fall in the purchasing power of sterling would increase exports (autonomous credits) and reduce imports (autonomous debits). If the authorities by contrast stood ready to support the price of its currency on the foreign exchanges (as was demonstrated in Fig. 5.2(b)) then the authorities will in effect accommodate for or offset in the accounts the total currency outflow (inflow) resulting from an excess (shortfall) of autonomous debits over credits by withdrawing from (adding to) official reserves. (The use of reserves, i.e. the provision of financial assets, is a credit in the accounts, while the addition to reserves, i.e. the acquisition of assets, is recorded as a debit.) When exchange rates are managed, therefore, the possible need for accommodating flows of funds poses a policy problem.

Unfortunately our analysis thus far has drawn an over-simple pic-ture of the nature of international payments and transactions. We have assumed that autonomous transactions are restricted to current trans-actions or exchanges of goods and services (items 1, 2, 3 in Table 5.1), and that accommodating capital transactions are restricted to the use of official reserves (i.e. the settlements items 10, 11 in Table 5.1). We have ignored items 5 and 6 in Table 5.1. Private capital flows are in fact a problematic area in balance-of-payments analysis. The problem is one of isolating autonomous from accommodating capital flows.

Private borrowing and lending activity across national frontiers may take a variety of forms. A capital inflow, for instance, may take the form of the purchase by a foreigner of short- or long-term government bonds, and of stocks and shares of domestic firms. Alternatively the capital inflow may take the form of the build-up of foreign-owned deposits or balances at domestic banks (or the run-down of externally held balances). For recording purposes it is possible to distinguish between the type of capital transaction involved, but it is less easy to identify the motivations behind each transaction. Long-term external borrowing or lending for direct investment purposes may on many occasions be an autonomous transaction, motivated purely by considerations of commercial profitability. But given central government control over the direction of investment, in for example the public sectors of economies, then a policy decision may be taken to borrow abroad rather than at home in part at least for balance-of-payments reasons. Similarly, shorter-term borrowing in the form of increases in foreign-owned domestic balances (or reductions in domestically owned foreign balances), may be a passive or accommodating transaction which finances an autonomous trade imbalance. That is to say that an excess of UK-imported goods from (over exports to) the US may be paid for by adding to the sterling balances of US exporters in London (or by reducing UK-owned dollar balances in the US). This will be recorded in the accounts as a balancing capital inflow. Changes in such short-term balances are however also generated (as we have already seen) by changes in interest rate differentials and expectations of the future course of exchange rates; factors which may or may not be independent of the overall payments situation.

How then do we give analytical and operational significance to the often-used terms surplus and deficit in the balance of payments? The accounts are an *ex post* record of international transactions which pose two major problems to the analyst. On the one hand, how do we separate or draw the line between autonomous ('above the line') and accommodating ('below the line') transactions? On the other hand, to what extent does the actual balance on the appropriate set of transactions diverge from the desired balance? It is to these issues that we now turn our attention.

5.3 The nature of imbalance

Accounting concepts

Where we choose to draw the line in the actual classifications of the payments accounts will determine whether there is apparent imbalance, i.e. surplus of autonomous credits over debits or vice versa. For analytical and policy-formulation purposes we need to identify the extent to which transactions are undertaken for their own sake or are in response to some other transaction elsewhere in the accounts. In practical terms it is only possible to satisfy this analytical requirement if we can attach distinct motives to sets of transactions as recorded within the accounts. Given the absence of this happy coincidence we can then organise the accounts in a variety of ways to produce alternative, proxy measures of imbalance (see Veil, 1975). The usefulness of each proxy is likely to vary with time and between countries as circumstances and policy-makers' concerns change. Indeed we may go so far as to argue that it is impossible to describe the balance of international transactions with a single figure, in an analytical sense that is, and that therefore accounting balances should not be used. This recommendation was in fact made by the US Advisory Committee in 1976 (see the Report of the Advisory Committee, 1976).

The fact that countries record transactions or organise their accounts differently means that international comparison is often difficult. With the aid of Tables 5.2 and 5.3(*a*) and (*b*) we will seek to compare the UK and US recording methods, and the changes in US procedure since 1976.

'Settlements' concepts Since the balance of 'above-the-line' and 'below-the-line' transactions must net out to zero, we can identify surplus or deficit situations by considering the type of transactions we place either side of the line. One obvious approach to measuring the extent of accommodating transactions used to deal with excess demand for or supply of foreign exchange (or domestic currency) is to draw the line just above the settlements entries. The balance on official settlements focuses attention on the balance of transactions which the monetary authorities undertake to support the exchange rate. In its more extreme formulation it only includes below-the-line changes in official reserve assets and net direct government borrowing of foreign currency, from the IMF or foreign central banks or the private money market, i.e. items 10 and 11 in Table 5.1. For a fuller coverage of official transactions, we should include net changes in liquid liabilities to foreign official reserve agencies, i.e. item 8 in Table 5.1. An excess supply of domestic currency on to the foreign exchange market which arises out of autonomous transactions, may not require financing from reserves or borrowing in whole or part, if other central banks are willing to hold the currency concerned in their own reserves. This is in fact a particularly significant measure of payments deficit for a currency which is commonly used as a reserve asset. The US concept used before 1976, the 'balance on official reserve transactions' shown in Table 5.3(*a*), approximated closely to this broader idea of settlement, although it also included changes in non-liquid liabilities to foreign official reserve agencies. In the UK case, with the allocation of Special Drawing Rights (SDRs) from the IMF included below the line, official financing corresponds above the line with the 'total currency flow'

Table 5.2 UK balance of payments (1972–7) (in £ million)

	(£ million) 1972	1973	1974	1975	1976	1977
Current transactions						
Net visible balance	− 722	− 2 383	− 5 235	− 3 236	− 3 589	− 1 709
Net invisible balance	+ 857	+ 1 384	+ 1 644	+ 1 381	+ 2 452	+ 1 998
Current balance	+ 135	− 999	− 3 591	− 1 855	− 1 137	+ 289
Transfers		− 59	− 75			
Investment and capital flows (net)						
Official long term*	− 255	− 254	− 276	− 288	− 158	− 291
in UK public sector	+ 120	+ 175	+ 252	+ 43	+ 203	+ 2 182
in/by UK private sector	− 588	− 90	+ 1 169	+ 416	+ 95	+ 737
borrowing/lending by UK banks	+ 471	+ 525	+ 294	+ 235	− 106	+ 384
change in sterling liabilities	+ 196	+ 154	+ 1 558	+ 67	− 1 152	+ 1 452
trade credit and other capital flows	− 613	− 345	− 712	+ 61	− 1 588	− 54
Net capital flows	− 669	+ 165	+ 1 697	+ 278	− 2 896	+ 4 410
Balancing item (recording errors)	− 731	+ 122	+ 323	+ 112	+ 404	+ 2 662
Total currency flow	− 1 265	− 771	− 1 646	− 1 465	− 3 629	+ 7 361
allocation of SDRs	+ 124					
Official financing						
change in reserves† (withdrawals (+)/additions (−))	+ 692	− 228	− 105	+ 655	+ 853	− 9 588
Government foreign currency borrowing‡		+ 999	+ 1 751	+ 810	+ 1 792	+ 1 114
net transactions with overseas monetary authorities	+ 449				+ 984	+ 1 113

*Not under exchange cover scheme
†From July 1972 transactions with IMF affecting reserve position in the Fund are included in changes in reserves
‡Including public sector borrowing under exchange cover scheme
Source: adapted from UK Balance of Payments 1967–77, Tables 1.1 and 1.3. (HMSO, Sept. 1978)

Table 5.3(a)   US Balance of payments (1972–4): old basis

	($ million) 1972	1973	1974
Current transactions			
Net merchandise trade	− 6 912	+ 471	− 5 277
Net services	+ 2 302	+3 856	+ 9 107
Net private transfers	− 1 570	−1 943	− 1 721
Net official transfers	− 2 174	−1 933	− 5 461
Balance on current account	− 8 353	+ 450	− 3 357
Investment and capital flows			
Long-term capital: private	− 152	+ 62	+ 1 119
Long-term capital: official	− 1 339	−1 538	− 8 463
Balance on current account and long-term capital	− 9 843	−1 026	−10 702
Short-term, non-liquid capital: private	− 1 637	−4 276	−12 936
(Allocation of SDRs	+ 710		
errors and omissions)	− 3 112	−2 303	+ 4 698
Net Liquidity balance	−13 882	−7 606	−18 940
Change in liquid private claims	− 1 234	−1 944	− 6 267
Change in liquid private liabilities	+ 4 776	+4 246	+16 810
Balance on official reserve transactions	−10 340	−5 304	− 8 397
Financed by:			
Change in reserves (withdrawal (+)/addition (−))	+ 32	+ 209	− 1 434
Changes in total liabilities to foreign official agencies	+10 308	+5 095	+ 9 831

Source: Survey of Current Business, Dec. 1973, 1974 and 1975, Table 1

concept recorded in Table 5.2. In 1976 for instance the total currency outflow of £3 629 million was 'officially' financed by drawing £853 million from foreign currency reserves, and by borrowing £1 792 million in the private money markets and £984 million from the IMF and other overseas monetary authorities.

Since the end of 1972 UK official settlement or financing may be seen within a wider context. The line between official or non-official financing has become more blurred. Since this time balance-of-payments deficits have been 'indirectly' financed in part, by borrowing on the private international money markets by other public-sector agencies (local authorities and nationalised industries), under the exchange guarantee scheme. Under this exchange cover scheme the Treasury protects the borrower from any rise in the sterling value of the foreign currency debt due to a depreciation of sterling. In 1976, however, borrowing under this scheme was redefined as official borrowing, and included therefore as official financing. In addition to the growth of this less direct official settlement activity, we may also consider to what extent non-official capital flows (borrowing and lending activity) should be viewed as accommodating settlement. Thus

Table 5.3(*b*)   US international transactions (1975–7): revised basis

	($ million) 1975	1976
Exports of goods and services	+148 410	+163 265
Imports of goods and services	−132 141	−159 668
US military grants: net	− 2 232	− 386
Unilateral transfers	− 4 620	− 5 023
US assets abroad (net) (increase/capital outflow (−))	− 31 131	− 42 959
US official reserve assets	− 607	− 2 530
Official assets, other than reserve assets	− 3 463	− 4 213
US private assets	− 27 061	− 36 216
Foreign assets in US (net) (increase/capital inflow (+))	+ 14 879	+ 34 520
Foreign official assets in US	+ 6 336	+ 17 945
other foreign assets in US	+ 8 544	+ 16 575
(Allocations of SDRs)		
Statistical discrepancy	+ 4 602	+ 9 866

Source: Survey of Current Business, Sept. 1977, Table I, p. 40

far we have placed all private capital flows above the line. In our consideration of interest-arbitrage we demonstrated the sensitivity of capital to interest rate differentials. Given a deficit on autonomous transactions for instance, the authorities may help to attract (with relatively high interest rates) overseas funds into short-term assets in particular, such as bank deposits or government securities. Table 5.2 shows a current deficit of £3 591 million for the UK in 1974, for example. Official financing in the same year, however, was only £1 646 million, and it is reasonable to assume therefore that a significant element of the £1 558 million increase in sterling liabilities was induced by domestic financial policies.

For policy purposes, however, the authorities may remain concerned with official reserve transactions. Under a pegged exchange-rate system, official reserve transactions may measure direct foreign-exchange intervention. The size of the reserves is in fact an immediately measurable and frequently publicised economic variable. Reserves, acquired to resist revaluation for instance, are frequently seen as indicative of the strength of the currency and a country's external position. Once however the authorities cease to maintain the exchange rate on an irregular (a 'dirty' float) or a permanent (a 'clean' float) basis, the official settlements concept becomes a rather less meaningful indicator of currency market conditions. Under a 'clean float' for example official settlements should tend to zero. The US decision to drop a measure of intervention activity is explained for instance by the advent of a floating dollar. (The factors accounting for this change in exchange-rate policy are considered in Chapter 8.)

Since floats are likely, however, to be 'managed' rather than 'clean', the transactions of the official monetary authorities may remain of significance. Concern for the primary reserve position is likely to remain with anything less than freely floating exchange rates. Reserves (and credit) are finite, and the authorities are unlikely to be able to permanently 'neglect' the value of their currency on the foreign-exchange markets. Indeed, maintenance of confidence in the external value of the currency may be particularly important where a currency is widely held by foreigners for the financing of trade or in official reserves. This is the case for the US and to a lesser extent the UK.

Where such liabilities exceed official reserves, their potential liquidation has an important bearing on currency market conditions. Although privately held liabilities do not represent a direct threat to reserves in the same way that officially held and therefore immediately convertible liabilities do (in principle), they do represent an indirect threat where the authorities stand committed to maintaining the value of the currency through support buying.

In the case of a reserve currency such as the dollar, the threat is magnified if countries other than the US accumulate dollars in their official reserves in order to avoid appreciation or revaluation of their own currencies. The intensification of this direct and indirect threat to US official reserves forced the US to suspend dollar convertibility in 1971. (See Chapter 8 for further discussion of this issue.)

Liquidity considerations The official-settlements concept has therefore some important limitations. By equating accommodation with the direct capital transactions that official agencies fulfil, it ignores that the authorities, by means of interest-rate policies, can indirectly influence the pattern of short-term capital flows for balance-of-payments purposes. It also ignores the potential threat to reserves that liquid liabilities of private foreigners present, especially for reserve currencies.

The US 'net liquidity balance' in Table 5.3(a) (the case for which was first argued by Lederer, 1963) was in fact an attempt to measure the authorities' capabilities in defending the exchange rate. This, Lederer argued, depended upon the liquid resources available to the financial authorities for use in the foreign-exchange market, and upon the liquid claims that may be made against those reserves. The US concept therefore sought to measure all the liquid liabilities which accrued to foreigners as a result of above-the-line transactions. Below the line it combined changes in reserve assets with net changes in dollar liabilities to both official and private foreigners.

This concept was fundamentally a pragmatic response to the problem of distinguishing between autonomous and accommodating short-term capital flows (namely not to bother trying!), and to dealing with the unique problems facing the dollar as a reserve currency of the pegged exchange rate system of the 1950s and 1960s. In just the same way, however, that not all capital flows are acts of accommodation, not all externally held claims on reserves are immediate liabilities. Since the floating of currencies, for example, increases in liabilities to foreign official institutions may not reflect pressure against that currency – rather they may reflect a deliberate portfolio decision to add this currency to the reserves as a result of confidence in the particular currency. In fact a country willing to fulfil the reserve asset function (with the rest of the world's approval) may wish to pursue a policy of deliberately contributing (in net terms) to world liquidity by increasing official foreign holdings (Salant, 1969). Similarly, increases in privately held liquid liabilities may also reflect an increase in the demand for working balances (i.e. for the financing of trade) rather than an increase in interest-sensitive balances. Short-term lending may in effect become long-term in nature if it is repeatedly renewed. By contrast foreign portfolio investment is defined as non-liquid and long-term in nature for balance-of-payments purposes. It is therefore recorded above the line, but may on occasions be sensitive to both interest and exchange rate variations. Both portfolio and direct investment may be volatile and responsive to domestic policies.

Given the subjectivity of the liquidity concept and the suspension of dollar convertibility, the US have decided to discontinue publication of a net liquidity balance (compare Tables 5.3(*a*) and (*b*)).

Measuring basic forces   Nevertheless the justification for drawing the line so as to derive the balance on current account and long-term capital or the 'basic balance' (the first five items in Table 5.1) is based upon the premise that this captures above the line the stable and predictable forces within an accounting framework. By extension the more transitory and volatile elements remain below the line. This arrangement is as we have suggested not without its difficulties (see Kindleberger, 1969). Long-term capital flows are statistically identified by the original maturity of the assets bought or sold (i.e. greater than one year). Bonds, long-dated at issue, may however be purchased near maturity or sold again quickly. The statistical distinction does not capture therefore the extent to which capital flows are reversible. Doubts, in fact, about the validity of including all 'long-term' capital while excluding all 'short-term' capital from the basic balance led the UK authorities to abandon the concept in 1970. The US briefly reconstituted this balance at this time (see Table 5.3(*a*)), but also abandoned the concept in 1976.

Despite these difficulties this measure may be an indicator (albeit crude) of underlying trends in the pattern of international payments. A persistent current deficit which is matched for instance by an inflow of long-term capital may be acceptable to policy-makers. If the inflow raises productive capacity, encourages exports and reduces import dependence, then the long-term capital inflow may help to reduce the current deficit. In the absence of such stable long-term inflows of capital or of the political willingness to increase foreign dependence, the alignment or equality of the value of a country's imports and exports may be a focus of attention.

The current balance, i.e. the sum of the balances on goods, services and unilateral transfers (items 1, 2 and 3 in Table 5.1), is the most regularly monitored payments measurement. (The US have in fact retained the merchandise trade balance and the balance on goods, services and remittances as memoranda items in their summary of international transactions.) The appeal of the current balance is that it is immediately compatible with the traditional national income framework, and since concerned largely with visible and invisible trade it is subject to generally more predictable forces, i.e. factors such as domestic and global incomes and prices. As a guide to economic policy it indicates whether or not a country is absorbing goods beyond its current income (if unilateral transfers are included), or at least whether there has been a net inward or outward transfer of real resources if such transfers are excluded.[6] It is to whether or not (or at least under what conditions) underspending (a current surplus), or overspending (a current deficit) in relation to current income is a desirable external target, that we must now turn our attention.

Policy concepts

Living beyond a country's present income (a current-account deficit) contrary to popular belief (the 'puritan ethic of international trade' – Scitovsky, 1966) can not in itself be automatically considered harmful or undesirable. Each payments situation must be examined in relation to the prevailing conditions. Those conditions will include for example the prevailing levels of domestic activity, and the country's ability to draw upon past savings (reserves) or foreign savings (through borrowing). A country may wish to stimulate domestic activity, and therefore to use in effect a current payments deficit as a vehicle for encouraging expansion of the economy. That there is an interdependence in the movement of domestic and external policy variables in fact raises two important issues. First there is the problem of deciding about the length of time over which we wish to specify that equilibrium or balance should be achieved. Second we must consider to what extent policy targets and equilibrium concepts for the balance of international payments are compatible with each other.

Flows of autonomous transactions and therefore the demand for and supply of currency will obviously be subject to short-term disturbances. Awareness of the existence of erratic or seasonal forces which may generate temporary imbalances, does not simplify the problem of attaching precise values to economic time periods. Given for instance the seasonality of economic activities, then the minimum period within which there can be self-correction is one year. There is a less obvious period of self-correction for erratic influences. Similarly, cyclical influences may well not be self-correcting within one year. The duration of the business cycle would therefore seem to set a limit on the period of time required to identify fundamental or underlying patterns of external (im)balance. Nurkse (1945) suggested a period of five to ten years based on the average duration of the business cycle, while Dasgupta and Hagger (1971) identify the long term as being up to a decade. Cohen (1969) however, in view of the variability of the length of cycles and of the analytical difficulty of separating the cycle from trend influences, argues that imbalances which persist for more than one year may in fact be indicative of fundamental disequilibrium. As analysts therefore, we may by necessity remain imprecise, but the policy-maker is likely to have more definite time horizons imposed upon him by the finite nature of reserves and borrowing.

In reality the probability is that governments will be motivated by short-term (e.g. electoral) considerations, and will set targets for 'actual balance' (Meade, 1951) on a particular set of *ex post* transactions. Although this actual balance may correspond to an accounting equilibrium (i.e. an equality of autonomous credits and debits), there is still the problem of deciding whether it also corresponds to a desired equilibrium position. Our earlier discussion has shown that there is a continuous interaction between changes in policies and all types of international transactions. Cooper (1966) argues that actual (im)balance effectively varies as policies at home and abroad vary. We must decide therefore on the arrangement of economic policies and targets which we wish to see prevailing alongside the 'actual' balance (however measured).

External targets   External targets are frequently expressed so that actual balance should be achieved without recourse to less than full employment or to trade and payments restrictions. The viewing of actual balance achieved at less than full employment levels of domestic incomes and output, or with the aid of restrictions, as hidden disequilibrium, draws on the traditions of the 'true' or 'potential' balance concepts of Nurkse (1945) and Meade (1951) respectively. The basic Keynesian proposition, however, that full employment is not a unique equilibrium situation,[7] suggest that Nurkse and Meade were providing a target balance of external payments (or what Machlup (1950) calls a 'programme balance' of hopes and desires), rather than a strict equilibrium concept. That is to say that if adopted, it provides an indication of the programme of objectives which in the policy-makers judgement is most desirable, rather than the analytical requirements of economic modelling.[8] The 'market balance' concept (Machlup, 1950) is analytically more rigorous since it seeks to compare the demand for and supply of foreign exchange under alternative and hypothetical future incomes, prices and interest rates.

It is perhaps more operationally relevant to express external equilibrium or balance within a framework which assumes that governments use certain instruments to achieve certain targets. However, the requirement of unrestricted trade and full employment is based as much on value judgements as objective considerations. Similarly, the suggested trade-off between price inflation and unemployment (in the short-run at least), poses problems for analytical objectivity. In fact the subjectivity of, and therefore lack of homogeneity of attitude between countries towards the trade-off between unemployment and inflation in an interdependent world, is an important source of difficulty in reconciling external equilibrium and full employment and relative price stability for a country acting in isolation. Without the problem of interdependence, the mutual achievement of internal and external targets is still not without its difficulties. Experience has shown that the achievement of internal targets for full employment has in practice often been at the expense of external imbalance. It is to this potential source of external imbalance and others that we must now turn our attention.

5.4 The sources of imbalance

Although the identification of external imbalance is not without its difficulties, any discussion of the possible sources of imbalance or disequilibrium tends to be even less precise. This is because we must begin to place the balance of payments within a theoretical framework. Unfortunately 'general theories' in economics are not without their competitors, and are usually less than general in their approach. Balance of payments theorising is no different.

If, however, we adopt Johnson's framework (Johnson, 1958b) we can view the balance of payments as the difference between the aggregate receipts (R_A) of the residents of one country and the aggregate payments (P_A) by those residents. Thus we can seek to examine the factors which influence aggregate receipts and payments, and the way in which the balance of payments responds to those changes.

Stock and flow imbalance
The inequality of R_A and P_A may result from either a decision to alter the composition of the community's asset holding, i.e. a once-and-for-all decision to substitute between money and other assets; or a decision to spend in excess of current receipts. The former is a stock decision, the latter a flow decision (Johnson, 1958b). (Of course, if the exchange rate is perfectly functioning, i.e. the elasticity conditions are satisfied, imbalance will only arise if the exchange rate is not free to adjust.)

A stock decision is therefore inherently temporary since any aggregate decision to reduce money balances over a certain stock adjustment period in order to increase holdings of real goods (leading to current imbalance) or of securities (leading to capital imbalance) will only generate imbalance over that particular period. The stock imbalance therefore will only pose a policy problem if reserves are insufficient to finance the imbalance.

A flow imbalance may however imply a worsening of a country's economic performance and thereby pose a policy problem if self-adjustment forces are absent, insufficient or frustrated, or if again reserves are inadequate. Theoretical analysis is generally concerned with flow 'deficits' or 'surpluses' since they are not inherently temporary.

External imbalance as a monetary phenomenon

An external deficit by definition implies an excess of payments by residents over receipts to residents which must, *ceteris paribus,* result in a run-down in the community's cash or money balances. Take the situation where under some managed exchange-rate system domestic money is transferred abroad. The increased spending and payments deficit which corresponds to this domestic dis-hoarding necessarily implies an increase in the velocity of circulation of domestic money (v), if the money supply is not replenished. This is not of course compatible with 'monetarist' philosophy, which stresses monetary determinacy and therefore constancy of v. If on the other hand v is constant, then balance-of-payments deficits must result from monetary expansion. We will shortly consider the role of the monetary authorities in generating monetary sources of imbalance. At this stage we must stress that although we can establish the immediate monetary form of imbalance and argue that 'balance of payments deficits and difficulties are essentially monetary phenomena' (Johnson, 1958b), it is important to emphasise that there may be other ultimate or initiating sources of imbalance to which the money supply passively adjusts. These may include, for instance, real income changes and changes in relative prices.

The income approach to imbalance

If we concentrate on the current balance (exports (X) minus imports (M)) and ignore unilateral payments, then it is possible to place balance of payments analysis within a national income framework which is essentially Keynesian in spirit. An income-expenditure model for an open economy (without government intervention) will take the following form:

$$Y = C + I + X - M$$

where Y is national income, C is consumer spending and I is investment spending.

To simplify our analysis we must assume that prices are constant and that there are idle resources in the economy. This will allow us to examine real income adjustment only, in response to external imbalance. We will also adopt simple linear relationships.

It is usual to assume in these basic models that spending on imports, like the rest of consumer spending, is positively related to national income itself (i.e. $M = M_0 + mY$, where m = marginal propensity to import), while exports are independent of the level of domestic income ($\bar{X}$). These relationships are demonstrated in Fig. 5.3, and combined to

Fig. 5.3 Simple import and export functions

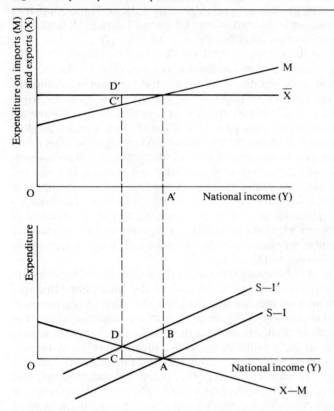

Fig. 5.4 Equilibrium in an open economy

provide the inverse relationship between the balance of trade $(X - M)$ and income shown in Fig. 5.4.

If we apply the condition for equilibrium in the closed economy, namely that injections equal leakages, then the equilibrium condition for this open economy is:

$$X + I = S + M$$

This can be rearranged to establish that the balance of trade is equivalent to the difference between saving and domestic investment:

$$X - M = S - I$$

This condition is diagramatically represented in Fig. 5.4. The $S - I$ function is upward-sloping because savings (S) are assumed to be directly related to income, while investment is exogenously determined and assumed therefore to be invariable with income. The diagram shows that the balance of trade $(X - M)$ is zero at the level of national income at which the X − M schedule cuts the income axis (equivalent also to income level A′ in Fig. 5.3). In Fig. 5.4 point A initially corresponds to a situation of external balance (X − M = 0) and to one of internal equilibrium (X − M = S − I).

It is possible to examine the relationship between income and the balance of payments by considering shifts in either the S − I or X − M functions. But since our aim is to demonstrate the impact of income change on the balance of trade, let us consider a shift in the S − I function to S − I′. (This may result from a reduction in autonomous consumption or investment.) The size of the fall in domestic spending at income level A is shown by the distance AB in Fig. 5.4. This fall in spending will have downward or reverse multiplier effects on income, which will in turn reduce both the level of imports and saving. The fall in income will continue until leakages (S + M) have fallen by the same amount as the initial fall in injections. In Fig. 5.4 a new equilibrium is established at income level C (corresponding to the intersection of X − M and S − I′ at point D). At this new equilibrium position there is a current surplus represented by the distance CD (which is equivalent also to the distance C′D′ in Fig. 5.3).

The degree of imbalance generated in this simple model by spending changes depends therefore on the size of the multiplier effects of spending changes on income (i.e. ΔY) and the value of the marginal propensity to import (i.e. $\Delta M = m \, \Delta Y$). In other words the smaller the value of m and the change in income, the smaller the change in imports and therefore in the balance of trade. We must remember, however, that we are assuming that exports remain constant. In reality, changes in one country's imports will alter other countries' income levels and their ability to import from the first country. There are likely therefore to be feedback effects on a country's exports of changes in its imports. The existence of these international linkages serves in part to reduce imbalance by spreading the effects of income changes, but it also serves to provide a further, potential source of imbalance.

The international transmission of imbalance

The effects of expansions or contractions in autonomous expenditure in one country will be transmitted to other countries as a result of the effect that changes in income will have upon the initial country's imports (or other countries' exports). If for example there is a domestic investment boom in one country, there will be spillover effects to other countries. Although the leakage of income through increased imports acts as a constraint on expansion in the country initiating expansion, the corresponding injection of spending into other economies in the form of exports serves to transmit the process of expansion abroad (and correspondingly external imbalance).

The degree of this spillover effect will depend upon the relative size of the country transmitting expansion or contraction, and upon its marginal propensity to import. (The absolute size of cyclical changes in income of a country like the US has been a significant source, or potential source, of external imbalance for its trading partners, despite its relatively low dependence on imported goods.) Given, however, the increasing interdependence or interrelatedness of economies in the post-war period it is not always possible to identify the country initiating boom and slump. It may actually be more accurate to talk in terms of a world cycle, which reflects the increasing synchronisation of national cycles. Nevertheless the grouping of countries in Fig. 5.5 to provide a two-case model serves to illustrate the process of international transmission, where the exchange rate is fixed.

The increase in autonomous investment in America which shifts the $(S - I)_A$ function outwards towards $(S - I)'_A$ increases income in America (to income level B) and imports from the rest of the world

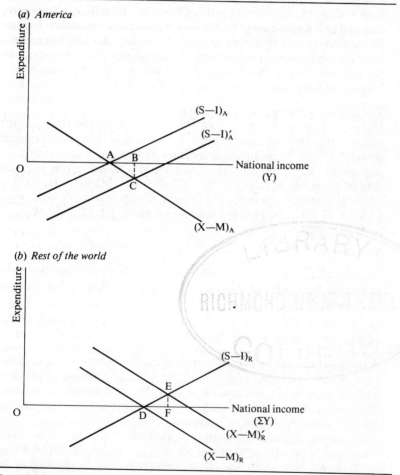

Fig. 5.5 International transmission of imbalance

(ROW), providing capacity is available. This increase in the rest of the world's exports to America (the outward shift of $(X - M)_R$) raises the level of real income in the ROW to income level F. The immediate consequence of these initial income adjustments is to generate a trade deficit of BC in America, and a corresponding surplus of EF for the ROW. There may of course be some further feedback effects which tend to reduce the (foreign trade) multiplier effects of spending and income changes, and therefore the degree of imbalance, but it is likely that further policy adjustment by America or the ROW will be necessary if imbalance is to be removed.

In terms therefore of the income approach to external imbalance, we may conclude that although spending changes will generate payments imbalance, the income changes will themselves tend to move the balance of payments back towards equilibrium. These automatic forces of income adjustment will not, however, be sufficient to remove external imbalance except under very unusual circumstances. Income fluctuation is likely therefore to generate the need for other automatic forces of adjustment or further income adjustment through discretionary policies. (For a fuller coverage of the income approach to the balance of payments see Scammell, 1974, Ch. 13.)

The income—absorption relationship

If we continue to abstract from the impact of capital flows on the balance of payments, then we are able to establish some useful general principles from the income-expenditure analysis just examined. If we reconsider the basic national income model, including this time the role of government (i.e. $Y = C + I + G + X - M$) then the level of national income is equivalent to the sum of expenditure or absorption (A), i.e. $C + I + G$, plus the balance of trade (B), i.e. $X - M$.

Algebraically:

$$Y = A + B$$

We can rearrange this to establish that the balance of trade (B) is the difference between the level of real national income and the sum of real absorption,

i.e. $B = Y - A$
and $B \gtreqless 0$ as $Y \gtreqless A$.

A trade deficit occurs therefore when domestic absorption exceeds the level of national income, and a surplus when absorption is less than national income. In other words a 'flow' deficit is a problem of over-absorption, and a surplus of under-absorption in relation to the current level of national income or output.

We have already considered a possible explanation for non-alignment of real absorption and real income. In Keynesian terms we have shown how over- or under-absorption may be generated by autonomous increases in spending which may for example reflect a change in the attitude towards current and future consumption. In this approach we did not give attention to changes in relative prices, although they are unlikely in reality to remain unchanged. In the income-expenditure model in fact we specifically considered real change and assumed that excess capacity and price rigidity prevailed. In the full employment conditions of the post-war period neither of those assumptions appear realistic. Changes in price competitiveness in domestic and foreign markets may in fact be an important source of imbalance.

Changes in relative prices

There are obviously many non-price features of competitiveness (e.g. design, after-sales service, etc.), which in practice are difficult to quantify. Our analysis will focus attention on how the general pattern of relative prices may influence the overall payments position. We may reason in fact that current deficit (surplus) is associated with a rise (fall) in the relative prices of exportables or traded goods, which reduces (increases) competitiveness in domestic and foreign markets. In the **absence** of exchange-rate flexibility, changes in relative prices result from variations in rates of domestic inflation.

Suppose, for example, the price of traded goods increased more rapidly in the UK than in other industrial countries due to a growth of money wages in excess of real productivity growth. The result would be an excess of spending in money terms over output, which would push up the price of UK traded goods in relation to foreign traded goods.[9] In consequence, there would be a deterioration in the UK's current balance as imports grew and exportables were diverted to the home market. Classical theories of adjustment suggest that falling employment in the UK resulting from this decline in international competitiveness would tend to depress money wages, and to bring about therefore a readjustment of relative prices. We may be pessimistic, however, whether under modern conditions money wages will fall, and people may in fact compensate for rising prices by pressing for even further increases in money wages. Relative prices may therefore remain in disequilibrium, especially if rapid productivity growth in excess of money-income growth is occurring in other countries. Thus in the absence of complete domestic factor and product price flexibility, and of adjustment of relative prices through exchange-rate adjustment, a growth of imports in excess of exports may persist.

The reader may wish to work through the situation arising out of a fall in relative prices.

The monetary approach reconsidered

Are the explanations of over- (and under-) absorption so far considered, namely the income flow and relative prices approach, genuine sources of imbalance or merely alternative manifestations of the actual monetary cause? Viewed within a monetary framework, balance-of-payments surpluses and deficits (and movements in exchange rates) are the result of a disparity between the demand for and supply of money (see Johnson, 1976). When a disparity exists monetary theorising suggests that spending units will attempt to draw down (build up) their money balances through the purchase (sale) of real or financial assets. Suppose for example the monetary authorities increase the money supply in America, then *ceteris paribus* this may cause an increase in the demand for goods, services and securities in America and other countries. This increase in demand is also likely to increase the price of real and financial assets (and therefore lower interest rates) in America relative to foreign markets. As a result residents in America will reduce spending on domestic assets in favour of foreign assets, while domestic producers will be encouraged to concentrate on the home market at the expense of foreign sales. Foreign spending units and producers will be motivated to act in the opposite manner. All these factors would generate a deficit on current and capital transactions as the import of real and financial assets increased and exports of the same fell. Under a fixed or managed exchange-rate system (and if we accept this monetary transmission mechanism), monetary expansion will reduce America's reserve holdings as the accumulated money balances of foreigners are converted into their own currencies.

We will consider in Chapter 6 the long-term, automatic adjustment forces that such changes in primary reserve assets may generate. At this stage our aim is to establish the possibility of a monetary explanation of imbalance, or at least of a contributory, monetary source of imbalance. As we have previously argued, this may lay active responsibility for external imbalance against the monetary authorities if we view the money supply as being exogenously determined by them. It may however be the case that we are merely identifying passive, endogenous adjustment of the money supply to the real forces that have generated spending changes. Many readers will in fact be familiar with the conflicting views in macroeconomic literature on the role of money and of the channels of monetary influence.

Other sources of imbalance
We have concentrated our investigation of possible sources of imbalance in broad aggregate terms. Before leaving this issue it is worth mentioning that we could approach this topic in a more disaggregated manner. A more detailed examination of import and export functions and of the structure of the economy would identify other real influences on or sources of imbalance.

We may for instance identify capacity deficiencies in certain industries or sectors which generate a 'ratchet effect' to import growth with each upturn in domestic activity. (For the UK economy, see Milner, 1977.) Similarly we may discover 'structural imbalance' in an economy whereby the pattern of goods produced is not consistent with domestic and global patterns of demand. (Again for the UK economy, see Panić, 1975.) Finally we may identify deliberate policies to perpetuate imbalance, i.e. trade discrimination of a tariff or non-tariff nature on an industry-by-industry or economy-wide basis.

Where in fact other countries pursue policies designed not to generate or to prevent a return to external balance, then that will itself impose imbalance on other countries. (The problem of international inconsistencies is considered again in Chapter 6.) These inconsistencies may occur because countries either do not know how to reconcile internal and external policy targets or cannot agree on common and compatible objectives. It is to this fundamental policy problem in balance of payments analysis and potential source of imbalance that we turn our discussion.

5.5 Imbalance as a policy problem

Policy conflict
We can illustrate how the achievement of external balance may be constrained by consideration of internal balance by reference to Fig. 5.6. This particular representation of the policy problem draws upon the work of Swan (1963).

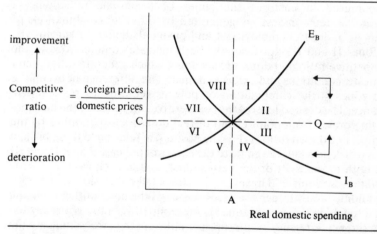

Fig. 5.6 Internal and external conflict

If we adopt domestic employment as a proxy for the internal target and current balance (X = M) as a proxy for external balance, then we can argue that each target is dependent on both the level of real domestic expenditure, and the international price competitiveness of domestic goods. Figure 5.6 indicates that the achievement of internal balance requires an improvement in the competitiveness of domestic goods as the level of domestic expenditure decreases. By contrast, as the competitive ratio improves, external balance will only be maintained if it is accompanied by an increase in the level of domestic spending. In crude terms the model is assuming that improvements in competitiveness reduce imports and increase exports and therefore employment and vice versa, while increased domestic expenditure stimulates imports and employment. Thus the slopes of Iʙ and Eʙ (the loci joining combinations of the competitive ratio and domestic expenditure generating internal and external balance respectively) indicate that full employment is achievable with a combination of high export and low domestic demand or vice versa, while external balance can be achieved at low levels of export and import demand or high levels of each.

The model clearly demonstrates potential conflict since twin balance is only possible at a unique combination of the competitive ratio (C) and real domestic spending (A). The model illustrates in fact potential divergence from one or both of the targets of economic policy. Positions to the right of the Iʙ curve represent over-full employment (inflationary) conditions, and to the left under-full employment (deflationary) conditions. Positions to the right of the Eʙ curve represent deficit situations and to the left payments surplus. (The reader may in fact wish to check the reasoning behind this and to reinforce his understanding of the model by considering the policy problems encountered in each of the zones of 'economic unhappiness'. 'Economic unhappiness' as generated by differing combinations of over- or under-full employment and payments deficit or surplus.)[10]

Zones II and III, for instance, both indicate combinations of the competitive ratio and domestic spending which generate inflationary domestic conditions and external deficit. The difference between the two zones is the combination of policies required to restore twin balance. The desired level of the competitive ratio is set by the horizontal line drawn from point C and of real domestic expenditure by the vertical line drawn from A. It is the position in relation to these broken lines which provides the guide to the choice of policies. Zones II and III are both to the right of the vertical line, and in both cases domestic deflation is required. However, the zones fall either side of the horizontal line, and while in the case of zone II the competitive ratio will need to fall, in the case of zone III the competitive ratio is already too low and needs raising by appropriate policies (the arrows indicate the direction of adjustment required). The Iʙ and Eʙ lines therefore divide the area according to the nature of the problem or the symptoms, the broken lines according to the policy response or remedy required. In most instances the policy-maker will need to adjust both the competitive ratio and the level of real domestic spending to restore twin balance (assuming in the short term, at least, that changes in domestic spending will not influence the competitive position). Where, however, the circumstances are represented by a position on a broken line, e.g. point Q in Fig. 5.6, then a single policy adjustment will serve to move the economy back towards both policy targets. In our example a reduction of domestic spending will serve to remove both domestic inflationary conditions and the external deficit.

There are of course limitations to this particular treatment of the policy problem. It does for instance abstract from the possible conflict between internal targets of full employment and price stability, and more significantly it fails to represent conditions typified by high unemployment and inflation. It also ignores feedback effects or the reactions of other countries to changes in domestic spending. Similarly, one might question the implications of ignoring capital transactions, since an increase in real expenditure with a fixed money supply will raise interest rates and probably the inflow of capital. Nevertheless the model does graphically demonstrate the potential imbalance that is threatened by target conflict.

Policy options

We considered in Section 5.3 the economic implications of alternative external deficit and surplus situations. Whether for instance over- or underspending in relation to current output is desirable or not, was dependent, we argued, upon the prevailing domestic and global conditions. A sustained deficit or surplus may however pose a problem for policy in any event, because of the need to finance the imbalance. We shall argue in subsequent chapters that there is likely to be a differential burden between surplus (accumulating reserves) and deficit (decumulating reserves) countries. Both solutions do, however, pose problems. The run-down of reserves to finance an external deficit poses a speculative threat as liquid reserves are used up and a deflationary threat as income and monetary reserves are transferred abroad. By contrast the accumulation of reserves poses an inflationary threat.

These inflationary and deflationary pressures are of course automatic adjustment forces, i.e. changes in relative prices and incomes that will bring about equilibrating reallocations of resources. The balance of payments remains a problem, however, for economic policy because these automatic adjustment forces may be inadequate or too slow and costly. We have demonstrated that given some form of managed exchange-rate system the restoration of balance between autonomous payments and receipts by automatic movements in incomes is likely to be inadequate. Similarly, rigidities in domestic prices under modern conditions may reduce the opportunity for relative price adjustment. Of course the exchange rate may provide a complete and automatic means of removing imbalance. Nevertheless, even if a freely flexible exchange rate provides a complete adjustment force, the authorities may wish to supplement or replace this mechanism if it is slow and/or costly.

The adjustment process is likely to be costly, for example, if it includes increasing the level of unemployment, and conflicts therefore with internal policy targets. We have already shown that the balance of payments must be seen within the broader policy problem of achieving multiple objectives with the available policy instruments. The target-and-instrument approach to economic policy (pioneered by Meade, 1951 and Tinbergen, 1952 and further developed by Mundell, 1962) indicates that full balance requires that there usually be as many instruments as targets, and that instruments are appropriately allocated to specific targets. (We shall return to this issue shortly.)

Adjustment versus financing   Crudely expressed, the authorities when faced with external imbalance can choose either to reinforce or resist the market adjustment forces. It will shortly become clear, however, that these are not necessarily mutually exclusive courses of action. In the short term for instance, the authorities may wish to minimise the adjustment costs by resisting or slowing down the adjustment process, while pursuing a long-term policy of active or passive reinforcement.

Our earlier analysis has demonstrated that market pressures for movement of the exchange rate from its managed level must be resisted if the rate is to remain pegged. Alternatively expressed in terms of the payments accounts, the imbalance must be accommodated for or financed in some way. In the case of a deficit for instance, it must be financed from reserves, by borrowing, or by induced short-term capital inflows. These accommodating capital flows do nothing directly, however, to reallocate resources and to bring therefore the intersection of the desired (*ex ante*) demand and supply schedules for the currency within the managed range of values. Financing is in that sense an alternative to adjustment. Since there are limits imposed on financing activities (in the case of deficits by the size of reserves and sources of borrowing), we can view financing as a form of balance of payments stabilisation (see Cohen, 1969); stabilisation that is for a shorter or longer period of time depending on the immediacy of those reserve or borrowing limits. Even where the power to resist market pressures is weak, the internal costs of adjustment provide an incentive for stabilising or delaying actions. Thus it would be preferable to view financing activities and adjustment as complements rather than alternatives (see Kenen, 1966). For analytical purposes, however, we will consider each separately.

Alternative forms of adjustment
We have established that the balance of trade (B) is the difference between real income or output (Y) and real expenditure or absorption (A). The removal of imbalance through adjustment requires therefore that the equality of Y and A be re-established. The authorities can seek to influence either expenditure or output. In the case of a deficit for instance (i.e. over-absorption in relation to current output) the

authorities can seek either to reduce absorption relative to output through deflationary fiscal and monetary policies (expenditure-reducing policies), or to increase output relative to absorption. We are of course distinguishing between the initial effects since it is ultimately impossible to change expenditure or income in isolation as they are interdependent. (Provided, however, that the **marginal** propensity to absorb current production is less than unity, any increase in output or decrease in expenditure, for example, will always increase a payments surplus or reduce a payments deficit.)

To increase output it is necessary to increase the foreign or home demand for that output. If we wish to achieve this with the existing level of domestic absorption, it is necessary to influence the distribution of that spending between domestic and foreign production. In other words it is possible to increase output by switching expenditure of residents and foreigners from foreign to domestic output (expenditure-switching policies). The switch by residents will reduce imports, while the switch by foreigners will increase exports.

This distinction between expenditure-changing and expenditure-switching policies provides us with a framework for considering the range of instruments available for dealing with payments imbalance. Expenditure-changing policies in the form of domestic monetary and budgetary manipulations – deflationary (inflationary) for a deficit (surplus) – seek to reinforce the automatic income-adjustment forces that we suggested imbalance generates. If the reader refers back to our earlier discussion of managed exchange rates he will appreciate that in a deficit situation deflation should tend to bring about a backward shift in the supply schedule for domestic currency, and to restore the equilibrium nature of the managed or pegged rate of exchange. This would appear to be an alternative to or a means of resisting the expenditure-switching effects of currency realignment. Our detailed analysis of devaluation in the next chapter will however demonstrate the need to release resources to meet the switch in demand to home production induced by devaluation or depreciation of the currency, which frequently makes expenditure reduction a complementary strategy to devaluation.

In any case it is possible to achieve expenditure switching without the use of currency realignment. Domestic financial policies and prices-and-incomes policies may in the longer term for example alter the price competitiveness of a country's goods and therefore foreign and domestic patterns of demand without the need to change the rate of exchange. Similarly, import controls will have the effect of switching domestic demand away from imports towards the home market.

Some economists feel that trade restrictions and exchange controls are not legitimate mechanisms of adjustment. Machlup (1965) argues that they are merely compensating corrections and that genuine adjustment is restricted to domestic prices and incomes and the exchange rate. We have already brought into question the legitimacy of the classical emphasis on unrestricted trade in our consideration of the nature of external balance. We will delay no further over the issue. The more pressing need, given the problem of achieving both internal and external balance, is to consider how to combine or mix the instruments available.

The mix of policies for internal/external balance

The literature on the factors influencing the choice of instruments, and on the way in which they are assigned to specific objectives, concentrates on the 'classical' tools of adjustment, i.e. the exchange rate and domestic financial policies. Both of these instruments, however, have an impact on internal and external balance. Meade (1951) in his pioneering work on the assignment problem assumed that usually the adjustment of the exchange rate would be used to remedy external imbalance, and financial policies to restore internal balance. Without formulating a general solution to the conflict problem, Meade had incorporated in his analysis what Mundell (1960b) was to rationalise in his 'principle of effective market classification'. Given that there are relative costs and benefits in terms of the impact on variables such as employment, growth and distribution of using particular instruments, the principle establishes that net costs are minimised and a stable system possible if policy variables are paired with the objectives on which they have the greatest relative impact. This prescription is usually seen to support the assignment of the exchange rate and financial policies to external and internal targets respectively.

As we shall see however in subsequent chapters, for much of the post-war period the prevailing orthodoxy placed a resistance on the use of exchange-rate variations, and much of the burden therefore of reconciling internal and external targets fell on to expenditure-changing financial policies, i.e. apparently on one instrument. A solution to this restriction was offered by Mundell (1962). He argued that financial policy is in fact made up of fiscal and monetary policies, which initially we may assume to be independent of each other. Although the two types of expenditure-changing policies may often be mutually reinforcing in the direction of impact on internal and external targets, their impact is not identical. It is in principle therefore possible, Mundell argued, to establish an appropriate mix of the two policies to achieve twin balance.

Fiscal and monetary policy mix   The possibility of twin balance at any one competitive ratio (i.e. for a given set of exchange rates and price levels) is seen to arise out of the impact of monetary policy on the capital-flows element of the balance of payments which we have tended so far to ignore. We have established earlier that capital flows are affected by changes in interest-rate differentials between countries. Since the domestic rate of interest, and therefore the interest differential (if interest rates in other countries remain constant) depends on the mix of fiscal and monetary policies, it is possible to alter

Fig. 5.7 Policy mix for internal–external balance

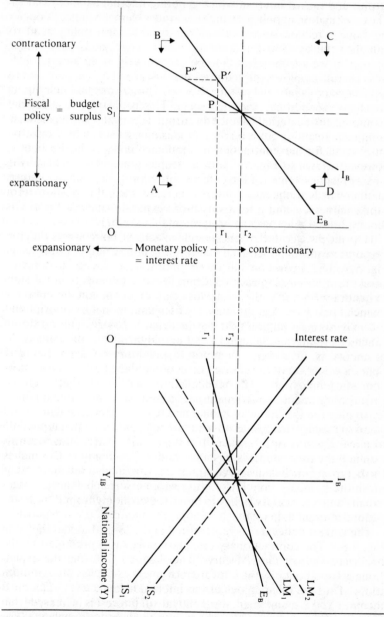

Fig. 5.8 An IS–LM Model of policy mix

the flow of capital in accordance with the imbalance on current transactions, while at the same time maintaining internal balance.

We can demonstrate this principle with the aid of Fig. 5.7. Both I$_B$

(the locus of those combinations of policies, proxied by the budget surplus and rate of interest, which generate internal balance) and E_B (the combination of policies which generate external balance) slope in the same direction since both monetary and fiscal policy tend to influence the demand for domestic and foreign goods in a similar manner. If we assume exports to be exogenously given, internal balance or full employment requires that fiscal policy becomes more expansionary as monetary policy becomes more contractionary in its effect on expenditure, and vice versa. This is also the case for the maintenance of external balance on current transactions – the increase in imports resulting from a more expansionary fiscal policy must be offset by a further contraction of monetary policy. The E_B line is, however, drawn in Fig. 5.7 with a steeper gradient to indicate the greater responsiveness of the external situation to the rate of interest. In other words, as the rate of interest increases the inflow of short-term capital increases, and a relatively more expansionary fiscal policy is required to increase imports and maintain external balance.

The model suggests that it is possible to achieve both targets with the appropriate mix of policies, i.e. interest rate r_2 and budget surplus S_1 in Fig. 5.7. The arrows on the figure indicate the direction of policy adjustment required in each quadrant to move towards twin balance. In quadrants A and C the authorities can set a common direction for financial policy (in A contractionary fiscal and monetary policies and in C expansionary policies). At P in quadrant B, however, the economy is achieving internal balance or full employment but the balance of payments is in deficit. Common expenditure-reducing financial policies would serve to remove the external deficit at the expense of domestic employment. The Mundellian prescription is that given the correct assignment of instruments, i.e. a contractionary monetary policy to increase the inflow of capital and restore external balance, and an expansionary fiscal policy to maintain full employment, it is possible to move towards twin balance. If, by contrast, instruments are mis-assigned then the model is unstable, and the economy in fact moves further from twin balance. A contractionary fiscal policy would tend to move the economy from P to P' (to restore external balance), and an expansionary monetary policy to move the economy from P' to P'' (to restore internal balance).

The correct policy mix is represented in the IS–LM model shown in Fig. 5.8.[11] The contractionary monetary policy is represented by the backward shift of the LM curve from LM_1 to LM_2 and the expansionary fiscal policy by the outward movement of the IS curve from IS_1 to IS_2. Thus the full employment or internal balance level of national income (Y_{IB}) is maintained, while the rate of interest is increased from r_1 to r_2. It is in fact possible to incorporate an external balance (E_B) function into the IS–LM model, to represent precisely the movement from r_1 to r_2 required in Fig. 5.7 to move the economy from position P to twin balance. This function represents combinations of Y and r, which for any given level of exports, generate external balance; any increase in Y and therefore in imports requires that the inflow of capital is increased by a rise in r, if external balance is to be maintained. (For a fuller discussion of this representation of the policy-mix approach, see Wrightman, 1970.)

This is clearly then an ingenious method of attempting to reconcile internal/external conflict, where the exchange rate is pegged.[12] We could question the validity of some of the assumptions underpinning the shape of the functions adopted. A more important limitation, however, is to view the approach as a long-term solution to balance-of-payments problems. There may be serious doubts about the extent to which capital is consistently sensitive to interest differentials, and therefore a reliable policy variable. Interest rates are in any case influenced by global conditions and we may question the extent to which countries can operate independent interest-rate policies. In addition there are likely to be domestic political and economic constraints on raising interest rates to very high levels, and dangers of domestic and international misallocation from externally orienting interest rates for long periods of time. Similarly, there are political and administrative constraints on making short-term, budgetary manipulations.

Perhaps a more fundamental criticism is that fiscal/monetary mix is a means of stabilising rather than actually adjusting payments imbalance. It is a financing activity similar to the use of official reserves which does nothing to directly influence the pattern of autonomous transactions through resource reallocation.

Payments financing has nevertheless an important complementary role to play in balance-of-payments policy, while the authorities perhaps try to achieve the appropriate mix of genuine adjustment tools (exchange-rate variations, financial policies, incomes policies and perhaps trade restrictions). The choice adopted by individual countries is not, however, only influenced by the relative efficiency of particular instruments, but by the degree of international consistency and cooperation and by the distribution of the adjustment burden between countries. It is in fact dependent upon the nature of the global monetary arrangements, and it is to a consideration of alternative, global adjustment systems and their impact on individual countries that we will turn our attention.

Notes

1. For a rigorous examination of the elasticity conditions required for exchange market stability, see pp. 170–4 in Chapter 6.
2. For an analysis of spot and forward rate determination under alternative market conditions see Stern (1973), pp. 47–61.

3. In the UK the Bank of England operates the Exchange Equalisation Account on behalf of the Government.

4. Under the Bretton Woods system, the authorities were also permitted under Article IV of the IMF Charter to influence the rate for forward transactions. No precise relationship between the spot and forward rate was laid down. For a discussion of forward intervention, see Cohen (1969), pp. 81–7.

5. Countries were required under the Bretton Woods agreement to maintain exchange rates within 1 per cent either side of par (or pegged) values. The band was raised to $2\frac{1}{4}$ per cent either side of the par value following the Smithsonian agreement of 1971. Subsequently the Joint European Float, arranged in 1973, restricted total variation on cross rates to 50 per cent of that permitted by the new IMF rules. The arrangement became known as the 'snake within the tunnel'.

6. Advanced industrialised countries may in fact seek a current surplus to finance the appropriate level of foreign aid.

7. Modern monetarist debate has in fact questioned the consistency of full employment with the equilibrium or natural rate of employment.

8. Cohen (1969) suggests that equilibrium is achieved when all the variables in the model achieve a new state of mutual compatibility. For a detailed consideration of equilibrium concepts, see Machlup (1958).

9. Bernstein (1956) termed this a 'price and cost disparity' as opposed to the 'current inflation' problem that over-absorption in real terms generates.

10. For attempt to operationalise the Swan model for the UK economy, see Graham (1977).

11. For a derivation of IS–LM functions see Westaway and Weyman-Jones (1977), and for a more precise, four-quadrant analysis of the impact of interest rate movement on capital flows and the external balance, see Johnson (1967b).

12. For a consideration of the nature of the policy mix when the exchange rate is flexible, see Mundell (1960b) or Stern (1973).

Chapter 6

Balance of payments adjustment

6.1 Introduction

Having seen what is implied by balance-of-payments imbalance, and examined its possible sources, we now turn our attention to the removal of imbalance. Such correction is usually referred to as balance-of-payments adjustment.

Balance-of-payments adjustment has been defined as 'a marginal reallocation of productive resources and hence of exchanges of goods, services and investments under the influence of changes in relative prices, incomes and/or exchange rates' (Cohen, 1969, p. 90). The means of attaining such a 'marginal reallocation of resources' depends crucially on our conception of the nature and causes of imbalance. Thus imbalance may be seen as the inevitable result of a divergence between the prices of traded and non-traded goods, or as a direct consequence of over-absorption, perhaps induced by a divergence between individuals' desired money balances and their actual money balances. As we will see presently, these are essentially different ways of looking at the same thing.

Our aim in this chapter will therefore be threefold. First, we will examine two views of the balance of payments which suggest that imbalances may be self-equilibrating, i.e. so-called automatic adjustment processes. Having seen why these processes may not operate or at best may function imperfectly or incompletely, we will proceed to examine the means of, and likely consequences of, discretionary adjustment. These will then form the basis for the study of alternative forms of exchange-rate regimes (or adjustment systems), and the problems of policy formulation given different constraints.

6.2 Automatic adjustment processes

There are several views of the balance of payments which suggest mechanisms whereby balance-of-payments adjustment will be automatic. We have for instance already considered in Section 5.4 the process whereby linkages in countries' national incomes may stimulate automatic adjustment forces. Later we will consider freely fluctuating exchange rates. Here we will consider two further views of the balance of payments which suggest that under certain circumstances, payments imbalance will be self-correcting. (Chronologically these represent the earliest and latest contributions to balance-of-payments theorising.)

The price–specie flow mechanism
Implied in the definition cited earlier is the suggestion that the marginal reallocation of resources necessary for balance-of-payments adjustment, can be achieved via changes in relative prices. The classic price–specie flow mechanism, first formalised by Hume (1752), outlines the process by which changes in relative prices between trading nations automatically correct payments imbalances. The system of payments relations which existed in the late nineteenth and early twentieth century, the International Gold Standard (IGS), is frequently characterised as a good example of a smoothly functioning price–specie flow mechanism.

Certain preconditions are necessary for the successful operation of such a system. First, since in theory gold would be the only form of internationally acceptable money, domestic monies must be freely convertible into gold in order to permit international trade. Second, individuals must have complete freedom to import and export gold. The precise significance of this condition will become apparent presently. Third, Central Banks must stand ready to buy and sell unlimited amounts of their own currency at a fixed gold price. Finally, each country's gold stock has to form the reserve base of its domestic money stock, thereby ensuring that domestic financial policies are dependent on any gold inflows and outflows.

Each country in the system would have a fixed gold price for its currency. Exchange rates between different currencies would therefore be automatically determined. If for example, the UK fixed the price of £1 at 112.982 grains of pure gold, whilst the US authorities set $1 = 23.2 grains, then the sterling–dollar exchange rate would be £1 = $4.87 (i.r. 112.982/23.2). This would be the *mint par rate*. On either side of this value would be a *gold import point* and a *gold export point*. The precise locations of these points would be determined by the costs of shipping gold bullion. Suppose the costs of shipping gold amounted to one new penny per £1 worth, i.e. 1 per cent, then the gold import point would be $4.92, the gold export point £4.82.[1] The sterling–dollar exchange rate would be kept strictly within these limits by the profit-seeking activities of arbitrageurs. An example will help to illustrate how this would be accomplished.

Assume for instance that an excess supply of sterling temporarily pushes the exchange rate to $4.70 in London. Under such circumstances, it would profit an American arbitrageur to convert $4.70 into £1, use the £1 to purchase 112.982 grains of gold from the Bank of England, then resell the gold to the US treasury at the fixed price $1 = 23.2 grains. For his 112.982 grains, the arbitrageur would therefore receive $4.87, which yields him a net profit of 12 cents on the transaction (17 cents less 5 cents costs incurred in transporting the gold from London to New York). The incentive for arbitrageurs to shift gold from London to New York remains, so long as the transport costs involved are less than the price differential between the two markets. Thus when the price of sterling reaches $4.82, the incentive is removed. The reverse situation would occur if for any reason the price of sterling in London exceeded $4.92 (the student should check this reasoning for his/herself).

Thus the authorities do not intervene in the foreign-exchange market, they merely stand ready to buy and sell domestic money at a fixed gold price; it is the profit-seeking activities of gold arbitrageurs which maintains the exchange rate between the gold import and export points. Consider Fig. 6.1.

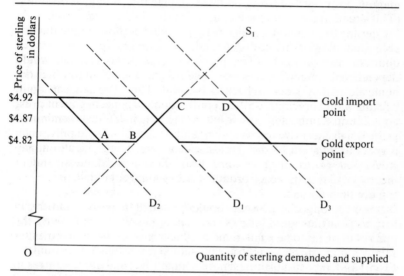

Fig. 6.1 Exchange-rate determination under a gold standard

Initially, the market for sterling is cleared at the mint par rate of $4.87 since at this price D_1 and S_1 intersect. Suppose now a decreased demand for UK exportables shifts the demand schedule for sterling from D_1 to D_2. Any tendency for the price of sterling to fall below $4.82 provides the incentive for arbitrageurs to ship gold from London, since they can clearly profit by converting dollars into sterling, purchasing gold from the Bank of England and reselling this gold to the US Treasury.

The role of the Bank of England is merely to sell gold at 112.982 grains per £1 in exchange for an amount of sterling approximately equal to the distance AB in Fig. 6.1. If an autonomous increase in the demand for UK exportables resulted in the demand schedule for sterling shifting from D_1 to D_3, then the converse would occur. Upward pressure on the sterling–dollar exchange rate would provide the incentive for arbitrageurs to import gold into the UK, the Bank of England standing ready to supply CD of sterling in exchange for gold.

In summary then, exchange rates remain fixed within narrow bands due to the profit-seeking activities of arbitrageurs, the role of the Central Bank being confined to buying or selling domestic currency at the fixed gold price. We must now pose the question: What implications does this have for balance-of-payments adjustment? Since we have already stated that the domestic money supply must be backed by gold, clearly any gold inflows and outflows must have repercussions for the domestic economy.

Take the situation where a nation is in payments deficit. There would be an excess supply of domestic money on the foreign exchange market, downward pressure on the exchange rate, and gold outflows. (This situation would be analogous to the shift in the demand schedule for sterling from D_1 to D_2 in Fig. 6.1.) This gold outflow should then be able (and allowed) to slow down additions to, or even contract, the domestic money stock. (The precise degree of contraction would depend on the 'fractional reserve standard', i.e. the extent to which the domestic money stock is backed by gold. Thus 100 per cent gold backing would precipitate a 1 : 1 contraction, 50 per cent gold backing a 1 : 2 contraction, etc.) Any resultant increase in interest rates would provide a disincentive to investment and stockholding, and precipitate a general deflation of the domestic economy. In the idealised pre-Keynesian world of downward price flexibility, domestic factor incomes and thus domestic product prices should either fall, or rise less rapidly than abroad.

Since the opposite process should be simultaneously occurring in surplus countries (gold inflows stimulating monetary expansion), the end result ought to be a fall in the product prices of the deficit country relative to the surplus country. This should make the deficit country's export and import substitutes more competitive, and ultimately result in an improvement in the trade balance and an increase in the overall level of activity, as domestic factors are re-employed in export and import substitute industries.

Thus, given no accommodating finance, no central bank offsetting policies, and factor and product price flexibility, we have an adjustment process which operates automatically for both deficit and surplus countries.

The IGS experience   Was such a blueprint adhered to under the IGS? In reality even in the heyday of the IGS (usually taken as being sometime after 1870 up to 1914), both deficit and surplus countries alike tended to frustrate the operation of the mechanism somewhat by employing policies designed to cushion the domestic economy from the full impact of any gold inflows and outflows ('offsetting' or 'sterilisation' policies, whereby the central bank engages in open market operations to replenish or decrease the domestic money stock). Furthermore, product and in particular, factor prices probably did not exhibit sufficient downward flexibility for a fully operative and efficient price–specie flow mechanism. Sustained payments surpluses and deficits were not uncommon therefore.

This does not mean that the adjustment mechanism was wholly frustrated. Subsequent research suggests, however, that any adjustments which took place were due as much to capital flows and income flows, as to changes in relative prices. Short-term capital flows that is, in response to interest rate differentials; and income flows generated by the action of foreign trade multipliers. Furthermore, although exchange rates between some of the main Western economies did remain remarkably stable, exchange-rate adjustments in the 'periphery' countries were not uncommon. (The interested student should refer to Triffin, 1964, and Yeager, 1966, Chs 15–17.)

The monetary approach and balance-of-payments adjustment
The most recent contribution to balance-of-payments theorising (and one which in many respects builds on the price–specie flow mechanism) is the extension of monetarist precepts and philosophy to the analysis of balance-of-payments problems. This too views balance-of-payments adjustment as an automatic process. As Johnson (1973) notes however, it differs from other approaches since, 'its essence is to put at the forefront of analysis the money rather than the relative price aspects of international adjustment'.

It is important to note that there exists no unified coherent statement of the monetary approach as such. Rather, what we have is a number of related theories which comprise 'the monetary approach'. Although they may differ in detail, they all have certain commonalities, such as their emphasis on the long run, their stress on monetary determinacy, and their analysis of the overall balance of payments. (A survey of the various elements can be found in Whitman, 1975; and Frenkel and Johnson, 1976.)

The monetary approach is a long-run theory of the balance of payments, which views any imbalance as being associated with reductions or accumulations of money balances, i.e. disequilibrium in the money market. The central postulate is that any disparity between actual and desired money balances manifests itself in international payments imbalance. This postulate is based on the familiar monetarist notion that the various forms of assets held by individuals are kept in a fairly constant relationship to each other. In other words, they hold a 'portfolio' composed of cash balances, time deposits, stocks and shares, consumer durables, and so on. Thus at any point in time, they have a given level of *desired* money balances. If for any reason individuals' *actual* money balances exceed their desired money balances (e.g. because the authorities create and circulate more money), this excess money will result in additional spending, including spending on imported goods and securities. Monetary theorists contend that the resulting effect on the balance of payments will be automatically corrected by the action of these same individuals in adjusting their actual cash balances back towards their desired level. Payments imbalance can only result from stock adjustments in the money market. As such, all imbalances must therefore be inherently temporary. Let us illustrate by example.

Take for instance the situation where the UK balance of payments is initially in equilibrium, and the authorities increase the domestic money supply. This will ultimately be transmitted into increased prices of goods, services and securities (the latter due to the downward pressure on interest rates). This tendency makes exports from the UK less competitive, causing both domestic and foreign residents to switch expenditure away from UK goods and securities. Given pegged or fixed exchange rates, such a movement implies a deterioration of the UK balance of payments. This deterioration essentially reflects the decisions of UK residents to exchange their excess money balances (which were created by the increase in the money supply) for real and financial assets from abroad. In the long run the foreign recipients of these money balances (i.e. importers into the UK) present them to their Central Bank, which in turn re-presents them to the Bank of England. The latter 'pays' for the money balances out of the country's stock of international reserves.

Since international reserves are assumed to be an uncontrollable element of the domestic money supply, any reduction in reserves should automatically result in a multiplied contraction of the domestic money supply (and an expansion abroad) towards its initial level. This mechanism should therefore automatically correct the UK payments deficit and reduce the surplus of her trading partners. Any intervention on the part of the authorities unless to reinforce and quicken adjustment is futile. If for example the authorities attempt to sterilise the effects of reserve loss, thereby preventing the domestic money supply from contracting, they merely perpetuate the inequality between actual and desired money balances and reinforce the need for adjustment. In other words, individuals will still hold excess money balances which they will exchange for foreign goods, and which will therefore serve to perpetuate the balance-of-payments deficit. Other policies have no more than a transitory effect. Thus Mussa (1974) argues that a tariff has little lasting effect on the balance of payments whilst Johnson (1973 and 1977) contends that devaluation has only a temporary effect.

The policy implications of the monetary approach are therefore relatively straightforward. Since balance-of-payments imbalance is always and everywhere a monetary phenomenon, policy should focus on control of the money stock. It is possible to criticise this view on several fronts (see for instance, Currie, 1976, and Tsiang, 1977). One could for example question whether the money demand function is stable, i.e. do individuals hold a fairly constant relationship between the assets in their portfolio, to ensure that the velocity of circulation will be stable? Furthermore, of what exactly is money demand a stable function? There is a certain amount of disagreement over the variables which enter into the demand for money function. As Tsiang notes:

Obviously much depends on the demand function for money, yet there does not yet seem to be general agreement among the proponents of the monetary approach about its precise specification, even though everyone would assure us that, whatever it is, it is stable in the long run at least.

(Tsiang, 1977, p. 321)

A second important point of contention is whether the supply of money is exogenously determined by the central monetary authority, or whether in fact it may be endogenous, and therefore determined by the level of economic activity. If this were the case then money supply could not be excessive or deficient at any point in time. This latter possibility Johnson (1977) dismisses as the 'old Banking School fallacy'.

A third point of debate is the validity and relevance of Walras' law, that excess demands and supplies in all markets net out to zero. This too is central to the analysis since excess supplies (demands) in the money market are ultimately transmitted into excess demands (supplies) in the goods and securities markets, with subsequent adjustments eventually restoring equilibrium. If markets do not function this smoothly then adjustment will be incomplete.

These are areas of serious academic debate, not only over the monetary approach to balance-of-payments analysis, but over monetarism as such. For our present purposes however, the essential point to note is that the monetary approach, like the price–specie flow mechanism, suggests that given time, international payments imbalances will be self-correcting.

If this assertion has any validity, why is the balance of payments usually such a headache for policy-makers? We can answer by reference to two considerations. First, automatic processes may not of themselves be sufficient to achieve necessary adjustments. Both the price–specie flow mechanism and the monetary approach assume smoothly operating and efficient world markets. Any price rigidities, especially in a downward direction, will tend to frustrate adjustment. Second, they may simply not be permitted to work because most governments are concerned with the potential costs of self-correction. Serious and persistent unemployment tends to be politically unpalatable. Automatic adjustment processes of the type examined here necessitate the sacrifice of internal balance in achieving external balance. As we have already seen, when one is concerned with the maintenance of both internal and external balance in the shorter run, the balance of payments becomes a policy problem.

6.3 Discretionary adjustment

When talking of discretionary adjustment it is usual to distinguish between expenditure-changing and expenditure-switching policies. This is a distinction we have already considered. It will be remembered that the former relies on the use of domestic financial policies to deflate (inflate) the domestic economy, as a means of eliminating a balance-of-payments deficit (surplus). Expenditure-switching policies, on the other hand, aim to switch domestic expenditure away from foreign goods towards domestically produced goods, and/or to switch foreign expenditure towards domestically produced goods. This result could be achieved via commercial policy, via the indirect effects of expenditure-reducing policies, or via exchange-rate adjustment. The last of these, by altering the relationship between the prices of traded goods, and the relationship between traded and non-traded goods, aims to switch domestic production and foreign consumption towards tradeables, and domestic consumption away from tradeables. Exchange-rate adjustment has had a prominent role in balance-of-payments analysis for many years now, and will occupy us for the remainder of this section.

For purposes of illustration take the case of a country which lowers the price of its currency in terms of foreign currency, i.e. it devalues its currency. The result of such a devaluation should be that domestic goods become cheaper in foreign currency, foreign goods more expensive in domestic currency. If this occurs the crucial consideration is: What factors determine whether or not the end result is a switching of domestic expenditure away from goods produced abroad, and foreign expenditure towards domestically produced goods? If we assume that spare productive capacity exists to satisfy increased demand then quite clearly it depends on the magnitude of the price changes and the response of domestic and foreign consumers to these price changes, i.e. on the domestic price elasticity of demand for imports, and the foreign price elasticity of demand for the devaluing country's exports.

Elasticities and devaluation

Let us illustrate this by examining the impact of a small (1 per cent) devaluation on the devaluing country's net foreign exchange receipts (and therefore on its trade balance). To isolate the role of elasticities we assume initially that the level of income is held constant (in order to eliminate the impact of any secondary income effects; that supply elasticities are infinite (thus spare capacity is available to meet any increases in demand following exchange-rate adjustment); and that import prices in domestic currency (Pm) rise, and export prices in foreign currency (Px) fall, by the full amount of the devaluation or depreciation.

Take first the effect of devaluation on domestic demand for imports. If the domestic price elasticity of demand for imports (dm) is relatively elastic, i.e. greater than 1, then we would anticipate a 1 per cent devaluation to result in a more than proportional decrease in the quantity of imports demanded (Qm). Conversely, if dm is less than 1, there would be a less than proportional decrease in Qm. Thus the higher the value of dm, the greater will be the effect of devaluation on Qm. In terms of Fig. 6.2, the more elastic the schedule Dm, the greater the contraction in the quantity of imports demanded as a result of the devaluation.

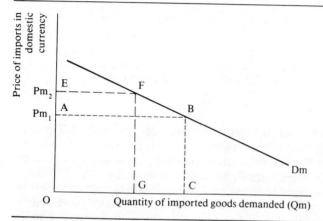

Fig. 6.2 Domestic demand for imports

Analogously, the effect of devaluation on foreign demand for exports (Qx) is dependent on dx, i.e. foreign residents' price elasticity of demand for the devaluing country's exports. The higher the value of dx, the more responsive will foreign consumers be to a fall in Px, and therefore the greater the expansion in foreign demand for exports. Thus the more elastic the schedule Dx in Fig. 6.3, the more responsive are foreign consumers to the change in Px following devaluation.

Referring to Fig. 6.2, the effect of devaluation on the devaluing country's foreign exchange requirements is approximately identified by the change from the area OABC to OEFG, i.e. the change in the amount of domestic currency offered for foreign exchange. The more elastic is domestic demand for importables, the greater will be the reduction in the area under the demand curve. By contrast, the change in foreign-exchange receipts which results from the fall in the foreign price of exports will increase the area OKLM in Fig. 6.3 if foreign demand is elastic, whilst reducing the area if demand is inelastic.

The changes in the areas under the demand curves in Figs 6.2 and 6.3 are not, however, directly comparable since the valuations are in different currencies. By attempting to focus on the change in foreign receipts and outlays, however, we are concerned with identifying the conditions under which the trade balance will improve as a result of a

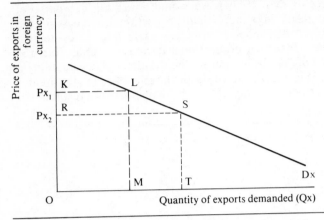

Fig. 6.3 Foreign demand for exports

devaluation. Thus when foreign exchange requirements fall (which they must do so long as the volume of imports falls), we wish to know when this fall will more than offset a possible fall in foreign-exchange receipts when foreign demand for exports is inelastic; or the fall which will best complement the benefits of an increase in receipts in the event of elastic foreign demand. These conditions are usually expressed by the well-known condition that for devaluation to improve a trade balance, the sum of the elasticities dm and dx must exceed unity (see Haberler, 1949). This is the so called 'Marshall–Lerner condition'. (A precise mathematical formulation of the condition can be found in Stern, 1973, pp. 64–69.)

The condition can be illustrated graphically in terms of the demand for and supply of home currency, by reference to Figs 6.4(*a*), (*b*) and (*c*). We assume the home country to be Britain, the rest of the world being represented by America. Exports from Britain generate a demand for the pound sterling (and a supply of the dollar), imports from America create a supply of the pound (and a demand for the dollar).

Figure 6.4(*a*) shows the position where we have a 'normal' negatively sloped demand curve. Thus as sterling depreciates, the consequent fall in Px will induce an increased demand for British exports and therefore an expansion of the demand for sterling. This combines with a positively sloped supply curve indicating that depreciation, since it reduces the British demand for imports from America, reduces the supply of sterling on the foreign exchange market. In other words what we have is a relatively high dm and dx resulting in stability in the foreign exchange market, in the sense that if the pound is overvalued (undervalued) a depreciation (appreciation) will re-establish a market-clearing equilibrium.

In Fig. 6.4(*b*) we have the same demand curve, but a negatively sloped supply curve. This implies that as sterling depreciates, the

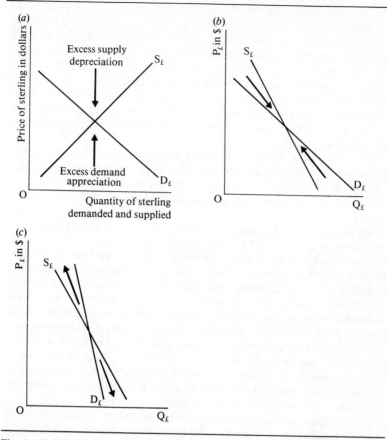

Fig. 6.4 Foreign exchange market stability and instability

supply of sterling will actually expand. This would be the case if Britain's dm were relatively low because of a lack of domestically produced import substitutes. If, for instance, imports into Britain were composed principally of raw materials, the lack of any domestically produced alternative would mean that as Pm increased domestic consumers would continue to purchase the imported goods. Therefore depreciation results in an increased supply of sterling to pay for the higher-priced imports. Despite this low dm, however, dx is still sufficiently high to fulfil the Marshall–Lerner condition so that an excess supply of sterling (balance-of-payments deficit) could be corrected by depreciation; an excess demand (payments surplus) by appreciation.

Figure 6.4(c) illustrates the possibility of instability. Again we have a negatively sloped supply curve indicating that dm is relatively low. On this occasion, however, dx is not high enough to counteract it and the Marshall–Lerner condition is not satisfied. Any movement away from equilibrium, rather than being corrected by depreciation/appreciation, is now exacerbated. In fact the policy prescription here would be to devalue to correct a surplus, revalue to eliminate a deficit! This occurs because the domestic demand for imports is so inelastic that sterling depreciation results in a less-than-proportional contraction of demand for imports, which actually expands the supply of sterling on the foreign exchange market. Similarly with exports. If the foreign demand for exports is highly inelastic, the decrease in Px following depreciation only serves to contract foreign exchange receipts because foreign demand for UK exports expands by less than in proportion to the price fall.

When we talk of the 'normal' effects of a devaluation or revaluation we implicitly have in mind the situation depicted by Figs 6.4(*a*) and 6.4(*b*). How likely is it, however, that the situation depicted in Fig. 6.4(*c*) would prevail, i.e. that we would have *elasticity perversity*?

Elasticity perversity and the 'real world'   Certain real-world tendencies diminish the possibility of perversity in the long run. For instance, a country's dx will be higher, the greater the competition it faces in world markets. In general world markets (particularly in manufactured and semi-manufactured goods) are highly competitive. The chief exception to this is where a country is the principal producer of a particular product, and so faces little or no competition, and where the product itself is in relatively inelastic demand. Many primary producer countries may fit this criterion, for example, Ghana with cocoa, Brazil with coffee, Malaya with tin, India and Sri Lanka with tea. These countries may face low dx's as a result of their market dominance.

Similarly with imports. Usually the existence of a domestic import-substitute industry tends to result in dm being higher than it otherwise would be. This, however, may not always be the case. The import of primary products by industrial nations is a good example of the lack of import substitutes resulting in low dm's (which was one of the factors contributing to the successful upward administration of oil prices by OPEC in 1973). Also, as we have already seen, many LDCs are heavily dependent on foreign supplies of manufactured and semi-manufactured goods whilst they are still developing their own secondary sector. Even when some manufacturing activity is carried out, LDCs are often dependent on imports of capital goods and intermediate inputs.

This provides us with two possibilities: firstly, certain LDCs may face exchange market instability because of low dx's and dm's; secondly, some industrialised nations may face the same prospect, principally because of low dm's. It is generally accepted, however, that where instability does exist, it is only likely to be a short-run phenomenon. It is most unlikely that instability would prevail in the long run since this would imply an ever-worsening deficit for a country whose currency was persistently depreciating. Clearly this is untenable since there will be a point where further increases in Pm will not result in an expanded supply of domestic currency (even if it is where the nation's entire national income is being devoted to imports!). Similarly, there will be some point beyond which dx will again become elastic. In the long run any unstable equilibrium will be bounded by stable equilibria, when the effects of depreciation/appreciation become 'normal' again. The situation is depicted in Fig. 6.5, where the unstable equilibrium E_2 is bounded by the stable equilibria E_1 and E_3.

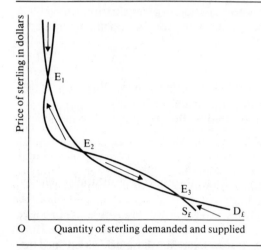

Fig. 6.5 Multiple equilibria in the foreign exchange market

Absorption and devaluation

Examining exchange-rate adjustment via elasticities was for some time the 'conventional wisdom'. Increasingly however, in the post-war years dissatisfaction with the approach grew. Alexander (1952) voiced this dissatisfaction by contending that to argue that the response of the balance of payments to exchange-rate adjustment depended solely on elasticities, amounted to no more than implicit theorising. He contended that if we use 'partial' elasticities we hold too many things constant, whereas if we use 'total' elasticities the stability conditions become tautological.[2] In addition it was argued that the approach was incomplete. As an explicitly partial approach, it ignored secondary multiplier effects of exchange-rate adjustment, and focused narrowly on the trade balance (see Meade, 1951). As an alternative the so-called 'absorption approach' to balance-of-payments analysis was developed (Alexander, 1952). This approach commences with the familiar national income identity:

$$Y = C + I + G + (X - M)$$
$$\therefore (X - M) = Y - (C + I + G)$$
$$B = Y - A \qquad (1)$$

which simply states that a country's balance of payments (B) is the difference between its real income (Y) and its expenditure or 'absorption' (A). A deficit is therefore the result of over-absorption, a surplus under-absorption. Take again the policy implications of a deficit.

To eliminate the deficit, income and absorption must be brought into line. Thus Y must be increased relative to A and/or A reduced relative to Y. Johnson (1958b) considers in some detail the alternative means by which this could be achieved. Alexander (1952), however, addresses himself primarily to the effects of devaluation.

Since absorption and income must be brought into line to eliminate the deficit it follows that

$$\Delta B = \Delta Y - \Delta A \tag{2}$$

We can envisage a twofold impact on absorption. First, the direct (negative) impact of a devaluation on absorption (d); second, a (positive) change in absorption induced by the positive change in income. Thus

$$\Delta A = c\Delta Y - d \tag{3}$$

where c is the marginal propensity to absorb. By substituting we have

$$\Delta B = \Delta Y - (c\Delta Y - d)$$
$$\therefore \Delta B = (1 - c)\,\Delta Y - d \tag{4}$$

Following Alexander we can now examine these effects on income, absorption and the propensity to absorb.

The most important direct effect of devaluation on income is the so-called 'idle resources effect'. If the effects of the devaluation are 'normal' and an increased demand for exports and import substitutes ensues, then presumably idle resources (in particular labour) will be put back to work and income will be generated. This will tend to increase Y relative to A. Out of this increased income, however, a proportion will be absorbed, i.e. some of the increased income will be used up for consumption and investment purposes. The amount of induced absorption will depend on the marginal propensity to absorb (c in equation 4). Ignoring for the moment the direct effects of devaluation on A, for the foreign balance to improve c must be less than 1. In other words additional consumption or investment has to absorb less than the full amount of any increase in income. If c is greater than 1 then the foreign balance merely worsens.

Alexander also points to a 'terms of trade effect' on real income. This is based on the presumption that a devaluation will result in a decline in export prices (in foreign currency), which will exceed any decline in import prices, thereby resulting in an adverse shift in the terms of trade and therefore a reduction in the devaluing country's real income. If this occurs there will be an accompanying reduction in absorption. As long as c is less than 1 the net effect will be a deterioration in the foreign balance. Only if c is greater than 1 would a deterioration in the terms of trade improve the foreign balance.

Certain direct effects on absorption are also posited. The most important of these is the 'cash balance effect'. Since devaluation will erode the real value of cash balances (because of the increased price of traded goods), individuals and corporate bodies will reduce their consumption or investment in order to maintain the former relation between cash balances and income. In the Johnsonian mechanism this same result is achieved by individuals selling securities, driving up interest rates and thereby inducing general disabsorption (Johnson, 1958b).

In addition there will be certain income redistribution effects. As idle resources are put back to work, Alexander argues that initially increases in income will go primarily to profit-earners rather than wage-earners. This would depress A relative to Y if profit-earners have a lower marginal propensity to absorb. Furthermore, given a progressive tax structure, government revenue will increase as prices and money incomes increase. Since the government generally has a low marginal propensity to absorb (in the short run anyway), this will tend to depress absorption.

None of these income and absorption effects appears to be very powerful, some are in fact downright dubious. The most potent are likely to be any idle resources and cash balance effects, but even the benefits from these may be transient. In the former the marginal propensity to absorb may be so high as largely to negate any positive impact; or quite simply there may not be any idle resources, i.e. the economy could be close to full employment. With the latter, the domestic money supply may expand to facilitate trade at the higher price level. This would merely serve to replenish any depletion in cash balances which had taken place, thereby counteracting disabsorption. Monetary expansion would also generate inflation which may result in a further tendency towards imbalance.

This doubt as to the general ability of devaluation to 'cure' a payments deficit highlights the need for devaluation to be accompanied by other policies. Thus, prior to any devaluation, idle resources should be made available so that full advantage can be taken of any income-increasing idle resources effects of devaluation. This would argue for disabsorption policies to precede any exchange-rate adjustment.

Historically the most successful devaluations appear to be those where domestic deflationary measures were taken prior to exchange-rate adjustment, e.g. the devaluation of the French franc in 1958 is usually deemed to have been such a marked success because of the disabsorption measures which preceded it.

Furthermore, the absorption approach would suggest that to enhance the chances of a successful devaluation, it should be accompanied by monetary restraint so as to allow cash balance adjustment to take place.

Money, absorption and elasticities

Before examining the problem of policy coordination under various exchange-rate regimes, we must ask ourselves one more question: How do these ostensibly different approaches to balance-of-payments adjustment square up to each other? A certain amount of effort has already been expended on the problem of reconciling the different approaches, in particular in synthesising the absorption and elasticities approaches (e.g. Alexander, 1959; Tsiang, 1961; Pearce, 1961).

We can perhaps best illustrate by considering how each approach views a payments deficit. According to the monetary view, this situation is created by excessive monetary expansion which results in stock disequilibrium in the money market. Eventually, the excess money balances are used abroad to purchase goods, services and securities. The absorption approach asserts exactly the same thing but commences from the other side of the transaction. It places direct emphasis on the excess goods, services and securities being imported, i.e. the over-absorption and its implications for the current balance. The elasticities approach focuses on the divergence of relative prices as the immediate cause of the deficit. This contrasts with the absorption and monetary schemas, where a divergence of relative prices between trading nations is merely a symptom of imbalance rather than the cause.

There is also a certain sympathy in their analyses of devaluation. The elasticities approach focuses on the initial impact effect of devaluation, whilst the absorption approach takes for granted an absence of elasticity perversity, and then attempts to take a more aggregate view of the process. Monetary analysis proceeds from a different angle by focusing attention on the money market. It can be reconciled, however, with elasticities considerations since the price of foreign exchange would be a variable in any fully elaborated demand for money function; and it can be reconciled with the absorption approach since the latter explicitly takes account of monetary consequences in analysing cash balance effects.

All this does not mean that the approaches are perfect substitutes for each other. Clearly they are not. They have differing conceptions of the balance of payments. The elasticities approach concentrates on the trade balance; the absorption approach on the current balance; and the monetary approach on the overall balance of payments.

Which approach is 'best' to start with will depend on the given situation at hand. Is for instance the persistent UK current-account deficit due to low productivity and therefore 'high' relative prices in a world where the Marshall–Lerner condition generally holds? Or is it because of a relatively high marginal propensity to absorb and relatively low propensity to save due perhaps to a high social discount rate on the part of UK citizens? Or is it the inevitable result of excessive monetary expansion? One could easily make out a reasoned case for any of these. Similarly with West Germany's payments surplus. Is it that the Germans are extremely productive and make goods cheaply for a world market where the Marshall–Lerner condition holds? Is it because the Germans have a relatively low marginal propensity to absorb and relatively high marginal propensity to save? Or is it the product of monetary restraint?

The problem could be an amalgam of all three elements at any given time, or equally well could be viewed as being due to one dominant 'cause', i.e. over-absorption, or excessive monetary expansion or perverse elasticities, etc. Kindleberger is most probably correct when he notes:

Fully elaborated, the elasticities, absorption and money supply effects merge into one another. For particular problems, however, one or the other may produce the most mileage. The skill of the economist is in making the right choice.

(Kindleberger, 1973, p. 385)

6.4 Adjustment systems and policy coordination

Attention has so far been concentrated on the possible mechanisms of adjustment to payments imbalance, and not on the relative costs and benefits of adopting a particular mechanism as the basis for a global system. Any particular system must be judged in terms of its efficiency in removing international imbalances, encouraging the maintenance of full employment and relative price stability globally, and facilitating the efficient allocation of resources, and the growth and distribution of world trade and output.

It is important to emphasise from the beginning that the fixed-versus-floating exchange rate debate should not be divorced (although it often is) from a consideration of either the efficacy of domestic policies in achieving price and income stability, or the degree of international coordination of policy that prevails. It is for instance too simplistic to argue that flexible exchange rates encourage weak government or that fixed exchange rates impose a burden of external adjustment on the domestic economy. Of course it is possible to interpret the post-1972 depreciation of sterling as the price paid for rapid domestic monetary expansion, and the pre-1967 reluctance of the authorities to devalue sterling as an unnecessary restraint on domestic stability and expansion, and thereby to give some substance to these arguments. Governments, however, may feel just as motivated to protect the foreign-exchange value of the currency, as they do the international reserves through appropriate domestic policies. The public may see either as an indicator of the success of stabilisation policies.

It is in fact the case that with flexible exchange rates any mistake in domestic policy will fall completely on the exchange rate, whereas under a system of fixed exchange rates, the direct link between countries' price levels means that some of one country's policy misjudgement will be passed on to other countries through the balance of trade and the foreign trade multiplier. Similarly, although under a system of fixed exchange rates greater coordination of policies and targets is required, it is not the case that the existence of an equilibrating force (assuming that this is provided by the exchange rate) will remove imbalance if countries continually seek mutually inconsistent goals. Recent global experiences of payments imbalances, trade recession and price inflation during a period of floating exchange rates emphasises that countries are no less under pressure to cooperate with each other. Deficit countries in particular have been anxious to impress upon the major surplus countries the need to reflate their economies in order to offset the deflationary impact of, for example, the oil price rises.

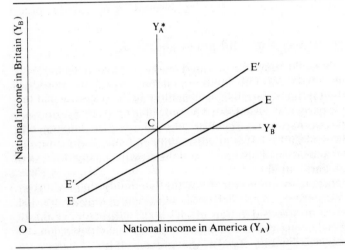

Fig. 6.6 Goal and policy coordination – a two-country model

The problem of reconciling internal and external balance in a world of highly interdependent, but autonomous nations or currency areas can be illustrated in the simplified two-country representation in Fig. 6.6 (see Swoboda, 1973). The positive slope of the EE locus (i.e. those combinations of national income which generate external balance), indicates that any increase in incomes in Britain (Y_B) and therefore spending on America's exports, requires a corresponding growth in America's spending on Britain's production in order to maintain a balance of the trade between the two countries. Any points or combinations of national income above the EE locus generate a surplus for America and therefore a deficit for Britain. (The roles are reversed for points below the EE locus.) The reconciliation of national income targets for internal balance or full employment ($Y_A{}^*$ and $Y_B{}^*$) with external balance requires therefore, either the movement of intersection point C towards the EE locus through the resetting of internal targets, or the existence of some equilibrating force which will shift the EE locus towards point C. Any tendency, however, for an equilibrating instrument such as the exchange rate to shift the locus towards $E'E'$ may be hindered if the surplus country, America, revises its domestic target, in order to maintain external surplus.

Experience of the post-war period has in fact given support to the argument that external balance is not always the objective of countries. This experience and our simple model serve to illustrate the dangers of oversimplifying the arguments in the fixed-versus-floating exchange rate debate, and of isolating the exchange rate decision from consideration of the efficacy and international consistency of domestic policies. The fixed-versus-floating exchange rate argument is in any case complicated by the need to relate the hypothetical and extreme possibilities to how 'fixed' and 'floating' systems are operated in practice.

'Equilibrium' exchange-rate systems

Mundell (1968) has described the 'adjustable peg' exchange system instituted under the Bretton Woods agreement as an 'international disequilibrium system'. It is often against this particular system that the benefits of flexible exchange rates are weighed. It is possibly misleading, however, to describe the system of adjustable pegs in this way. The fact that the authorities are committed to maintaining the prevailing par value of a currency within narrow limits, through support buying and selling if required, does not necessarily mean that the peg is not at an equilibrium value. The successful operation of other policy instruments, or international coordination of policy goals may ensure the maintenance of an equilibrium rate of exchange (see Meade, 1951). In any case the fact that the peg is adjustable means that equilibrium can be restored through devaluation or revaluation. It is in fact a question of the time scale over which we see the term 'equilibrium' as applying. The arguments are not simply concerned with the desirability of fixed and flexible exchange rates, but also with the benefits of discretionary as opposed to automatic exchange-rate adjustment. In operational terms 'fixed' and 'flexible' are not precise or rigid concepts.

The adjustable peg system which operated until 1971 did not for example correspond fully to either the fixed or freely fluctuating exchange-rate alternatives. It was in fact in the middle of a spectrum of possibilities, ranging from freely floating to permanently fixed exchange-rate regimes. Since governments were and remain unlikely to relinquish totally the right to intervene in the foreign-exchange market, argument has centred around the extent to which exchange-rate adjustment should reflect market forces. The advocates of 'managed flexibility' argue that the widening of the band of potential variation around the parity, or the existence of automatic rules for the steady and regular adjustment of the peg ('crawling peg' or 'sliding parity') over time would give the appropriate balance between market flexibility and administrative control (Halm, 1970). An adjustable peg system could in principle steer a similar compromise course. During the 1945–71 period, however, the authorities demonstrated a marked reluctance to adjust parities.

The case for exchange-rate flexibility

Given the downward rigidity of prices and wages it would seem unlikely that countries could indefinitely maintain a particular exchange rate at an 'equilibrium' level through control of domestic prices and incomes alone (especially in the face of differential rates of structural and technological change between countries). The viewing of any parity as sacrosanct may in fact give rise to adjustment, allocative and liquidity problems. It has already been mentioned that the need to maintain an exchange-rate parity may impose a discipline on domestic policy. Whether this form of discipline is desirable is more questionable. For a country with an inflation rate in excess of its major trading partners' and a tendency to move into external deficit, the one-way flexibility of wages and prices means that balance-of-payments adjustment will fall on domestic incomes and employment.

Exchange-rate flexibility therefore avoids this deflationary threat (provided that is, that the price elasticities are such as to make exchange-rate adjustment effective). Following a period of pessimism about the values and the reliability of empirical estimates, it is now generally accepted that elasticity perversity in the long run is exceptional.[3]

The greater possibility of releasing domestic policy tools for internal policy purposes will also tend to discourage the *ad hoc* or short-term nature of policy. In the British case, for instance, it is frequently argued that the *ad hoc* or 'stop/go' nature of policy during the 1960s was to a large extent a function of the attempts to maintain the parity of sterling (see Brittan, 1969). The reserve role of sterling of course, has heightened the sensitivity of the UK economy to external imbalance, but the existence of, and need for international reserves or liquidity is itself a function of the choice of exchange-rate system. In Chapter 7, the relationship between adjustment and liquidity will be examined in greater detail. At this stage we can accept the general proposition that the greater the degree of exchange-rate flexibility, the smaller in general will be the global reserve requirements.

International reserves are in fact a buffer against the need for immediate exchange rate and domestic adjustment. Under the Bretton Woods system however, where there were no operational adjustment rules or codes, reserves proved a more effective buffer for the surplus countries. It is relatively easy to accumulate reserves and thereby avoid revaluation or immediate reflation of the economy. A deficit country will, by contrast, be pressurised into a devaluation or deflation as its reserves diminish. Such asymmetry of adjustment burden is, however, as much an argument for reducing individual countries' discretionary powers as for allowing currencies to float.

In fact one could argue that there may be a depreciation bias under a system of floating exchange rates. On the one hand, given one-way wage flexibility, the more rapidly inflating economies will find it more difficult to reverse the process than the economies with relatively low rates of inflation. On the other hand, given the absence of supranational control and the existence of inherited reserves of international currencies, the opportunity exists for tactical intervention by the authorities on the foreign exchanges. Such potential limitations of exchange-rate flexibility do serve to re-emphasise the need to identify the appropriate conditions for the effective operation of a particular system of exchange rates.

Whether a flexible system is more efficient than a more managed system depends in part upon the potential costs of adjustment under flexible regimes and misallocation due to exchange rigidity. The adjustment process for instance provided by flexible exchange rates is more efficient when productive factors are domestically mobile. In these circumstances the export and domestic market oriented sectors of an economy can expand or contract without generating unemployment. Traditional demand management policies under a regime of fixed exchange rates would however face the same difficulty, namely, in trying to set a level of aggregate demand which would satisfy the needs of a dual economy. In fact for an economy with regions of high unemployment and others of high inflation and low inter-regional mobility, the separation of the economy and the establishment of a flexible exchange rate between the regions may be preferable. This question of factor mobility and the optimal arrangement of currencies by area will be re-examined in more detail later in this chapter. The number of currencies actually floating in relation to each other is, in any case, divorced from the case for flexibility, except to the extent that there may be a geographical arrangement of currencies for which flexible exchange rates will operate most efficiently.

To the extent therefore that there are no market imperfections, exchange-rate changes will bring about adjustment to trade imbalance through the reallocation of domestic resources. By contrast, where an exchange rate is pegged or fixed away from its 'true' equilibrium value, we can expect a loss of economic welfare from the misallocation of resources and the intertemporal distortion of consumption and import prices (see Johnson, 1966). There may also be welfare losses resulting from the distortion of international capital movements, especially if countries resort to capital controls or the external orientation of interest rates as a means of avoiding politically unacceptable domestic policies.

The case for the management of exchange rates
Rigidity or predictability of exchange rates is sometimes seen as a

means of minimising the costs of international transactions; the elimination of uncertainty being seen as an encouragement to world trade. Clearly, transactions in the forward exchange market allow the trader to avoid the risks of the exchange rate moving unfavourably. Where there are flexible rates, the difference between spot and forward rates is sometimes taken as a measure of the additional cost involved. More detailed examination of the motives and behaviour of traders reveals that forward covering may not be a risk payment, and in any case the issue is whether forward transactions are more expensive the more freely flexible the system is (see Machlup, 1970). The freedom of exchange rates to move does not necessarily mean that they are in actual fact highly variable. With pegged exchange rates for instance, the uncertainty of larger and less predictable administrative adjustments to the exchange rate may make the costs of transactions greater than under a system of steadier and more continuous adjustment. More rigid regimes in principle also require domestic prices to adjust or fluctuate in order to achieve adjustment. (Although it has already been established that the price–specie adjustment under the gold standard was far from complete in practice.)

Similarly, under the post-Second World War pegged system, adjustment via internal prices and the exchange rate was generally resisted. Given the surplus countries' ability to resist reflation and revaluation, deficit countries were generally unwilling (and possibly unable) to deflate to the extent of removing price increases. The result, contrary to the previously predicted deflationary threat of rigid systems, was a long-term inflationary bias; a bias in fact encouraged by the authorities' increasing realisation that exchange-rate rigidity and full employment could be accommodated without fundamentally adjusting for current external imbalance.

We have already referred to the policy-mix approach, whereby a deficit country could use expansionary fiscal policies to maintain full employment, and contractionary monetary policy as a means of raising interest rates to attract foreign funds required to finance the deficit. The theoretical neatness of this approach is appealing. However, the longer-term consequences for allocation and growth, of financing imbalances rather than adjusting, have been viewed more critically in recent years (see Fausten, 1975). In the case of Britain, however, it is clear that the external orientation of monetary policy has continued despite the floating of sterling.

Although the adjustment deficiencies of fixed exchange-rate systems remain, the supporters of such systems would claim for them the benefits of stability of exchange rates and domestic prices. The suggestion is on the one hand that 'free' foreign exchange markets increase speculative activity, which is in turn destabilising. On the other hand, it is argued that where the tradeable-goods sector is large, exchange-rate depreciation may lead to domestic inflation, which will also in turn offset the initial relative price adjustment of the depreciation. The image engendered is thus one of a feedback process of speculation-induced exchange-rate depreciation and cumulative inflation. This scenario is however open to some misgivings. Is speculative activity greater under a system of freely floating rates than, for instance, under a system of pegged rates which may be periodically adjusted? There is more often than not, only a one-way option for exchange rates under a pegged system, when the potential gains of a significant exchange adjustment may be large in relation to the potential gains under a floating system. The nature of the commitment to the peg by the authorities is crucial in determining the type of speculative activity. For example, pressure on sterling during the 1964–67 period was not solely the outcome of pure speculation. The 'leads and lags' effect was also important. This refers to the incentive for the UK importer to discharge foreign-currency obligations sooner rather than later, and the foreign importer to accumulate sterling debt in the expectation of the pound's devaluation. Such activity is better described an arbitrage decision of how to finance trade.

'Pure speculation' is concerned by contrast only with the difference between the current forward exchange rate and the expected, future spot rate. In these terms, the argument that speculation destabilises exchange rates is far from unequivocal (see Yeager, 1966). The empirical evidence will be examined presently.[4] There is now, however, a strong theoretical presumption that speculation will reduce exchange-rate variation (see Telser, 1959). Although we must acknowledge the difficulties of defining and isolating the 'speculative' transaction, thinking has been significantly influenced by the intuitive appeal of Friedman's remark that:

People who argue that speculation is generally destabilising seldom realise that this is equivalent to saying that speculators lose money, since speculation can be destabilising in general only if speculators, on average, sell when the currency is low in price and buy when it is high.

(Friedman, 1953, p. 175)

If we assume, as in Fig. 6.7, that in the absence of speculation the underlying market forces generate a regular, cyclical movement of the exchange rate, then Friedman contends that speculators will buy foreign exchange when the rate is relatively low and expected to rise, and sell when the rate is relatively high and expected to fall. The extent of the stabilising effect will depend on the degree of the speculators' foresight, the cost of exchange transactions and the level of competition among speculators.

Baumol (1957) has questioned the generality of Friedman's argument, whilst admitting that profitable speculation will be stabilising if, as we have assumed thus far, non-speculators respond only to the current exchange rate. If, however, non-speculators adjust their buying and selling of foreign exchange only after some time lag, the speculators have the opportunity to sell after the peak and buy after the upturn. As long as the speculators buy at lower prices than those at which they sell, then these activities can be destabilising (increasing the frequency and amplitude of cyclical movements) and remain profitable. Non-profitable speculation or apparently perverse, non-speculative behaviour, i.e. buying when the exchange rate is high and selling when low, are however usually presumed in theory to be exceptional. The weight of theorising in fact appears to point to the stabilising influence of speculation.

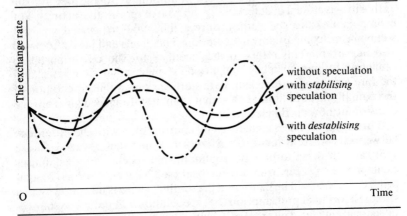

Fig. 6.7 The impact of speculation on the exchange rate

Empirical testing of that theorising is complicated by the difficulties of separating the impact of the actions of speculators during periods of floating rates from the effects of the authorities' frequently erratic domestic policies, and of identifying the hypothetical time path of the exchange rate in the absence of speculation.

The link between domestic prices and the stability of the exchange rate is equally problematic and equally difficult to separate from the effects of domestic stabilisation policies. There is clearly a two-way relationship between domestic prices and the exchange rate. One could argue, for instance, that under conditions of domestic price stability, foreign-exchange markets would be stable. By contrast, the recent inflationary experiences of the UK economy have been linked to the post-1972 depreciation of sterling, and viewed as a contributor to the spiral of cost-push inflation (see Wilson, 1976). To admit to the existence of a causal link between exchange depreciation and inflation is not necessarily to lay the blame on floating systems. Arguments in the inflation debate continue, but the monetarist would argue, for example, that a general rise in prices is only possible if the authorities are willing to fuel the rise through monetary expansion. The full implications of this type of argument are beyond the scope of this text, and an evaluation of this and the other issues in the exchange-rate debate must rest on the ensuing empirical evidence and further reading.

Some empirical assessments

The light shed on the arguments by the experiences this century of floating exchange rates is somewhat limited by the conditions prevailing during these periods. It was, for instance, against a background of global depression that the European countries experimented with floating exchange rates in the inter-war period. Similarly, the broad post-1971 collapse of the pegged system was made necessary by high and divergent inflation rates and the destabilising effects of oil price rises. Some evaluation of the current situation has been attempted (Hirsch and Higham, 1974), but possibly a more illuminating and well-documented experience is provided by the Canadian experiment with floating exchange rates during the relatively stable 1950–62 period. (For a detailed discussion of the Canadian experience, see Yeager, 1966.)

The Canadian dollar remained relatively stable and investigations indicate in general the stabilising influence of short-term capital movements. Canadian trade and the economy grew steadily during the 1950–56 period in particular. A slow-down after 1956 and the growth of unemployment has been explained in part by a downturn in the USA and the inappropriateness of domestic policies. The return to a pegged rate in 1962 has therefore been interpreted not as a sign of failure, but of the inappropriateness of conditions for effective functioning. Increasing intervention by the authorities on the foreign exchange market during the last years of this period, for instance, tended to heighten speculative activity. As such, Stern concludes of this episode that:

There would seem in retrospect to be little room for disagreement over the facts that fluctuating rates in Canada during the 1950s displayed none of the signs of excessive exchange risk, perverse speculation and resource waste that have frequently in the past been attributed to such rates.

(Stern, 1973, p. 107)

This of course does not necessarily mean that a freely floating system of exchange rates is superior to either a managed float or a more rigid system. In fact, while not attempting to make an overall evaluation, Hirsch and Higham feel that the post-1971 'messy floats' have not met up to expectations. They feel that fluctuations have been substantial and that the stabilising role of the speculator is far from proven. But these authors, too, stress again two aspects of exchange-rate policy – its interaction with domestic policy, and the problems of international management and coordination. Few commentators would see exchange-rate flexibility as a panacea for payments adjustment, and the reconciliation of internal/external conflict.

Thus we can conclude that the effective operation of a system of exchange-rate flexibility will be achieved when:

1. exchange rates and domestic prices are dynamically stable;
2. the costs of exchange-rate uncertainty are not excessive;

3. domestic policy discipline is maintained despite the greater leeway allowed by floating rates;
4. any 'management' of exchange rates is internationally coordinated.

This final condition which the adjustable peg system failed also to satisfy – deficit countries being burdened by the threat of reserve loss – has also not been formally satisfied by the recent managed float. No distribution of responsibility between 'strong' and 'weak' currencies about the decision to intervene has been agreed; an issue in fact which precipitated the collapse of the Bretton Woods system. The US desire to act the part of Mundell's 'redundant' nth country, by maintaining a fixed gold price for the dollar in order that the dollar remained the numeraire and currency for international trade and investment, required that the other $n - 1$ countries in the international economy were willing to maintain balance-of-payments equilibrium through either exchange rate or domestic adjustment – equilibrium in US balance of payments would therefore have been guaranteed (Mundell, 1968). The implications of this relationship will be discussed in more detail in Chapters 7 and 8, but at this stage our concern is whether as many as $n - 1$ countries with floating rates is optimal.

6.5 Monetary integration

An optimal level of exchange-rate flexibility

The desirability of a particular organisation of exchange rates (provided that the other conditions for the effective operation of the system prevail) appears to rest upon two further key variables; the level and spatial arrangement of factor mobility and the relative importance of tradeable and non-tradeable goods. Expressed somewhat differently, the suggestion is that given prevailing patterns of factor mobility and economic structure and of established political organisations, there may be an optimal arrangement of fixed and floating exchange rates.

Mundell (1961) has for instance been concerned with the issue of intra- and inter-regional factor mobility. We have already discussed the need for internal factor mobility to make flexible exchange rates effective. Taken one step further, the implication of this condition is that if factors are mobile between countries, flexible exchange rates are unnecessary. The conclusion of Mundell's analysis is in fact that floating exchange rates work best for regions between which factors are immobile. The region may of course be sub-national or it may cut across national boundaries, and in this case a political commitment to currency reorganisation would be necessary. A region and currency area is therefore identified in terms of geographical factor mobility according to Mundell's analysis.

McKinnon (1963) has suggested a somewhat different approach. He stresses the importance of tradeable and non-tradeable goods and argues that a system of fixed exchange rates may be more appropriate where tradeable goods are much more important than non-tradeable goods. The argument is based on the view that in situations of full employment, expenditure-reducing policies may be more effective in restoring equilibrium than the expenditure-switching effects of exchange-rate adjustment. This may in particular be the case if factors are relatively immobile between the non-tradeable and trade goods sectors of the economy. To the extent that mobility between these industrial sectors may correspond to a geographical pattern of mobility, the Mundell and McKinnon approaches may (but not necessarily) argue for a similar arrangement of fixed and floating exchange rates or of currencies. To quote Kindleberger:

A system of permanently fixed rates is equivalent to the existence of a single world money. A system in which exchange rates can alter on the other hand, divides the world into separate monies. How finely divided should the world be?

(Kindleberger, 1973, p. 420)

We shall turn now to the relationship between fixed exchange rates and currency unification: a practical answer to Kindleberger's question remains beyond the scope of this book (see Presley and Dennis, 1976).

Fixed exchange rates and currency unification
The Werner Report on European monetary integration argued that:

A unified monetary zone implies the convertibility of currencies, the elimination of the margins of fluctuation between parities and the complete freeing of capital movements. This can be achieved by keeping the existing national currencies or by establishing a common currency.

(Werner Report, 1970, p. 5)

It is a moot point, however, whether a bloc or global system of fixed exchange rates in practice secures the same benefits as a unified currency, and the associated supranational control of monetary expansion, for instance, provides a more efficient medium of exchange. It minimises transaction costs by removing the costs of currency conversion and uncertainty. This is particularly the case where the desire for national autonomy leaves the fixity of exchange rates in doubt. Similarly, the existence of supranational monetary authority removes the problem of coordinating the growth of separate national monies, while the adoption of a sole currency reinforces any commitment to monetary, economic, and political union. However, the danger remains that non-optimal currency arrangement will make some regions or countries susceptible to the crudeness of a common monetary policy. If there are market imperfections and regions are subject to wage and price inflexibility due to factor immobility, it is important that policies are adopted to increase the movement of goods and factors within the unified currency area, and that there is supranational power to redistribute income through some regional fund. The same proviso of course applies to the fixed-exchange-rate option, but here there is the added requirement that rates of inflation are consistent between member states.

In practical terms the discussions on European monetary integration have been conducted with the retention of national monetary symbols and autonomy much in mind (see Coffey and Presley, 1971). Progress has in general been hampered by the lack of homogeneity of attitudes towards the trade-off between unemployment and inflation and the best means of bringing divergent rates of inflation into line. Although the principle of monetary union appears to have received common acceptance as a method for overcoming recurring currency crises and of establishing a European counter-balance to the power of the USA and the dollar in the international economy, the means of achieving this goal has remained a source of dispute. The 'monetarist' viewpoint would be that a monetary union would impose monetary discipline and therefore greater price stability on members – the speedy adoption of fixed exchange rates or a common currency is the prerequisite, since divergent inflationary pressures are an effect, not a cause, of the failure to achieve monetary union (Parkin, 1976). The fear is of course that this would impose unacceptable levels of unemployment on some countries, without necessarily equalising inflation rates if we accept some cost-push explanation of price increase.

A deflationary threat to the deficit countries of the union can to some extent be constrained by automatic access to an adequate reserve fund. The funds to finance such short- and longer-term payments imbalances would presumably be provided by the surplus members. In the European deliberations it is not too surprising therefore that Germany has been more anxious to reach agreement on the coordination of short-term and growth targets and policies, if it was to furnish such financial aid. In the event, the joint European float launched in 1972 against the dollar (and in which Britain and Italy were in any case unwilling to fully participate) proved an unrealistic fixing of intra-Community parities given the continued divergence of growth and inflation rates. Whether the breakdown should be interpreted as a function of those divergences or as a symptom of monetary laxity remains a controversial issue. The proposals for development on two tiers, monetary union in the short run for the 'strong' currencies with membership for the 'weak' currencies at some later stage appears to accept the first of these alternative interpretations.

Any movement towards monetary union, it must be emphasised however, requires the creation of a reserve asset which the separate monetary authorities can buy and sell in order to maintain the fixed parities between their currencies, or which ultimately could be adopted as a common currency. Monetary conditions and policy, as under any rigidly fixed exchange-rate system (as was illustrated in the operation of the Gold Standard principle), become dependent on the supply of that reserve asset. The control of a supply of a European reserve currency (the so-called 'Europa') which would satisfy the divergent national demands for liquidity to avoid excessive domestic adjustment and for incentives to encourage balance-of-payments adjustment, would be as problematic as the regulation of the dollar proved during the post-war Bretton Woods system (see Cooper, 1972).

Thus far, however, members of the EEC have been unwilling to relinquish national autonomy, in particular over the control of domestic employment, but also to return to a dependence on the dollar as reserve currency and on US monetary policy through a pegged rate system. The result has been a movement towards global flexibility of exchange rates, and a possible impeding of the process of capital-market unification.

Integration and capital markets

Financial integration and the optimal arrangement of currencies, besides seeking to maximise the benefits of international trade, also seeks to maximise the international movement of capital and to take fullest advantage of the entire range of a nation's financial assets, for purposes of international payments adjustment. The intention is that everyone would have complete freedom to trade in securities and other financial claims across national barriers, with the result that the pressure of any external imbalance would be widely diffused throughout all financial markets, and not fall on the currency market only. The rigidity of exchange rates and the removal of capital controls would therefore make the movement of financial capital and securities highly sensitive to differences in interest rates or yields between countries.[5] The unification of capital markets does however reduce the influence of individual national monetary policies over the structure and level of interest rates. This threat to national governments, of the loss of influence over the direction of investment, may be heightened by the growth of multinational corporations. The removal of uncertainty involved in moving across national frontiers would increase the multinationals' abilities to influence the nature and spatial distribution of investment and therefore employment.

The loss of independence in setting national targets has in fact been encouraged in the post-war period by a general removal of exchange controls and closer integration of the capital markets of the major industrial countries. A particular feature of this process has been the emergence of the so-called Eurodollar market. The term 'Eurodollar' strictly refers to short-term deposits held with banks outside the US which are expressed in dollars. However, the extension of this type of international financial operation to currencies other than the dollar has resulted in the evolution of the 'Eurocurrency' concept, i.e. short-term deposits in European banks expressed in some currency other than the domestic currency, e.g. D-marks deposited at a London bank.

The Eurodollar was in part a non-official response to the liquidity/capital deficiencies of Europe, and in part encouraged by interest-rate restrictions on bank deposits in the US. The Eurodollar thus developed into an attractive alternative for foreign holders of dollars to sell to their central banks, and for central banks to hold as part of their reserves. So attractive, in fact, that the US restrictions were removed and the interest-rate differential between the US and other countries narrowed. (In recent years tight monetary policies in the US have in fact been circumvented to some extent by the repatriation of Eurodollars.) Nevertheless, the market has continued to grow despite the breakdown of exchange-rate rigidity, and to refine the process of matching international borrowers and lenders. (For a detailed consideration of the Eurocurrency concept, see McKenzie, 1976; and for a more light-hearted discussion, see Aliber, 1973, Ch. 7.)

The responsibility given to UK local authorities and nationalised industries to borrow directly on the Eurocurrency market in 1973 is indicative of the market's importance and level of sophistication. In effect, this facility allowed UK authorities to finance the payments deficit by a semi-official means, and thereby to reduce the burden on the official reserves. To that extent the Eurocurrency market has in an *ad hoc* manner contributed to the stock of international liquidity – the implications and desirability of which we will now turn our attention to in Chapter 7.

Notes

1. The precise values would in fact be $4.9187 and $4.8213. These have been rounded to $4.82 and $4.92 for the purposes of exposition.
2. With partial elasticities we assume other things to be equal, so that it is possible to focus on the effect of price changes on quantity supplied. This is considered an unsatisfactory assumption to make where exchange rates are concerned, since secondary price and income effects are omitted. Total elasticities take into account these secondary effects. The tautology here occurs because all direct and indirect, primary and secondary price changes are taken into account, and the whole exercise becomes an *ex post* rationalisation.
3. Estimates of price elasticities are to be found in Houthakker and Magee (1969) and OECD (1970).
4. Conventional wisdom was initially rooted in the self-intensifying nature of speculative movements, which freely fluctuating exchange rates tended to encourage. This view was based on the study of the inter-war period by Nurkse (1944).
5. The theory of capital flows and the mechanism of real resource transfer, the transfer problem, is somewhat incomplete. For an exposition of classical and modern theory, see Scammell (1974).

Chapter 7

Problems of liquidity

7.1 Introduction

So far we have studied the mechanics of international payments relations. We have examined the structure of countries' balance of payments, the implications of external imbalance, and the range of possible measures which can be taken in attempting to adjust any imbalance. In looking at international payments and adjustment we have taken one very important factor for granted, the existence and significance of international money.

The object of this chapter will be to redress this balance. First, we will elaborate on what we mean by such terms as international money, international liquidity, and international reserves. Second, we will examine in some depth the demand for international reserves. This will allow us to highlight the crucial interdependence between the form of adjustment system, and the need for international reserves. Third, we will investigate aspects of the supply of international reserves. Finally, we will consider the various criteria which can be used to assess the adequacy of reserve provisions. Once we have completed our discussion of international liquidity, we will be in a position to consider different forms of international monetary organisation.

What is international liquidity?

By international liquidity we usually mean the stock of internationally acceptable monies available for the ultimate settlement of debts between individuals, corporate bodies and trading nations. These international monies can take various forms, the qualifications for use being that they be liquid, easily transferable, and more important perhaps, that they are readily acceptable and have a stable and predictable value.

Broadly speaking, we tend to think of international money in three general forms – commodity money, fiat money and credit money. In the context of international trading relations, gold has been the principal form of commodity money. This relatively scarce and precious metal was acceptable in international transactions because it fulfilled the function of a medium of exchange and store of value. Over time, however, with a continuous expansion in world trade and a shortfall in gold supplies, the need to economise on existing gold stocks became increasingly apparent. Despite the obvious advantages of paper money (cheaper to produce, more convenient to hold in cash balances, etc.), international trust was not sufficient to accept it on its own. It was, however, quickly realised that the advantages of fiat money could be reaped, if it were 'backed' by something with intrinsic value. Consequently we had the development of fiat money backed by gold. The countries whose currencies were used were those which were important trading nations, had a stock of gold with which to back their currency, and were prepared to run balance-of-payments deficits in order to supply the rest of the world with such liquidity. Thus, prior to the Second World War the pound sterling was the principal form of fiat money, whereas since the Second World War the US dollar has dominated international monetary relations.

Increasing sophistication of, and confidence in, the domestic economy usually results in an increasing dependence on credit money. This is also the case with the international economy. Thus, over the past decade or so we have seen increasing use of credit money in the settlement of international debts. Confidence in the international economy is not of course sufficiently developed to permit the type of almost total dependence on credit money that most advanced economies exhibit, but the signs are that it may become more rather than less important.

We will be discussing these developments in much more detail in Section 7.3. The question we must ask now is: Why is it necessary to have stocks of international liquidity available? Most obviously, international money is required to facilitate international exchange, in much the same way as a medium of exchange is required in the domestic economy. We may term this the *transactions motive* for holding international money. Individuals, corporate bodies and national governments all require money to pay for purchases from abroad. In addition we can envisage a *speculative motive*. As we know from Keynesian liquidity analysis, speculative motives for holding money revolve around expectations of changes in interest rates and asset prices. We have already seen in Chapters 5 and 6 how speculators stand to profit from exchange-rate variations, simply by switching their holdings of international money from one currency into another. We will see later in this chapter that speculation can have important implications for both the demand for, and supply of international money.

Our main purpose in this chapter is not, however, to focus attention directly on either of these motives, but rather to concentrate primarily on the demand for international money on the part of central banks.[1] This demand is not strictly speaking a transactions demand but rather a *precautionary demand*. Central banks (on behalf of their political masters, of course) tend to hold 'reserves' of international money in order to finance trade imbalances and not trade itself. In other words, reserves are held so that any unanticipated excess of international payments over receipts can be met. Thus, when a nation faces a balance-of-payments deficit it must finance this deficit before under-taking adjustment measures in the shorter or longer term. Inter-national reserves are held so that every balance-of-payments deficit need not be accompanied by immediate and costly adjustment meas-ures, but can be met by accommodating finance. It is this aspect of reserve holding to which we will pay attention.

7.2 The demand for international reserves

It is possible to conceive of the demand for reserves on two levels. First, the global demand for reserves, i.e. what considerations affect total world requirements at any point in time? Second, what considera-tions affect the reserve holding behaviour of individual countries?

Determinants of global reserve requirements
When discussing the implications of different adjustment systems, we noted that alternative systems make alternative demands on world liquidity. As we have already seen in Section 6.4, in the extreme case of a regime of **perfectly functioning** freely floating exchange rates, there is no need for central banks to hold stocks of international reserves (unless for purely political motives). By definition, variations in the exchange rate automatically equilibrates demand and supply in the foreign exchange market, and balances the nations' payments and receipts. Contrast this with a system of pegged rates where the cur-rency's par value is bound by agreed support limits, and the central bank is obliged to intervene in the foreign-exchange market to main-tain the value of its currency within these limits. Thus, in the event of a balance-of-payments surplus, currency appreciation is avoided by foreign exchange accumulation. In the opposite situation of payments deficit, the central bank is forced to use its stock of reserves to prevent the exchange rate from depreciating. In terms of Fig. 5.2, p. 132, the central bank is entering the foreign-exchange market to satisfy excess demand. In so doing, it is financing the country's balance-of-payments deficit from its stock of gold and convertible currency reserves.

Other things being equal then, the degree of exchange-rate flexi-bility inherent in the adjustment regime will have a crucial bearing on global reserve requirements. We can perhaps envisage the situation represented in Fig. 7.1, where R_1 represents reserve requirements as a function of exchange rate flexibility. *Ceteris paribus*, the higher the index of flexibility, the lower are global reserve requirements. Con-versely, the lower the index of flexibility, the greater are requirements.

At one end of the spectrum would be a system of freely floating exchange rates. Associated with this would be reserve requirements approaching zero. The domestic currency is always 'correctly priced', inasmuch as any payments imbalance would be corrected by automatic exchange-rate variation.

As we get lower on our index of exchange-rate flexibility, the

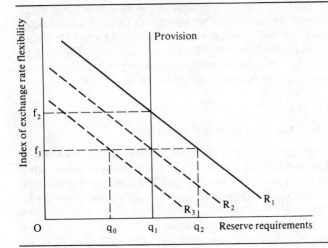

Fig. 7.1 Reserve provision and requirement under alternative exchange rate regimes

exchange rate is assumed to bear less and less of the strains of adjustment. The burden of adjustment is instead passed on to domestic incomes and prices. We again have a potential conflict between internal and external balance, and international reserves are required to reduce the urgency of (or completely avoid) adjustment. Other things being equal therefore, the more variable or flexible are exchange rates, the less will be the need for international reserves.

This question of adjustment regime brings us to a related factor influencing world reserve requirements, namely the ability and willingness of countries to engage in 'necessary' adjustments. In other words, when exchange rates are pegged or fixed, the main burden of adjustment is supposed to fall on domestic prices and incomes. When this is the case, how willing in general are countries to abide by the 'rules of the game'? Quite clearly, the less willing they are, the greater will potential reserve requirements be. The longer the time period over which deficit countries take to adopt suitable expenditure-reducing or expenditure-switching policies, the greater will be their desired stock of international reserves to finance their deficit. Similarly, if surplus countries find it unpalatable to engage in domestic reflation to eliminate or reduce their surplus, then a portion of world reserves becomes 'tied up' in their hands and is therefore immobilised.

This sort of impasse seemed to be a feature of the Bretton Woods system in the decade prior to its demise. Deficit countries (for example the UK and the US) felt they had borne a disproportionate share of the adjustment burden. Surplus countries on the other hand (e.g. Germany and Japan) seemed unwilling to inflate their domestic economies to the extent required to eliminate their surpluses. Quite clearly, if all countries in the system were to adopt this attitude, the demand for reserves would become infinite with ever-increasing stocks of reserves required to finance ever-increasing imbalance. (See Greenaway and Milner, 1978.) Thus *ceteris paribus*, the more willing are countries to participate in the adjustment process, the less will be global demands for reserves. Conversely, when countries are unwilling to make domestic adjustments, there will be increasing rigidity in the adjustment system, and increasing demands for international reserves.

Consultation and cooperation between countries may eventually result in the formation of international agencies which could have a bearing on this issue. For instance, it may be possible that through the forum provided by some international body, countries could devise and, more important, police a set of rules to facilitate and encourage adjustment. The International Monetary Fund (IMF) to some extent performs such a role. When deficit countries are running down their stock of international reserves and require assistance from the IMF (i.e. they have to draw on their *credit tranche*), certain conditions are laid down with the credit. For instance, in December 1976 the UK government negotiated a 'stand-by' loan of $3.9 billion. In order to obtain this loan, the UK authorities had to agree to certain conditions. Targets were set for the growth of the public-sector borrowing requirement and overall monetary expansion, in order that the authorities were seen to be taking some positive action to remedy the balance-of-payments deficit. In this way, pressure can be brought to bear on deficit countries to take some adjustment measures which will ultimately shift their demand and supply curves for foreign exchange, and reduce their reserve requirements.

In principle the IMF also possesses a weapon to stimulate surplus countries into action. The *scarce currency* clause of the Articles of Agreement can be invoked. This basically involves giving 'legal' backing to trade restrictions against any nation which persistently runs a balance-of-payments surplus and whose currency is declared 'scarce'. This scarce currency clause has not yet been used, however, and exhortation remains the main means of persuasion.

International cooperation may influence world reserve requirements in another way. If cooperation results in conflicts in national policies being minimised, then the primary source of payments disequilibrium could be 'controlled' in some small way. If divergent price and income levels between countries are seen as the proximate cause of payments imbalance, then the greater the magnitude of these divergences the greater the resultant imbalances, and thus the greater the global need for reserves.

Another factor which can have a crucial bearing on aggregate reserve requirements is the level and mobility of short-term capital. A glance forward to Table 7.5 illustrates the rapid growth of private liquidity holdings over the last decade or so. Such holdings are traditionally short-term (for instance a principal component of the column 'UK sterling liabilities' is UK Treasury Bills which mature within three months). Furthermore, they tend to be very mobile, shifting from one reserve centre to another in response to interest rate differentials, or in anticipation of currency realignments. These flows can increase deficit countries' reserve requirements. For instance in 1971 when devaluation of the dollar seemed imminent, official US short-term liabilities increased by $14.4 billion between the end of March and mid-August, as private dollar holders shifted into other currencies. Similarly, in the months prior to the 1967 devaluation of the pound sterling, over $1 billion in credits and short-term loans were made available to the UK government for use against speculative flows. It would seem that such flows only serve to aggravate the payments imbalance and increase reserve requirements.

On the other hand, however, capital flows may actually reduce reserve requirements by providing a source of accommodating finance. For example, in the early 1970s the UK government deliberately maintained interest rates at a relatively high level. This served to attract short-term capital flows which helped to fill the shortfall of foreign exchange and thereby 'finance' the balance-of-payments deficit. Clearly if this can be accomplished successfully the need for 'official' reserves is lessened. *Ceteris paribus* therefore, reserve requirements may be increased or reduced by private capital flows, depending on which of these conflicting tendencies predominate.

We can perhaps summarise these points overall, by positing that global reserve requirements will be dependent on the nature and mores of the adjustment system. Having discussed this interdependence between adjustment and liquidity, we wish now to become a little more specific and ask the question: What factors determine the amount of reserves which a particular country will demand at any point in time?

The national demand for reserves

As we would anticipate, there is a certain amount of overlap between the type of factors which help explain world reserve requirements, and those factors which may determine the reserve holding behaviour of individual countries. For example, the arguments developed relating to the type of adjustment regime and adjustment *mores* must of course provide the starting point for an analysis of individual country's reserve holding behaviour. In addition to this, however, we can develop a number of other factors relating more specifically to individual rather than aggregate demands.

It is possible simply to enumerate the type of variables considered relevant. Thus the size of a nation's foreign-trade sector would appear to be an obvious determinant of reserve requirements. The greater the size of its foreign-trade sector, the more significant the impact of any random disturbance, and therefore the greater the stock of reserves required.

The opportunity cost involved in holding reserves is another fairly obvious factor. Reserves are assets which traditionally yield relatively low interest payments. The yield on some forms may even be zero (or in the case of gold possibly negative, given storage and insurance costs). To hold a stock of international reserves therefore involves tying up resources in low-yielding assets when they could be (socially) more profitably used elsewhere, in either consumption or investment. Thus other things being equal, the greater this opportunity cost the lower the stock of reserves held.

Other important factors might be: considerations of the costs involved in taking adjustment measures (*ceteris paribus,* the costlier is adjustment in terms of output forgone, the greater the stock of reserves held in order to slow down the adjustment process); the speed at which adjustment takes place (*ceteris paribus*, the faster the adjustment process, the less is the need to hold reserves); the degree of correlation between demand and supply fluctuations (the greater this is, the more likely it is that movements will offset each other, possibly stabilising the trade balance). We could go on and state the whole gamut of possible influences. Alternatively we could fruitfully explore one of the number of models available which attempts to explain individual country's reserve holding behaviour within a rational optimising framework. This would allow us to examine the interrelationship between the relevant variables, and also the type of problems

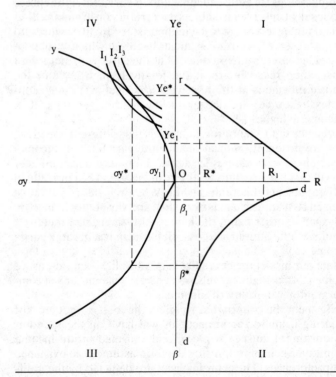

Fig. 7.2 A model of the optimum level of international reserves held by a country

which are faced when attempting empirical estimation. One such model is that of Clark (1970), a version of which is outlined in Fig. 7.2. (For a review of the literature, see Grubel, 1971.)

The model assumes that exchange rates are fixed, and therefore a given payments deficit can be eliminated by price and income adjustment, or accommodated by recourse to the use of foreign-exchange reserves. The R-axis represents the level of desired reserves. The country can select a target level of reserves, at the same time selecting a value for its adjustment parameter β. Thus, if its desired stock of reserves is relatively high (R_1), any payments adjustment can take place over a relatively long time period, and therefore β has a relatively low value of β_1. If on the other hand, desired reserves are set at the level R^*, then adjustment must take place over a much shorter time period, and the adjustment parameter takes the higher value of β^*. The curve dd in quadrant II traces out all combinations of desired reserves and their associated adjustment parameters.

The problem facing the individual country is to select the best possible target level of reserves, in the knowledge that the lower this level is, the greater the probability that reserves will quickly be depleted, and adjustment measures will be necessary. Since the amount of reserves held at any time, and the speed of adjustment, have important implications for future income and its variability, the choice of a desired level of reserves is subject to certain constraints.

It is assumed that reserves are low-yielding assets. In other words, to hold stocks of reserves, resources must be used which could be invested to yield greater future income. Thus the curve rr in quadrant I indicates that when reserves are at the relatively high level of R_1, expected future income is at the relatively low level of Ye_1. By contrast, when less resources are tied up in low-yielding reserves (R^*), expected income is higher (Ye^*).

The other constraint to be borne in mind is that different speeds of adjustment have different implications for the variability of income. Since adjustment is via domestic demand management, quicker adjustment will result in greater variability of income. The curve Ov in quadrant III represents this relationship. When the desired level of reserves is high (R_1), adjustment is slow (β_1), and variability of income is low (σy_1). On the other hand, the higher adjustment parameter β^* indicating quicker adjustment, has associated with it a greater variability of income (σy^*).

To complete our model the curve Oy in quadrant IV denotes, as we would anticipate, that higher levels of expected income are accompanied by a greater variability of income.

To optimise then, the country has to select the 'best' target level of reserves, bearing in mind the impact this will have on the speed at which any adjustment must take place, and expected future income and its variability. Such an optimising decision assumes the existence of a scale of preferences. These preferences are depicted by the indifference curves I_1, I_2 and I_3 in quadrant IV, higher indifference curves denoting greater levels of economic welfare. The shape and ranking of these indifference curves suggest that expected income is a 'good' (in the sense that more is preferred to less), whilst variability of income is a 'bad' (since less is preferred to more). As is obvious, welfare is maximised by the selection of R^* as the target level of reserves, since at this level indifference curve I_2 is tangential to Oy. I_2 is therefore the highest level of welfare attainable.

The model therefore graphically illustrates the trade-off between the stock of international reserves held, and the speed at which adjustment must take place. Furthermore, since there are costs involved in both holding reserves and taking adjustment measures, we can go on to explore the implications of a given target level of reserves for the level and variability of income. Like other models of a similar type it makes several testable predictions about individual countries' reserve holding behaviour.

It predicts for instance, an inverse relationship between a nation's marginal propensity to import (mpm) and its target level of reserves. A relatively high mpm requires a relatively mild deflation to correct a given balance-of-payments deficit, thus the target level of reserves need only be relatively low. Continuing this reasoning, a direct relationship between the speed of adjustment and the mpm would be predicted. *Ceteris paribus*, a high mpm would mean relatively quick adjustment. These relationships can perhaps be illustrated more clearly by reference to a simplified numerical example. Suppose a country faced a balance-of-payments deficit of £1 million. If its mpm were 0.5, the deficit could be eliminated by an income reduction of £2 million (ignoring feedback effects on exports). If, however, its mpm were 0.1, then a £10 million income reduction would be necessary to eliminate the deficit. Presumably in the latter case adjustment would take place over a longer time period, and the target level of reserves would therefore have to be much higher than in the former case.

An inverse relationship between the target level of reserves and their opportunity cost is posited. The greater the sacrifice in expected income through holding reserves, the lower will be the target level. If this is so then clearly the speed of adjustment will vary directly with the opportunity cost of holding reserves. The greater the opportunity cost, the greater the sacrifice in foregone income involved in holding reserves, therefore the greater the incentive to take rapid adjustment measures.

Finally, the model suggests a direct relationship between payments variability and the target level of reserves. Greater payments variability will mean a greater probability of payments imbalance, and therefore a higher desired level of reserves. This also implies an inverse relationship between payments variability and the speed of adjustment. A greater variability of payments would provoke a slower adjustment process, since a higher level of reserves would be held.

Some empirical evidence on the demand for reserves   These predictions are all plausible. *A priori* plausibility is not, however, the sole *raison d'être* of theorising. Ultimately the objective of most model building is to yield predictions which are borne out by empirical research. The question we must now ask ourselves then is: How does this model and models like it perform empirically? (For a useful survey of the empirical evidence, see Williamson, 1973, pp. 691–697.)

Various optimising models persistently point to a number of explanatory variables amenable to empirical investigation. These include: the opportunity cost of reserve holding, payments variability, the marginal propensity to import, and *per capita* income. Empirical studies have not, however, been wholly conclusive, with the evidence on most variables being conflicting. Some studies offer some support for the *a priori* predictions of the models (Kelly, 1970; Clark, 1970; Iyoha, 1976), whereas others can find no meaningful results (Flanders, 1971). This does not necessarily mean that the variables we have been discussing lack explanatory power. It is important to note that the statistical problems which the empiricist faces are considerable. In the absence of widely accepted measures of payments variability, or the opportunity cost of reserves, etc., proxies of varying degrees of quality have to be employed. Part of the lack of wholly conclusive evidence could therefore be due to the fact that poor proxies are being used. In addition, the wide range of proxies used is not conducive to consistent results. For instance, no objective measure of the opportunity cost of reserves exists since we can never be entirely certain how the resources held in reserves would have otherwise been employed. One could contend they would have been used for domestic investment or consumption, and proxy the opportunity cost by the growth rate. Alternatively one could opt for more overt 'market-related' proxies, such as the rate of return on long-term securities, or the rate on government securities. All of these (and several others) have been used. It is perhaps unsurprising then that results are not uniform.

Furthermore, one must bear in mind that the explanatory variables themselves tend to be interrelated and interdependent. The statistical technique most often used is multivariate regression, which attempts to explain movements in a dependent variable by reference to movements in a number of independent, or explanatory variables. Ideally, each independent variable ought to be truly independent, and make a separate contribution to the overall explanation. Often, however, the independent variables influence each other as well as influencing the dependent variables. Thus for example, although the marginal propensity to import and payments variability may both be related to the demand for reserves (our dependent variable), they may also be related to each other. In these circumstances it is often extremely difficult to separate out the relative importance of the different independent variables, because of the large standard errors involved in estimating their coefficients.[2]

We must be aware of these difficulties and the problems they can cause for empiricists. We must also remember that some support has been adduced. The alternative would seem to be to follow the lead of more than one distinguished economist, in arguing that countries' reserve-holding behaviour defies rational explanation (Flanders, 1971). Indeed, Fritz Machlup was moved to suggest that central bankers' motives for demanding reserves are no more complex than his wife's motives for demanding new clothes – a simple desire to have more! (Machlup 1966a.) Whilst clearly an extreme stand to adopt, this despairing conclusion is perhaps indicative of the intractability of some of the difficulties faced in this area.

7.3 The supply of international reserves

Having surveyed the type of factors likely to influence the demand for reserves, it is now necessary to consider the more widely documented area concerning the supply of international reserves.

We saw earlier that to qualify as international money, a particular type of reserve asset must satisfy several criteria – it must be liquid, acceptable and transferable. In the history of international monetary relations several types of assets have satisfied these criteria and come to be regarded as sources of international reserves. We can consider each asset separately under the headings: central bank gold holdings; convertible foreign currencies; IMF drawing rights and special drawing rights; 'other' sources. The changes in the relative importance of these components in the total world supply of international reserves are illustrated in Table 7.1 and Fig. 7.3.

Central bank gold holdings

The use of gold as a monetary unit antedates recorded history. For centuries the metal has been used in both the domestic and international economy. Following the demise of the International Gold Standard, the role of gold in international monetary relations went into secular decline. Its role was however reasserted at Bretton Woods, despite Keynes's protestations about the metal being a 'barbarous relic'. It was felt that the presence of gold at the heart of the system would maintain confidence in it and ensure its longevity. Consequently gold was valued at $35 per ounce and it was envisaged that this price could be maintained by central bank intervention in the bullion markets, operating a buffer stock policy.[3]

The role of gold has however continued in its secular decline. The supply of gold only increases slowly. Furthermore, as well as performing a monetary function, gold has industrial and artistic uses, and provides an excellent hedge against inflation for private hoarders. The attractiveness of gold as an 'investment' steadily increased in the post-war years because its price was fixed at $35 per ounce. Persistent

Table 7.1   Post-war level and composition of international reserves, 1948–78*

Year	Total Reserves (SDR billions)	Gold (SDR billions)	Fund positions (SDR billions)	SDRs (SDR billions)	Foreign exchange (SDR billions)
1948	49.5	34.5	1.6		13.4
1950	50.3	35.3	1.7		13.3
1952	51.8	36.9	1.8		14.2
1954	55.4	38.1	1.8		16.7
1956	58.2	38.0	2.3		17.8
1958	57.6	38.0	2.6		17.0
1960	60.2	39.3	3.6		18.6
1962	63.1	40.8	3.9		19.9
1964	69.9	40.9	5.4		23.7
1966	72.6	40.9	6.3		24.4
1967	74.3	39.5	5.7		29.0
1968	77.4	38.9	6.5		32.0
1969	78.2	39.1	6.7		32.4
1970	92.6	37.2	7.6	3.1	44.6
1971	123.2	35.9	6.3	5.9	75.1
1972	146.7	35.6	6.3	8.7	95.9
1973	152.2	35.6	6.2	8.8	101.7
1974	180.2	35.5	8.8	8.8	126.9
1975	194.5	35.5	12.6	8.8	137.4
1976	222.1	35.3	17.7	8.6	160.4
1977	262.4	35.5	18.1	8.1	200.6
1978	262.2	35.8	17.3	8.1	205.9

Notes 1. Figures are for end years except for 1978 (March)
2. Totals may not add precisely due to rounding
3. SDR Valuations

1948–70	SDR 1 = $1.00
1971–2	SDR 1 = $1.08
1973	SDR 1 = $1.20
1974	SDR 1 = $1.22
1975	SDR 1 = $1.17
1976	SDR 1 = $1.16
1977	SDR 1 = $1.21
1978	SDR 1 = $1.22

Source: Compiled from *International Financial Statistics* (Various Issues)

world inflation ensured that at $35 per ounce it was undervalued. Thus the private demand for gold inexorably increased and only small proportions of newly mined gold became available for monetary use. Thus, we can see from Table 7.1 that between 1948 and 1968, central bank gold holdings increased by less than 13 per cent from SDR 34.5 billion to SDR 38.9 billion.

Because of the pressure of demand for private uses, it was decided in 1968 to separate the market for gold into two tiers. One tier would be for dealings for official monetary use. In this market the price was to be maintained at $35 per ounce. The second tier comprised 'private' dealings only, where the price of the metal would be freely determined by the interaction of demand and supply. Despite revaluations of the

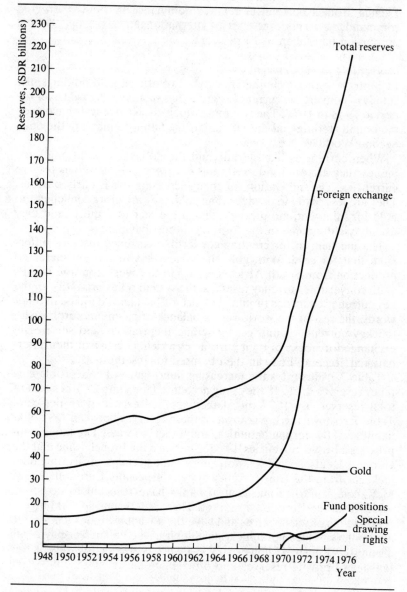

Fig. 7.3 Level and composition of international reserves

official price to $38 per ounce (December 1971) and $42.22 per ounce (February 1973), the free market price increased to a much greater extent, reaching a peak of almost $200 per ounce in late 1974. Clearly, in these circumstances central banks were not prepared to use gold for settlement purposes, and gold stocks became effectively immobilised.

Thus, from a position of relative dominance in 1948 when gold commanded a 70 per cent share of international reserves, by 1977 the proportion had fallen to 14 per cent.

Convertible foreign currencies

In contrast to the declining importance of official gold holdings, the supply of convertible currency reserves has steadily increased over the period 1948 to 1977. The two most widely used currencies have been the pound sterling and the US dollar, the latter dominating the post-Second World War period.

When currencies like sterling and the dollar act as international money they are often referred to as *key currencies* as well as reserve currencies. The motivation for their increasing use is fairly obvious. They are less costly to produce than gold, they are more convenient to hold for intervention purposes, they are easier to acquire, and they usually yield income in the form of interest payments.

The mechanism for creating convertible currency reserves differs from that for gold. With gold the system has to rely on increased production from South Africa, or sales to the West from the USSR. With convertible currency reserves, the system relies primarily on the key currency countries running balance-of-payments deficits. In other words, the rest of the world runs a balance-of-payments surplus with the key currency countries, by selling them goods and services in exchange for stocks of their currencies which, because of their international acceptability, can then be used for reserves.

Table 7.1 illustrates the increasing importance of convertible currency reserves. In 1948 they only accounted for some 27.1 per cent of total reserves. By 1977 this percentage had exceeded 75 per cent. Table 7.2 shows the breakdown of these reserves between US dollar liabilities, UK sterling liabilities, and 'other' sources. The latter comprise lesser-used currencies, like for instance the French franc and the German Deutsche mark. More important perhaps, it also includes leakages from the Eurocurrency system, especially Eurodollars (see McKenzie, 1976). Some central banks have resorted to acquiring assets from the Eurodollar market. These assets tend to yield higher returns than official sources and have the advantage that such reserve accumulation does not appear as a debit in the balance-of-payments accounts. (Recently, however, the IMF has sought to prevent this leakage of private reserves into official holdings.)

IMF drawing rights and special drawing rights

When a country becomes a member of the IMF it is given a *quota*.[4] This quota provides the basis upon which voting rights and drawing rights are assessed. Each member pays a subscription to the Fund equal to the value of its quota; 25 per cent of this is paid in gold, the remaining 75 per cent in the country's own currency.

Table 7.2 Composition of convertible currency reserves, 1950–77*

Year	US liabilities (SDR billion)	UK liabilities (SDR billion)	Other (SDR billion)	Total (SDR billion)
1950	3.8	9.6	n.a.	13.4
1952	4.9	7.0	2.3	14.2
1954	7.0	7.6	2.1	16.7
1956	8.3	7.4	2.1	17.8
1958	9.4	6.7	0.9	17.0
1960	11.7	7.0	0.9	19.6
1962	12.7	6.2	1.0	19.9
1964	15.4	6.5	1.8	23.7
1966	14.9	6.1	3.4	24.4
1967	18.3	4.8	5.9	29.0
1968	17.3	4.3	10.4	32.0
1969	16.0	5.2	11.2	32.4
1970	23.8	5.7	15.1	44.6
1971	46.6	7.3	21.2	75.1
1972	56.6	8.0	31.3	95.9
1973	55.4	6.5	39.8	101.7
1974	62.6	8.2	56.1	126.9
1975	68.8	6.3	62.3	137.4
1976	79.0	3.2	78.2	160.4
1977	103.7	3.3	78.6	185.6

*Notes 1. Figures are for end years, except 1977 (September)
      2. Totals may not add precisely due to rounding
Source: compiled from *International Financial Statistics* (Various Issues)

The IMF therefore acquires stocks of currencies from its members, which it can subsequently lend to nations facing balance-of-payments difficulties. Any country facing payments difficulties can borrow an amount of foreign currency from the Fund up to the value of the currency component of its quota (i.e. up to 75 per cent of its quota). The loan (plus service charges) is repaid over a specified time period (three to five years). These are the country's *drawing rights* and their importance can be seen by reference to the column headed 'Fund positions' in Table 7.1. The use of fund positions forms a relatively small percentage of total reserves. Since, however, they can be automatically activated whenever a country feels itself to be under payments pressure, they are still important sources of international reserves.

It is noticeable that there has been a steady increase in fund positions due to the periodic reassessment of, and increases in, member nations' quotas.

In addition to these automatic drawing rights, any member can further draw on its *credit tranche*. Here the member can borrow up to 125 per cent of its quota in five slices or 'tranches'. The first drawing (the 'reserve tranche') is unconditional. The remaining four tranches are, however, conditional, the conditions imposed becoming more stringent with each successive drawing. Because of the conditionality element, these are not usually included in calculations of countries' foreign exchange reserves.

The IMF's role in reserve supply was further extended by the creation of *special drawing rights* (SDRs). Their creation was approved by the Fund in 1967 and they became active in 1970. SDRs are completely new reserve assets. They are created by the Fund and issued to members in proportion to their quotas. Any member can draw on its allocation of SDRs if and when it pleases, so long as it maintains an average of 30 per cent of its initial allocation over a five-year period. Drawings can then be used to purchase foreign exchange from any other member, since all members of the Fund are obliged to accept SDRs up to a maximum holding of 300 per cent of their initial allocation. Countries using SDRs are charged a rate of interest of 5 per cent, whereas countries receiving SDRs are paid the same rate of interest. Since SDRs never have to be repaid, they constitute a net addition to world reserves, unlike ordinary drawing rights in the Fund's General Account (see Polak, 1971).

Initially SDRs were valued at SDR 1 = $1 US; since July 1974, however, valuation has been on the basis of a weighted 'basket' of currencies.[5]

Allocations of SDRs can be increased at any time so long as any proposed increase has the approval of 80 per cent of the Board of Governors. As can be seen from Table 7.1, allocations were increased in 1971 and 1972.

'Other' sources

It was fairly widely agreed that reserve growth in the latter 1950s and early 1960s was inadequate (see Chapter 8 for more detail). In response to this liquidity shortage, countries resorted to various agreements by which they could assist each other when in balance-of-payments difficulties. Thus, many countries negotiated bilateral 'swap agreements'. These are agreements whereby central banks swap quantities of their currencies for a specified period of time. Although introduced in 1962, many of these agreements remain. In 1976 the US Federal Reserve Bank still had reciprocal credit facilities with some fourteen other central banks.

In the same year as the swap network was instituted, the 'General Agreement to Borrow' (GAB) was negotiated. The GAB was an agreement whereby the Group of Ten provided the IMF with $6 billion of their currencies on which deficit countries could draw.[6] A similar agreement is in operation at present, whereby oil producers are using some of their accumulated reserves to provide a credit line for nations facing pressure due to 'oil deficits', the so called 'Oil Facility'.

These types of arrangements do not actually constitute increases in the total supply of reserves. Like IMF drawing rights, they assist in economising on the existing stock of reserves. One could perhaps even say that they operate to increase the velocity of circulation of a given stock of reserves (see Tew, 1977, Ch. 10).

These then are the primary sources of international reserves. Having analysed the post-war level and composition of reserves, our next task is to consider whether the type of reserves supplied, and the total level of reserve provision, have been adequate from the point of view of encouraging the post-war development of the international economy. Adequacy of reserves is a difficult notion to analyse. Any attempt must however consider adequacy in two conceptually separable, but nevertheless interrelated senses:

(a) The technical suitability of particular assets as international reserves.

(b) The adequacy of supply in satisfying demand.

7.4 The suitability of reserve assets

According to Professor John Williamson (Williamson, 1973), the suitability of a particular reserve asset should be assessed with regard to three broad considerations: 'confidence', 'stabilisation', and 'seigniorage'.

The confidence problem

The confidence problem arises from the simultaneous use of more than one form of reserve asset. In these circumstances, whenever doubts arise regarding the acceptability of any one asset, the possibility exists that reserve holders (both official and non-official) may substitute that asset for another with the result that strains are placed on the system. The problem can perhaps best be illustrated by reference to experience under the Bretton Woods system.

As we have noted the growth of gold reserves was insufficient to support the expansion of world trade. Given the post-war strength of the US economy and its huge gold stocks, the US dollar was regarded as being 'as good as gold'. US dollar liabilities were after all backed by gold on a greater than one-to-one basis. Countries therefore accumulated dollar reserves supplied through a US balance-of-payments deficit. Since, however, the US was under no obligation to maintain a fixed relationship between its gold assets and its dollar liabilities, her liquidity position steadily worsened; 'thereby undermining the objective basis for confidence by the rest of the world in the unlimited convertibility of their dollars into gold' (Johnson, 1967b). In other words, creditors became suspicious of the ability of 'the Banker' to meet her obligations.

This 'long-run confidence problem' has been neatly characterised by Johnson and can be illustrated by reference to Fig. 7.4.

Quadrant I depicts the reserve positions of countries outside the US, world reserves of R_1 comprising only gold and dollars. Quadrant IV

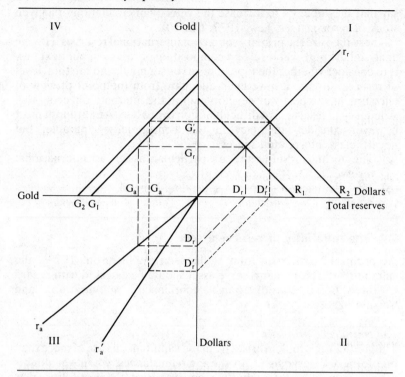

Fig. 7.4 The long-run confidence problem

shows the total world gold stock of G_1, G_a of which is held by the US, G_r by the rest of the world. Quadrant III therefore shows the overall liquidity position of the US, D_r of outstanding dollar liabilities backed by G_a gold reserves. Hence we have a gold : dollar reserve ratio given by the slope of r_a.

Consider now the situation where world monetary gold increases from G_1 to G_2 but, at the same time total reserves demanded by the rest of the world increase from R_1 to R_2. If the rest of the world wishes to maintain the same gold : dollar ratio as before (r_r in quadrant I), its dollar holdings would have to increase to D'_r, whilst US gold reserves fell to G'_a. The US liquidity position thereby deteriorates (from r_a to r'_a) and the process continues so long as the growth of demand for reserve assets exceeds the growth of supply of gold.

This is the so-called 'long-run confidence problem' which Triffin so lucidly analysed (Triffin, 1961). The US is faced with a fundamental dilemma. If in response to a growing world demand for reserves it runs the required balance-of-payments deficit, then its own liquidity position will deteriorate, and ultimately must result in doubts about the ability of 'the Banker' to meets its obligations. If on the other hand it does not run the required deficit, the growth in the supply of reserves will fall short of the growth in demand, and may generate a deflationary bias in the world economy.

The US deficit did in fact persist. How much this was due to choice on the part of the US and how much it was due to the Western European nations consciously running a payment surplus with the US in order to acquire dollars, is extremely difficult to say.

Whatever the reason, however, the deficit did persist and the growth in dollar liabilities duly outstripped the growth of gold holdings. The result, as Table 7.3 shows, was a decline in the US assets : liabilities ratio.

Table 7.3   US ratio of reserves : liquid liabilities : 1950–77

Year	Reserves : liquid liabilities	Year	Reserves : liquid liabilities
1950	2.73	1964	0.58
1952	2.38	1966	0.50
1954	1.84	1968	0.41
1956	1.59	1970	0.31
1958	1.34	1972	0.16
1960	0.92	1974	0.14
1962	0.71	1976	0.22
		1977	0.23

Source: compiled from *International Financial Statistics* (Various Issues)

Inevitably confidence in the liquidity position of 'the Banker' was undermined, and this manifested itself in two ways. First, several central banks converted their dollar holdings back into gold (which of course helped exacerbate the US liquidity position by worsening the asset : liability ratio). Second, there was asset switching on the part of private speculators. A dollar devaluation seemed possible. This appeared to be the obvious way of both eliminating the deficit and improving the ratio of gold to dollars. Thus speculation against the US dollar (and the pound sterling which was in a parallel situation) was quite common. This type of speculative activity (as we have already seen in Section 7.2) serves to place further strains on the reserve centres.

The full implications of the confidence problem for the development of the Bretton Woods system will be examined in more depth in Chapter 8. The important issue to grasp at this juncture is that where an international monetary system is founded on the use of more than one type of reserve asset, problems of confidence in the system may ultimately result.

It would seem that the key to preventing such confidence crises would be to rely on a single form of money, be it commodity or fiat. Clearly when there is only a single form of money the possibility of substitution is eliminated.[7] For this reason some commentators have argued for a return to a full gold standard (Rueff, 1961; Morgan and

Morgan, 1977). Such a proposal would undoubtedly solve the confidence problem, but we must remember that other considerations, namely stabilisation and seigniorage, are relevant.

Stabilisation

Stability characteristics are important considerations in assessing the efficiency of any monetary system. In the international context, ideally the quantity of money ought to be sufficient to facilitate a sustained growth in world trade. It ought not to be excessive otherwise world inflation may be generated and fuelled. Nor should it be deficient, in which case deflationary tendencies may predominate. We could go further and say that ultimately, what would be most desirable is a situation where it would be possible to actually control the volume of liquidity in a counter-cyclical fashion. Thus if inflation were threatening, world liquidity could be contracted, whereas tendencies to recession could be countered by reserve expansion.

From the stabilisation point of view the liquidity arrangements of the post-war Bretton Woods system seem to have been inadequate. Liquidity provision was by no means planned. With the 'official' price of gold being held at $35 per ounce while mining costs increased, supplies for monetary use grew very slowly. The supply of convertible currencies was primarily dependent on the size of the US balance-of-payments deficit. There is a considerable amount of debate over whether the size of the deficit was primarily dependent on US monetary policies, or whether the main determinant was the Western European nations desire to accumulate dollars. Both factors have undoubtedly contributed, and although the size of the US deficit was not entirely *ad hoc,* the amount of dollars being pumped into the world economy was far from being deliberately planned. Nor was liquidity provision counter-cyclical. At times it may even have been construed as being pro-cyclical. For instance, domestic monetary expansion in the US in the later 1960s (to finance the war effort in South East Asia), worsened the balance of payments and resulted in more dollars being exported. It is quite widely accepted that this contributed in no small way to the acceleration of world inflation in the later 1960s and early 1970s (Fand, 1975; Heller, 1976; and Chapter 8).

In the interests of stabilisation, the 'ideal' would appear to be a central monetary authority which could perhaps identify trends in the world economy and plan liquidity provision accordingly. For this reason it is often argued that an SDR system, under the auspices of the IMF, would provide the best prospects. As we will see later, however, this is far from being a panacea.

Seigniorage

The final consideration is the *seigniorage* problem. Seigniorage accrues whenever paper money replaces commodity money. The production of commodity money has a genuine resource cost in terms of output forgone. Thus if the world were on a gold standard, increases in the world money supply can only be achieved by the surrender of real resources to the goldmining industry. Paper money can however be produced at a very low cost to society, and its face value is usually considerably in excess of the resources used in its production. This difference in the face value of paper money, and the opportunity cost of actually producing it, is referred to as seigniorage and accrues to the producer of the paper money.

In the domestic economy seigniorage creates no difficulties. Indeed it is taken for granted as being the prerogative of the sovereign or government. In the context of international monetary relations, however, seigniorage accrues to those countries issuing reserve currencies and this is not regarded as their prerogative. Any country wishing to increase its stock of international reserves may have to do so by running a payments surplus with the US (or the UK). In other words by yielding real resources it must forsake the opportunity of investing or consuming those resources in exchange for paper dollars, the rate of return on which may be either zero, or relatively low. Many countries (in particular France and most of the less developed nations) have strongly objected to this seigniorage accruing principally to the world's richest nation. Periodic cries of 'dollar imperialism' succinctly summarise their objections.

The only way to eliminate the problem entirely would be to rely on some sort of commodity money. Thus some economists would use this as a further argument in favour of a return to a full gold standard. Presumably however, it is desirable to reap the available resource saving by substituting paper money for commodity money. The problem then becomes how precisely to distribute the seigniorage equitably.

Suitability and assets currently in use
In discussing Williamson's three facets of suitability or, as he calls them, the 'desirable characteristics of reserve assets', we have occasionally used assets currently in use for purposes of illustration. Although we may be repeating ourselves to some extent, perhaps we can summarise by considering more specifically the suitability of the assets currently in use by reference to the issues of confidence, stabilisation, and seigniorage.

With regard to gold, clearly the confidence problem would be solved if gold were the only form of international money. If, however, the metal coexisted with other forms of asset, as it did under the Bretton Woods system, then the incentive and means for switching would remain. The stabilisation issue is more problematic. As we have already seen in Section 6.2, if the monetary system were based on a full gold standard, if domestic monies were backed by gold, and if countries abided by the 'rules of the game' in adjusting to balance-of-payments imbalance, then a counter-cyclical supply of gold would be possible. World recession would reduce mining costs (in relative terms), thereby creating the incentive for increased gold production. World inflation on the other hand would increase mining costs and reduce the incentive to produce. The preconditions for such a stylised state of affairs are, however, very stringent, besides which the potency of such a counter-cyclical force is most questionable. Furthermore, two other difficulties remain with regard to stabilisation. First, it is unlikely that a planned long-term increase in the rate of gold supply would be feasible. Second, the possibility of periodic monetary shocks exists, for example through the incidence of new discoveries.

Since gold is a commodity money there would strictly speaking be no seigniorage problems. If, however, a return to the gold standard were accompanied by official gold revaluation (i.e. an increase in the dollar price of gold), then economic rents would accrue to the principal holders of gold (the Western European nations and the US) and the primary producers (South Africa and the USSR) (see Williamson, 1977a).

If international trust were sufficiently developed to accept the dollar as the sole form of international money, then presumably the confidence problem would be solved. A dollar standard would however raise some quite serious issues with regard to stabilisation and seigniorage. To achieve a counter-cyclical growth of reserves, the US would have to gear her domestic financial policies to the conditions prevailing in the world economy. It is more than likely that this would be politically unpalatable. It is equally unlikely that a planned rate of increase would be possible since the world would be relying almost entirely on the US deficit. In other words, we would be indirectly relying on the monetary policy of a country which may have a vested interest in seeing world inflation increase. The US has made substantial seigniorage gains from the use of the dollar as international money.[8] These gains must increase with increases in inflation, since with inflation, increasing amounts of dollars would be required. There would then be a certain 'moral hazard' in relying entirely on US dollars.

To many commentators special drawing rights appear to show the most promise. These have been referred to as 'paper gold' since, although they are no more than book-keeping entries, they have the backing of the IMF. Thus an SDR standard could presumably solve the confidence problem.

Since reserve creation would be in the hands of an international body a counter-cyclical supply mechanism would in principle be feasible. In practice, however, given problems of identification of trends, etc. (which are intractable enough in the national economy), counter-cyclical provision would probably not be realistic to aim for. Since, however, the provision of SDRs is in the hands of the IMF, and since an 80 per cent majority of the Board of Governors must approve any increase in supply, it would seem that monetary shocks could be avoided. The question of provision of a sustained long-run growth is somewhat more problematical. On the one hand prospects would seem to be better than with either a gold or dollar standard; on the other hand, as we have noted, an 80 per cent vote is necessary to alter supply. This means that the US on its own, or the EEC voting as a bloc, can exercise the veto over any proposed change in supply. The notion of what exactly constituted an 'adequate' long-run growth could then be very much dependent on the views of the industrialised West. A glance forward to Table 7.6 confirms that these countries traditionally command the lion's share of the stock of reserves. Their views on any proposed increases are likely to differ from those of the less developed countries, whose stocks of reserves are very much lower.

Since SDRs are only book-keeping entries, seigniorage would be reaped. Prospects would appear to suggest a more equitable distribution than under a dollar standard. Seigniorage gains could be distributed either via interest payments, or perhaps via initial allocations of SDRs. There have in fact been several proposals to specifically 'link' the creation of SDRs with aid to the developing countries, so that the 'Third World' countries would enjoy the benefits of seigniorage from the use of SDRs. Fleming (1971) provides a useful introduction to the subject, and Bauer (1973) and Kahn (1973) more detailed reviews of the salient issues.

From our discussion of the issues it would seem that the SDR satisfies our 'desirable characteristics' better than gold and the dollar. This would perhaps argue for a more pervasive role for the SDR in a reformed international monetary system. This prospect is something we will take up again in Chapter 8. A further discussion of the issues can be found in Greenaway and Milner (1978).

7.5 Adequacy in meeting demand

We have already commented on the difficulties faced in specifying a meaningful demand-for-reserves function. Quite obviously then, it is somewhat more difficult to say with any certainty how adequately the supply of reserves has met the demand for reserves. In the absence of any objective measures of adequacy, the question is usually considered from two angles. First, from a global point of view, has overall liquidity grown too quickly, too slowly or at roughly the correct pace? Second, has this growth in the stock of liquidity been 'properly' distributed?

Aggregate demand and supply

The first question, 'has the growth of liquidity been too slow, too fast or just about right', must beg the question, 'too slow or too fast in relation to what'? We contended in the previous section that in the interests of stabilisation, liquidity ought to grow rapidly enough to support a growing world economy, but not too rapidly or too slowly, such that inflationary or deflationary tendencies would be induced. Often then it is argued that the stock of reserves should grow in line with world trade, since world trade dictates reserve requirements or 'needs'. In converting this into an operational proxy, the level of imports can be regarded as representative of external transactions. This line of reasoning is followed by the IMF. Thus in its annual assessment of world liquidity developments, the IMF takes the ratio of reserves to imports (R/M) as its principal proxy of reserve adequacy (see for instance IMF, 1976). Furthermore, in assessing the adequacy of conditional liquidity (i.e. IMF credit tranches), the ratio of quotas to imports (Q/M) is regarded as being of significance.

Table 7.4 shows the R/M ratio for a sample of 60 countries over the period 1952–75. The ratio shows an almost continuous decline, from 75 per cent in 1953 to 29 per cent in 1970. With the explosive expansion of foreign exchange reserves in the early 1970s, the ratio increased for a few years, but has since declined. In addition to this the Q/M ratio has declined from over 10 per cent in the 1950s and 1960s, to less than 5 per cent in 1974 and 1975.

These declines, especially the persistent decline in the R/M ratio, are often invoked as evidence of reserve deficiency and therefore of a need to supplement existing reserves. We must, however, regard the R/M ratio with extreme caution. Since strictly speaking reserves are held to finance imbalances rather than to finance trade, the ratio cannot be used in isolation. The level of imports is only one of a number of factors influencing payments imbalance, and the demand for reserves.

The IMF itself only uses the R/M ratio as a first approximation to reserve adequacy, analysing reserve ease or reserve stringency in more detail by reference to such factors as exchange-rate changes, willingness of countries to borrow to finance imbalance, trade restrictions, and so on. Thus if we look at the 1960s, Table 7.4 tells us that the R/M ratio has declined from 75 per cent in 1953 to 51.5 per cent in 1962, and 38.6 per cent by 1966.

Prima facie this would suggest some degree of reserve stringency, and events would tend to bear this out. Although trade restrictions in general were being liberalised, there was a marked reluctance on the part of both deficit and surplus countries to alter their exchange rates, preferring instead to finance any imbalance, and possibly pursue some domestic adjustments. In order to supplement the stock of reserves to finance imbalance, countries had recourse to 'private' arrangements such as the GAB, currency 'swaps', stand-by credits, and so on.

Contrast this with the more recent period of the middle and early 1970s, when a much lower R/M ratio, rather than implying further reserve stringency, may even be consistent with excessive liquidity. The R/M ratio is now under 30 per cent, as opposed to a ratio in excess of 50 per cent in the early 1960s. This does not, however, permit us to draw the inference that reserve shortages have grown more acute. Circumstances have changed radically.

The world has drifted towards a system of floating exchange rates,

Table 7.4 Ratio of reserves to imports (%) 1952–75

	Industrial countries excluding US	United States	Other developed countries	Less developed countries	Total, 60 countries
1952	35.5	209.3	43.0	60.3	70.5
1953	39.7	203.3	51.5	77.4	75.0
1954	42.7	208.4	50.7	64.5	73.9
1955	40.7	183.3	43.2	61.1	67.2
1956	37.6	166.1	41.2	57.5	62.0
1957	34.8	165.9	39.9	47.4	57.6
1958	42.4	162.0	40.0	46.2	62.5
1959	43.9	129.5	40.8	43.7	58.9
1960	42.0	124.8	36.0	39.0	53.7
1961	45.0	119.2	37.6	36.8	53.7
1962	45.0	100.6	42.1	34.2	51.5
1963	42.9	90.6	42.8	34.8	48.7
1964	40.1	81.0	41.5	33.6	45.1
1965	39.3	66.6	35.8	34.5	42.3
1966	37.3	49.9	32.4	34.6	38.6
1967	35.6	40.2	31.3	35.3	36.6
1968	32.2	34.2	32.7	35.6	33.0

	Industrial countries	Primary producers			Total world
		More developed	Oil exporters	Less developed	
1969	30.0	30.0	43.0	28.0	30.0
1970	28.0	28.0	43.0	29.0	29.0
1971	33.0	33.0	52.0	28.0	32.0
1972	37.0	48.0	63.4	32.0	33.0
1973	31.0	47.0	59.5	34.0	34.0
1974	21.0	29.0	78.0	25.0	26.0
1975	22.0	26.0	93.0	23.0	28.0

Sources: 1952–68, *IMF Annual Report,* 1969, Table 5, p. 22
1969–75, *IMF Annual Report,* 1976, Table 16, p. 40

which ought to have reduced the demand for reserves. Two caveats are perhaps in order. First, exchange rates are not in general completely market determined. As we shall see in Chapter 8 they are to some extent managed. Therefore some reserves will still be held for intervention purposes. Second, widely divergent inflation rates, plus the Western world's 'oil deficits', have resulted in imbalances greater in absolute terms than a decade or so earlier. *Ceteris paribus*, this would imply a greater demand for reserves in the event of any exchange-rate management. In addition to this, as Table 7.5 indicates, private liquidity holdings have more than doubled since 1964. Again conflicting tendencies are suggested. On the one hand, reserve requirements may

Table 7.5   Estimated private international liquidity, 1964–73

Year	Total (SDR billion)	UK external sterling liabilities	US external dollar liabilities
1964	24.4	4.7	11.1
1965	27.3	4.9	11.5
1966	32.9	4.7	14.2
1967	36.9	3.8	15.8
1968	49.5	3.5	19.4
1969	71.6	3.4	28.2
1970	74.4	4.0	21.8
1971	70.6	5.7	13.9
1972	88.5	5.5	18.2
1973	104.5	4.4	19.7

Source: adapted from *IMF Annual Report*, 1974, Table 18, p. 44

be eased, since central banks or corporate bodies may have access to these funds (an example of which might be UK public-sector borrowing from the Eurodollar market). On the other hand, such increased funds could possibly increase reserve requirements, if they are used for speculation against exchange-rate movements.

A further factor which complicates assessment of the current situation is the uncertain position of gold. For some time the official price of gold has been SDR 35 per ounce (or around $40 per ounce). The free market price of the metal (February 1978) is $175 per ounce. Thus, if the dollar price of gold were increased towards its market value (which one assumes would depress the market value), then central bank holdings would automatically increase. If, for instance, the price were raised to SDR 100 per ounce (about $118 per ounce), central bank holdings would increase from just over SDR 35 383 billion to over SDR 101 000 billion. This would constitute an increase in world reserves of almost 30 per cent.[9]

Such considerations have led many commentators to believe that far from being less than adequate, the current stock of reserves with a system of floating exchange rates is more than adequate (Fand, 1975; Heller, 1976). The IMF itself has noted:

Although inflation has many and complex causes, the lack of success in curbing global inflation may in part reflect the effect of reserve ease in relaxing the pressure on countries to pursue anti-inflationary policies, and in intensifying expansionary influences from trading partners.

(IMF, 1974, pp. 45–46)

Estimated Eurodollar liabilities	Other estimated Eurocurrency liabilities		
	Deutsche mark	Swiss franc	Other
6.8	0.5	0.6	0.7
8.8	0.6	0.7	0.8
11.4	0.7	0.9	1.0
14.2	1.2	1.0	0.9
21.5	2.2	1.7	1.2
33.6	2.8	2.5	1.1
37.8	5.2	3.8	1.8
37.1	7.3	4.2	2.4
46.6	9.7	4.9	3.6
55.5	12.6	7.5	4.8

The distribution of reserves

To some extent it is artificial to talk of the **global** adequacy of reserves. How can we really suggest that liquidity provisions are more than adequate, if the countries which have the greatest need for a stock of reserves are also those countries with the lowest share? In other words, the distribution of reserves is pertinent to any assessment of adequacy. We can elaborate by reference to Table 7.6.

Several very striking trends are apparent from Table 7.6. The most immediately striking fact perhaps is the position of the industrialised countries as a whole. In 1950 their share of total world reserves amounted to 73 per cent. By 1960 this had increased to over 79 per cent, and by 1971 still exceeded 72 per cent. Since 1973 there has been some redistribution in favour of the less developed countries, primarily as a result of the oil-consuming countries' deficit with the oil producers.

One could of course respond by claiming that the industrialised countries as a whole have a greater 'need' for reserves. This, however, is a difficult position to sustain. At the simplest level, as Table 7.4 demonstrates, their R/M ratio is no worse than the LDCs (although, when one excludes the US it is certainly no better). If anything, the LDCs have a greater need for reserves. As Table 4.3 shows, by virtue of their economic underdevelopment they are more susceptible to payments variability than the industrialised nations. Possibly then, they should have a higher level of reserves relative to their external transactions. We must bear in mind, however, that the maintenance of a relatively low level of reserves on the part of the LDCs might in fact be a conscious policy decision. The opportunity cost of reserve holding is undoubtedly greater for LDCs than for industrialised countries. LDCs hold reserves at the expense of increasing their productive capacity, thus as Morton and Tulloch argue:

Despite the difficulties and disadvantages of relying on external credit to finance payments deficits, LDCs as a group keep their reserves relatively low.

(Morton and Tulloch, 1977, p. 280)

Some interesting 'facts' emerge when we examine more closely the distribution of reserves **within** the industrialised nations and within the LDCs.

In 1950, the US and UK together commanded almost 80 per cent of the industrialised countries' stock of reserves. By 1976 this had fallen to 17.5 per cent. Meantime the reserves of most other industrial countries has steadily increased. Most striking perhaps is the position of West Germany and Japan. Over the period in question the West German share increased from 0.5 per cent to over 27 per cent, whereas the Japanese share increased from 1.5 per cent to a little over 12 per cent. Most of the increase in both countries' stocks have taken place since 1960, as a consequence of their persistent balance-of-payments surpluses. If as we have argued throughout, reserves are necessary to finance non-synchronised imbalances between payments and receipts, the mere fact that some countries have been running persistent surpluses and accumulating the 'lion's share' of the stock of reserves, whilst other industrialised countries have faced persistent deficits (the US, UK and Italy), would suggest that reserves are not distributed in accordance with 'need' between the industrialised nations. We have already confronted this problem in a different guise in Chapter 6 when we discussed the asymmetries in the incentives to adjust between surplus and deficit countries. We shall be linking this with the adequacy-of-reserves question when examining the breakdown of the Bretton Woods system, and the possibilities for reform of the system in Chapter 8.

The final aspect of distribution which we must mention here, but again will develop more fully in Chapter 8, is the distribution of reserves within the LDCs. The position of the LDCs relative to the rest of the world hardly changed between 1950 and 1972. In this time their share of total reserves increased marginally from around 19.5 per cent to just over 20 per cent. Since 1973, however, there has been a dramatic increase in this share to over 40 per cent of the total. This is of course due to the increased prices of primary products, in particular oil. The OPEC cartel's upward administration of prices following the Middle East conflict of October 1973 has resulted in a massive surplus for the oil exporters' economies, and this surplus has manifested itself in an accumulation of reserves. Again it is extremely difficult to argue that reserves are strictly speaking distributed according to need, and

Table 7.6 Distribution of reserves, 1950–76*

	1950	1960	1970	1971	1972	1973	1974	1975	1976
Industrial countries									
United States	24.3	19.4	14.5	12.1	12.1	11.9	13.1	13.6	15.8
United Kingdom	4.8	5.1	2.8	8.1	5.2	5.4	5.7	4.7	3.6
Subtotal	29.1	24.5	17.3	20.3	17.3	17.3	18.8	18.2	19.4
Austria	–	0.7	1.8	2.2	2.5	2.4	2.8	3.8	3.8
Belgium–Luxembourg	0.8	1.5	2.8	3.2	3.6	4.2	4.4	5.0	4.5
Denmark	0.1	0.3	0.5	0.7	0.8	1.1	0.8	0.7	0.8
France	0.8	2.3	5.0	7.6	9.2	7.4	7.2	10.8	8.4
West Germany	0.2	7.0	13.6	17.2	21.9	27.5	26.5	26.5	30.0
Italy	0.7	3.3	5.4	6.3	5.6	5.3	5.7	4.1	5.7
Netherlands	0.5	1.9	3.2	3.5	4.4	5.4	5.7	6.1	6.4
Norway	0.1	0.3	0.8	1.1	1.2	1.3	1.6	1.9	1.9
Sweden	0.3	0.5	0.8	1.0	1.5	2.1	1.4	2.6	2.1
Switzerland	1.6	2.3	5.1	6.4	7.0	7.1	7.4	8.9	11.2
Subtotal (Continental industrial Europe)	5.2	20.1	39.0	49.1	57.7	63.8	63.4	70.4	74.8
Canada	1.8	2.0	4.7	5.3	5.6	4.8	4.8	4.5	5.0
Japan	0.6	1.9	4.8	14.1	16.9	10.2	11.0	10.9	14.3
Total, industrial countries	36.8	48.5	65.8	88.8	97.5	96.0	97.9	104.1	113.5
Primary producing countries									
More developed,									
Other European	1.5	2.3	5.6	8.0	11.7	13.4	12.4	11.2	11.8
Australia, New Zealand, South Africa	2.0	1.3	3.0	4.2	7.6	6.5	5.0	4.2	4.0
Subtotal (more developed primary producers)	3.5	3.6	8.5	12.1	19.4	19.9	17.3	15.4	15.8
Less developed countries									
major oil exporters	1.3	2.3	5.0	7.8	10.0	12.1	38.4	48.3	56.1
Other less developed countries									
Other Western Hemisphere	2.4	2.2	4.5	4.5	7.5	10.0	9.7	8.6	13.1
Other Middle East	1.1	0.7	1.7	2.0	2.7	3.6	3.9	4.4	5.0
Other Asia	3.7	2.7	5.8	6.3	7.8	8.8	10.5	11.2	16.1
Other Africa	0.5	0.9	2.0	1.7	1.9	2.2	2.4	2.4	2.6
Subtotal (other LDCs)	7.7	6.6	13.9	14.5	19.9	24.5	26.5	26.6	36.7
Subtotal (all LDCs)	9.5	9.0	18.9	22.3	29.9	36.6	64.9	74.9	92.9
Total, primary producing countries	13.0	12.6	27.4	34.4	49.3	56.5	82.2	90.2	108.7
Total	49.7	61.2	93.2	123.2	146.8	152.6	180.2	194.3	222.1

*See original source for detailed breakdown of country groups
Source: IMF Annual Report, 1977, Table 11, p. 42

we will delay a final assessment until Chapter 8. There are many facets to the problems caused by the increased oil prices which have wide-ranging consequences for international monetary reform. It is these questions we will now turn to, since a final assessment of adequacy of reserve provision will only be possible within the framework of an overall appraisal of the international monetary system.

Notes

1. For a more detailed analysis of the transactions motive and speculative motive, see Chrystal (1977) and McKenzie (1976) respectively.
2. The problems one faces are the statistical difficulties of multicollinearity and auto-correlation. The former occurs when the explanatory variables are strongly inter-related, which can result in difficulties in disentangling the separate effects of these explanatory variables on the dependent variable. The latter occurs when the dist-urbance values for different observations are not independent, which amongst other things can result in overconfidence in one's empirical findings. For a more rigorous analysis see Common (1976).
3. The role of price maintenance was initially 'informally' handled by central bank intervention on the London bullion market. In November 1961, however, the 'Gold Pool' was created to operate the buffer stock. The Gold Pool comprised the central banks of Belgium, France, Germany, Italy, the Netherlands, Switzerland, the UK and the USA, and it operated until March 1968. Since the price of gold was being maintained at an artificially low level, the Pool invariably engaged in support selling. This selling reached a height in the period of uncertainty following the sterling devaluation of November 1967, when the Pool converted $3 000 million of gold in six months; its activities finally ceased in March 1968.
4. The quota was assessed by reference to the country's national income, its stock of foreign exchange reserves, and other indicators of its relative economic importance.
5. The composition of the basket is:

Currency	Percentage weight	Units in one SDR
US dollar	33.0	0.40
German Deutsche mark	12.5	0.38
Pound sterling	9.0	0.045
French franc	7.5	0.44
Japanese yen	7.5	26.0
Canadian dollar	6.0	0.071
Italian lira	6.0	47.0
Dutch guilder	4.5	0.14
Belgian franc	3.5	1.6
Swedish krona	2.5	0.13
Australian dollar	1.5	0.012
Danish krone	1.5	0.11
Norwegian krone	1.5	0.099
Spanish peseta	1.5	1.1
Austrian schilling	1.0	0.22
South African rand	1.0	0.0082

See Polak (1974) and Dreyer (1975) for a consideration of alternative valuation proposals.

6. The Group of Ten comprises the principal industrialised nations, namely: Belgium, Canada, France, Germany, Italy, Japan, the Netherlands, Sweden, the UK and the USA.

7. It has been suggested (Lutz, 1963) that a multiple currency system might solve the problem by providing a large number of assets and therefore broadening the monetary base.

8. Seigniorage gains are notoriously difficult to estimate. Grubel has however put the gain to the United States at \$1.8 billion in 1961 alone (Grubel, 1964).

9. Provision was made at the IMF Annual Conference in Jamaica (1976), to free central banks from having to buy and sell gold at the official price of SDR 35 per ounce. Whether this results in market-related values being adopted by central banks, and whether gold stocks will subsequently become remobilised remains to be seen. Chapter 8 considers this question in more detail.

Monetary disorder and reform

8.1 Introduction

The previous three chapters should have provided an understanding of the analytical tools required to make a broader consideration of global monetary arrangements. Inevitably, we have been forced to analyse the problems of 'adjustment', 'liquidity', 'confidence', 'stabilisation' and 'reserve distribution' in isolation. We need now to draw together these interrelated problems into a general overview and assessment of prevailing conditions. Assessment, that is, in relation to the system's impact on individual countries and in relation to some global objectives.

Monetary relations in context
In the last decade we have witnessed recurring evidence of the potential breakdown of monetary order in international relations. The sterling crises, the gold crisis, and finally the dollar crisis, were all manifestations of the underlying weaknesses of the prevailing 'rules of the system'. The breaking of the rules, and the collapse of the system as it had been formalised at the Bretton Woods agreement in 1944, has not however resulted in chaos. Admittedly the move towards the general floating of currencies has been disorderly, and common rules about the form and degree of official market intervention absent. Nevertheless, this so-called current 'non-system' (see Williamson, 1976) has survived the pressures of massive oil price rises, large and divergent rates of inflation, and a general downturn in activity rates.

It would in fact appear that crisis and inertia are part of the process of *ad hoc* evolution which typifies international monetary relations. The conduct of international monetary transactions is demonstrably as much the outcome of private bargaining between individuals and national governments as it is dependent upon the existence of international institutions and the international extension of the 'rule of law'. In fact, the organising of a global monetary system within the context of separate nation states is clearly a political process in which dominance and cooperation are important themes. As such it is often difficult to isolate normative issues in international economics from political realities.

Nevertheless, the ultimate objective of this final chapter will be to examine proposals for the reform of international monetary relations, which range from the pragmatic, *ad hoc,* or piecemeal approach to the fundamental and sweeping restructuring of a system. Before we can consider ways of restoring monetary order, however, we must establish what problems confront the system, i.e. the nature of the disorder. The current problems include world inflation, the 'dirty' floating of currencies, oil surpluses and the changing economic order of countries. In addition, we can identify problems which have been 'inherited' from the past – the dollar 'overhang', the liquidity problems of the less developed countries, and the lack of central or supranational control. To understand these inheritances, it will of course be necessary to consider the recent history of international monetary relations. It seems reasonable therefore, to begin our overview with a consideration of the attempts to reconstruct monetary order after the Second World War, at the Bretton Woods conference.

8.2 The Bretton Woods system

Background to the agreement
The designers of the post-war monetary system were confronted with two major technical problems. On the one hand, they had to cope with the problems that were seen to have caused the collapse of monetary order between the two World Wars. On the other, they had to create conditions which would enable a rapid post-war reconstruction of trade that was not to be hampered by the indebtedness that war and reconstruction can generate.[1] (Indebtedness and its settlement had proved a source of difficulty, and a constraint, on the re-introduction of the gold standard after the First World War.[2])

The inter-war period had seen the final demise of the gold standard, and the collapse of a multilateral trading system. The 1930s had in fact been typified by unilateral actions (competitive devaluations, payments restrictions and trade barriers) undertaken to minimise the impact on individual countries of the global depression. Any post-war monetary system needed therefore to restore confidence in international payments, and to remove the threat of deflationary (high unemployment) conditions generated by payments imbalances under fixed exchange rates. This was essential if multilateral and unrestricted trade was to be a realistic aim.

The interlude of war did provide the circumstances for a general redesign of monetary relations. However, we must appreciate that some of the characteristics of the post-war system were inherited from before the Second World War. We outlined in Chapter 7 the historic reserve role of gold. The established use and existing distribution of (monetary) gold therefore imposed some constraints on the post-war design, if the role of gold was to be confirmed. Table 7.1 demonstrates the dominant position of gold in countries' reserve holdings immediately after the war; it also shows the substantial holding of convertible currencies in reserves. This economising in the use of limited gold stocks had its origins some time before Bretton Woods. In the absence of a demonetisation of gold immediately after the war, the further extension of the gold-exchange principle was inevitable as a 'dollar-hungry' Europe reconstructed and replenished reserves.

Alternative proposals

The extent to which the reformulation of the monetary system should break with the past was, in fact, the centre of much argument before the final agreement (see Harrod, 1951, Ch. 13). The institutional arrangements were primarily worked out by the US and the UK, a reflection of prevailing economic and political power. In the event, the more conservative (US) White Plan was adopted as the basis for the agreement, rather than the more ambitious (UK) Keynes Plan.

Given the concensus in favour of some form of relatively fixed system of exchange rates which would help to restore stability and confidence to international payments, the normative issues centred upon the form, quantity and management of international reserves or liquidity. On the one hand, the White Plan called for the continued underpinning of the monetary system by gold. To avoid the deflationary threat of payments deficits, the existing stock of gold could be more efficiently utilised by allowing deficit countries access to a stabilisation fund (to which member countries would contribute). On the other hand, the Keynes Plan called for a more fundamental break with the past. Rather than this central body merely acting as 'lender of the last resort' from member countries' gold contributions, Keynes wished to move away from gold and bestow powers of fiat-money creation on what would effectively be a supranational clearing bank.[3]

The fact that the dialogue was predominantly between the US and the UK is consistent with a pragmatic interpretation of international monetary relations. The 'key-currency' theory (Johnson, 1972) suggested that, as only a few currencies really matter in trade and payments, the essential problem is for these countries to behave responsibly. Whilst not stipulated, the White Plan was a passive acceptance by the US of the key-currency role, and continuance of the gold-exchange principle (though the Bretton Woods designers did not anticipate the extent of the shortfall in gold supplies that was to occur after the war). The Keynes Plan may be interpreted as the alternative and institutional approach to the shaping of international relations. In this approach, international management is seen to be achievable, not by the process of national bargaining, but by the extension of the 'rule of law' and rational economic management to the international community, on the assumption that all countries and currencies are equal. Johnson refers to this assumption as 'fictional equality' (Johnson, 1972). In reality of course, the essence of the UK proposal was a substantial increase in the stock of international liquidity. National interest would therefore have been served by reducing the constraint that post-war payments deficit and depleted gold reserves might impose on domestic policy targets.

The agreement

Agreement was eventually reached in July 1944, at the Bretton Woods Conference. With hindsight the package produced what may be interpreted in principle as a compromise between the 'key-currency' and 'institutional' approaches; a compromise nevertheless heavily weighted in favour of the former. The agreement drafted a system of 'adjustable' but 'pegged' exchange rates. Each member's currency was pegged in relation to the dollar and in turn to gold via the fixed dollar price of gold, namely $35 per ounce of gold. To support this pegged system a relatively small fund (the International Monetary Fund) was to be established. Countries could resort to the Fund when their currencies were under market pressure.

The IMF was an international institution that was unlikely to die, but it certainly did not represent a move towards supranational control of the international economy. The principle of national voting rights according to the then prevailing pattern of economic power, coupled with an 85 per cent majority requirement for change, which gave the US and the 'European' bloc an effective veto, made the IMF a microcosm of reality. The control of the international economy was to remain 'impersonal', and achievable in practice through national bargaining or international concensus. In practice therefore, the Bretton Woods agreement reaffirmed the historical emphasis on a key currency. The US had emerged from the Second World War with an overwhelmingly dominant economy, in terms of productive capacity and reserves of monetary gold, and to the rest of the world dollars became as desirable as gold. They were readily exchangeable into gold and brought a rate of interest to their holders.

The IMF started operations in March 1947. Its general aim was to promote international monetary cooperation and the expansion of world trade. More specifically, its task was to lessen the duration and degree of balance-of-payments imbalance, by placing the resources of the Fund at the disposal of member states. The use of the Fund's resources was intended as a means of riding out temporary deficits. Although the Fund was specifically required to promote exchange-rate stability, member countries could adjust their pegs or par-values in the event of (ill-defined) 'fundamental disequilibrium'. Members contemplating re- or devaluation of their currency were required to consult the IMF beforehand, and whilst in principle the Fund had no powers to object to small adjustments of under 10 per cent, it is doubtful in practice whether it would have tried to prevent larger realignments, had it so wished. In the event, adjustments were irregular.

Development of the system

The world developed, temporarily, a very successful gold exchange standard, not as we shall see as a result of the IMF, whose assets remained only a small part of total international reserves. (There is reason to believe, however, that as a source of information and arena for discussion, the Fund was a vehicle for encouraging cooperation.)

Thus, until the last years of the 1950s, the monetary system was functioning quite efficiently — whether measured by the avoidance of prolonged and severe recessions, the achievement of satisfactory domestic growth rates, the expansion of world trade and the steady diminution in reliance on exchange restrictions by the major industrial countries.

(Friedman, 1973, p. 355)

During this period, US balance-of-payments deficits were welcomed by a reconstructing Europe as a means of replenishing their stocks of international reserves with dollars. The stable operation of the monetary system, however, became dependent upon US willingness to run a deficit, and European willingness to hold dollars rather than gold. The resulting steady change in the US assets–liabilities ratio during the 1950s was therefore at the heart of the 'long-run confidence problem' that we examined in Chapter 7. Similarly, the liberalisation and integration of capital markets during the 1950s highlighted in the long run this loss of confidence in dollar convertibility as the mobility of short-term funds increased.

Uncertainties about the strength of the system were becoming evident by the beginning of the 1960s. Europe became increasingly doubtful about the size of the US deficit, and about the persistence of inflation (albeit at relatively low rates). From a stance of active encouragement, Europe became more reluctant to accept the reserve role of the dollar, unless the US behaved 'reasonably'. Short-term crises (evidenced by a shift back by Europe to the first-class currency, in this case gold) occurred whenever Europe doubted the reasonableness of US domestic policies. This was principally the product of the (unforeseen) growth in dollar liabilities, which by 1960 began to exceed US gold holdings. The seeds of the 'long-term confidence problem' had been sown.

It is, however, difficult to isolate the confidence problem from the liquidity and adjustment problems. They are in fact facets of a single whole. More rapid adjustment of exchange rates would have reduced the liquidity needs of the system as a whole, and therefore the growth of potentially destabilising dollar liabilities. Alternatively, more ample 'first-class' liquidity would have reduced the confidence problem and the need for adjustment. Whether the growth of liquidity up to the mid-1960s was inadequate, excessive or just about right is, as we saw in Chapter 7, a rather difficult diagnosis to make.

Alternative diagnoses   In Chapter 7 we took a rather pragmatic approach to the consideration of reserve adequacy. But the question 'adequacy in relation to what?' remains. In Fig. 7.1 (p. 196), for example, there is a shortage of reserves at level f_1 of exchange-rate flexibility (the quantity of reserves provided or supplied is assumed to be completely invariable with the exchange-rate regime adopted). This shortage may however be removed in a variety of ways. To increase the supply of reserves, from q_1 to q_2, is only one possible approach. The shortage may also be removed by increasing the degree of exchange-rate flexibility, from f_1 to f_2, which *ceteris paribus* should reduce the degree of payments imbalance, and therefore the quantity of reserves required from q_2 to q_1. Alternatively, reserve requirements and provision can be matched at f_1 degree of exchange-rate flexibility, by bringing about the appropriate backward shift in the requirements function. This can be achieved by increasing the extent to which price and income adjustment is used domestically to remove external imbalance.

These alternatives in fact neatly summarise the conflicting assessments made during the 1960s of the Bretton Woods system. Given the desirability of a relatively pegged system of exchange rates, the Triffin diagnosis (Triffin, 1961) was that there was a liquidity shortage (or at least at level of exchange-rate flexibility f_1 in Fig. 7.1, there was an *ex ante* shortage of the first-class currency, gold). This shortfall was in part removed by increasing the burden of imbalance on the domestic economy, i.e. a backward movement of the requirements function from R_1 to R_2, and by increasing the supply of the second-class currency, the dollar. It is possible in fact to interpret the emergence, during the first half of the 1960s, of attempts to economise in the use of existing global reserves by increasing their velocity of circulation (e.g. the 'swap' and borrowing agreements, referred to in Chapter 7) as evidence of such a liquidity shortage. Gold supply deficiencies were therefore seen as the root cause of the long-term confidence problem. By contrast the conservative diagnosis was that liquidity growth was excessive (e.g. see Rueff, 1967). In terms of Fig. 7.1 the 'optimal' or desired requirements function was perhaps R_3, and therefore at level of flexibility f_1 there was an *ex ante* excess of reserves. The excessive growth of liquidity was seen by this alternative diagnosis as reducing the discipline that governments should maintain over domestic prices and incomes in order to maintain external balance. The key-currency countries, the US and to a lesser extent the UK, in particular were able to finance deficits with their own currency, and to have 'deficits without tears'.

We will return to these normative issues in the final section. In more positive terms we can conclude that Bretton Woods had been devised to deal with the problems of the past; an adjustable-peg system of exchange rates to remove speculative crises and competitive devaluations, and IMF drawing rights to supplement gold supplies. The overall package was seen as a means of removing the deflationary bias of the gold standard. In a manner which encouraged *ad hoc* responses, however, all the problems reappeared in the post-war period – except that the deflationary bias was replaced with an inflationary one.

Adjustment problems and inflationary bias   Although automatic payments adjustment forces proved inadequate, further adjustment via domestic prices and incomes and the exchange rate tended also to be incomplete. It was not the rules of the system which made currency adjustments irregular. It was individual national resistance, often motivated by political considerations, which produced the resistance. The 1967 devaluation of sterling was for instance viewed at the time as a symbol of national and governmental weakness. Such resistance usually proved costly in terms of reserve use, as 'one-way' speculation intensified.

The surplus countries by contrast found it less costly to accumulate reserves, rather than decumulate them, and hence easier to avoid revaluation. This resistance to exchange-rate adjustment could in principle have been offset by a greater reliance on domestic adjustment. The deficit countries, placing a primacy on full employment, were only willing, however, to use temporary deflations and financing activities, in the hope that this would allow other countries' price levels to catch up with their own. Given that this catching-up process was temporary, and usually only partial, the surplus countries who sought continued growth, based on export surpluses, were willing to allow the slow inward slippage of inflation via their pegged exchange rates. The net effect was therefore an inflationary bias, which was increasingly heightened during the 1960s, as the US export of dollars and supply of international liquidity increased. Differential rates of inflation and exchange-rate rigidities tended to cause payments imbalances to persist.

It has been suggested in earlier chapters that the differential pressures imposed on governments by reserve loss, as opposed to reserve gain, mean that there is an uneven distribution of responsibility for initiating adjustment. In other words, only the deficit countries are required to adjust domestic prices and incomes or the exchange rate. Cohen (1966) also points out, however, that the country initiating the adjustment process need not necessarily pay the 'transitional costs' of resource reallocation. In fact, it may be that the expenditure-switching effects of currency devaluation, undertaken to remove external deficit, may impose a greater transitional cost on surplus rather than deficit countries. Certainly, this view of the distribution of adjustment costs is consistent with the reluctance of the surplus countries in the post-war period to lose the benefits of export-led growth, and with their willingness to supply credit to the deficit countries rather than force them to adjust. The credit packages provided by various central banks to support the lira in 1964 and sterling in 1965 for instance, may be interpreted as the surplus countries' discovery '. . . that bribes are less expensive than genuine adjustment' (Cohen, 1969).

This situation was produced, however, by the absence of rules (or of strong central control) over what should be the appropriate distribution of adjustment costs and over who was responsible for undertaking adjustment. From the individual country's point of view, the best distribution of the burden was the one which placed all the burden on other countries. It is of course a difficult issue to resolve, but under the Bretton Woods system exchange-rate adjustment was too infrequent, and perhaps because of this too costly when it occurred. Reserve loss and the accompanying speculative pressure eventually became unbearable. As in the inter-war period, there was a devaluation bias which was the product of periodic crisis conditions (see Yeager, 1966).

Crises of confidence Although there were, no doubt, competitive and structural factors which contributed to the UK's persistent balance-of-payments problems during the 1960s, the sterling crises also illustrate the special problems that accrue to reserve-currency countries. A long-term deterioration in the reserves/liabilities ratio, expecially when combined with a decline in relative economic power, is likely to produce periodic speculative crises which are the immediate manifestation of the 'long-term' confidence problem.

More central of course to the functioning of the post-war global system, was the strength of the dollar as a reserve currency. The dollar, increasingly during the 1960s, also began to face the problems of a gold-exchange or multiple reserve currency system. The long-term deterioration in the US asset/liabilities ratio produced periodic crises of confidence. Official and private holders of dollars would move out of what they saw as the second-class currency, into the first-class currency, gold (or into other 'stronger' currencies). The stability of the system was dependent upon the compatibility of the US assets/liabilities ratio, set by US domestic monetary policies, with the one that Europe required to achieve the desired global level of world prices and incomes.[4] In the event, the gold-exchange or gold-dollar standard proved a 'fair-weather' standard, which was subject to crisis whenever over-inflationary monetary policies in the US caused a deterioration in the US assets/liabilities ratio and an increase in the US deficit beyond that desired by Europe. The European response was to shift their reserve holdings back into gold in order to pressurise the US into pursuing what to them appeared a more stable monetary policy.

Increasingly, by the end of the 1960s doubts about the convertibility of the dollar and the possibility of currency realignment, especially revaluations by the surplus countries, intensified private speculative buying of the stronger currencies (e.g. D-mark and yen). As a result Europe became increasingly reluctant to use its gold reserves to effectively support the dollar. The surplus countries, however, remained reluctant also to reduce this pressure by revaluing their currencies.

Roots of the breakdown These short-term crises, heightened with the passing of time by the changing relative economic power of the US, Europe and Japan, were expressions of the long-term dilemma facing international relations governed by the following conditions. On the one hand, since gold was the ultimate store of value and its price must therefore be fixed in relation to the banker's currency, i.e. the dollar, it was only a happy coincidence that the supply of gold grew in line with the demand for reserves. On the other hand, the need for the reserve-currency country to run balance-of-payments deficits, to fill any short-fall in the growth of monetary gold, reduced the ability of the reserve-currency country to maintain the gold/dollar price relationship.

Of course, appropriate international cooperation on the part of the non-reserve countries would have reduced the dilemma. The US deficit was equivalent to the net surplus of the remaining countries. The US deficit could in principle, therefore, have been regulated by an appropriate exchange rate and domestic adjustment on the part of other countries. But as we have argued, the system was typified by adjustment rigidities, and there was little incentive for the surplus countries to reduce the size of their surpluses. If confidence in the reserve function of the dollar was to be maintained, then the US surrendered the right to use exchange-rate adjustment to regulate the size of their payments deficits. The satisfying of global liquidity and stability requirements necessitated, therefore, that the US was willing to use domestic policies to regulate the external situation.

The use after 1965, however, of expansionary/inflationary monetary policies, to finance the escalation of the Vietnam War (see Johnson, 1975; Zis, 1975), meant that the US deficit could not be manipulated to meet these requirements. The result was a rapid deterioration in the US assets/liabilities position and an emanation of inflationary liquidity from the US.

The introduction of SDRs in 1970 (agreed upon in 1967) indicated that there had been some official recognition of the problems of dependence on the dollar, and of liquidity shortage if the US deficit was reduced. There was, however, no strong collective view about an alternative standard, rather a feeling that inertia in the absence of crisis may suffice. World trade continued to grow and capital markets had become more sophisticated and integrated. Private capital flows and the access of central banks to these markets, e.g. the Eurodollar market, was a potential buffer to the use of official reserves.

The increasing mobility of private funds proved, however, also to highlight the underlying weaknesses of the system. Crisis, and doubts about the convertibility of the dollar at a fixed gold price could not be avoided. The gold crisis of 1968 was symptomatic of these doubts (see Johnson, 1969). The ability of the Gold Pool to maintain the fixed price of gold ($35 per ounce) in the face of a large-scale speculative rush for gold, was in part undermined. The decision was taken to end private convertibility into gold, with the formation of a 'two-tier' market for gold – a free, private market and a fixed-price, official market. Thus, though this shored up the system, not least because it discouraged the loss of gold to 'non-monetary' uses, it also indicated the reluctance of central banks (European in particular) to use gold reserves to keep the price of gold down.

8.3 Dollar crisis and collapse of the system

Mounting inflationary conditions and rising interest rates in the late 1960s led to the increased sensitivity of short-term funds to changes in purchasing power. The increased expectation of exchange rate adjustments was also typified by the speculative pressures against the franc and D-mark during 1969 – devaluation and revaluation respectively brought temporary relief. Despite a tightening of domestic policies the US deficit persisted and the outflow of funds from the US increased in 1970 in the expectation of further European revaluations. There was, however, a determination on the part of countries like West Germany to resist revaluation, or to reduce their competitive advantage through appropriate domestic measures. In the end West Germany was forced to close their foreign exchange market in May 1971, after a period of only two days which had seen a speculative inflow of $2 million.

The 'beginning of the end' was signalled by the floating of certain currencies, the Deutsche mark, guilder and Canadian dollar. Other countries did revalue to remain within the provisions of the IMF articles, but the size of the net adjustment reflected the reluctance of the non-key-currency countries to bear the full burden of the currency realignment, which the US was calling for. The imposition of a US import surcharge and the threat of a suspension of dollar convertibility were in fact used by the US as a bargaining weapon against European governments. The threat of the removal of official dollar convertibility proved inadequate, and in fact merely precipitated further immediate conversion of dollars by European central banks. Given the prospect of an untenable position, President Nixon suspended the convertibility of the dollar into gold in August 1971, and thereby technically brought the Bretton Woods system to an end.

Attempts at reconstruction
These momentous events, and the floating of the major currencies for several months, were not seen, however, as marking the end of a system based on the Bretton Woods-type rules. Rather they were viewed as a brief interlude after which 'normal' relations, albeit with a redistribution of responsibility, could be re-introduced. With the aim of paving the way for this, the Group of Ten met at the Smithsonian Institute in Washington in December 1971.

The outcome of the bargaining indicated no clear redistribution of responsibility. No operational rules for the adjustment of par values were established, rather a compromise and token realignment of exchange rates was agreed upon. The dollar was devalued by 7.9 per cent in terms of gold (the price of gold being raised from $35 to $38 per ounce), whilst there was a general, but equally small, realignment of the par values of other currencies (including a revaluation of the D-mark and yen in relation to gold).

Faith was reaffirmed in the principle of exchange-rate stability and in the implementation of reform via the IMF. In fact, shortly after the Smithsonian communiqué, the IMF announced that the margin of fluctuation allowable either side of par or central values was to be increased from 1 per cent to $2\frac{1}{4}$ per cent. This was an attempt to increase the degree of automatic exchange-rate adjustment. As a consequence this provision also increased the ability of the authorities to frustrate speculators. In the event, given the failure of the Smithsonian agreement to tackle the underlying causes of the dollar crisis and weakness in the Bretton Woods system, this increased margin of flexibility and the small realignments were insufficient to cope with increasing capital mobility, and more rapid and divergent inflation rates. This pattern of exchange rates, and the new arrangements, proved untenable and temporary.

Final breakdown
The brief calm at the beginning of 1972 ended with the floating of sterling in June 1972. (This was briefly copied by other EEC countries.) Despite a determined effort to defend their exchanges by continental central banks during the second half of 1972, the announcement of the largest US deficit in history in January 1973, and the subsequent speculative flight into the D-mark and yen, brought about the final collapse of pegged exchange rates during 1973.[5] A pegged system could not withstand global inflationary conditions at unprecedented rates (Johnson, 1975; Friedman, 1973).

The Swiss franc and the yen were floated in January and February respectively, and following the closure of foreign-exchange markets in Europe and Japan, a Joint European Float was announced in March 1973. The pegging of European currencies (excluding the lira and sterling) in relation to each other, whilst floating against the dollar, reflected the European preference for stable exchange rates and long-term commitment to monetary union. (Floating exchange rates also posed administrative problems for the EEC's Common Agricultural Policy.) Floating rates were seen as a short-term pragmatic response to world inflationary conditions, which had highlighted the smallness of the hastily approved Smithsonian realignments of exchange rates.

8.4 Monetary disorder: negotiation and inertia

Capital controls had proved of limited success in helping to maintain the existing pattern of exchange rates in the face of strong speculation.[6]

Floating exchange rates were therefore initially seen as an unavoidable, but temporary expedient; temporary that is, until the control of inflation permitted the restoration of a durable pattern of par values. The movement to a system of floating, albeit managed, exchange rates was not, however, the outcome of general agreement or conscious reform. It was rather the untidy product of a breakdown of the rules of the system.

Monetary disorder has nevertheless been accompanied by recurrent and active negotiation about reform between countries. This commitment to reform has also been via the vehicle of the IMF. Even at the height of the crisis, during 1972 and 1973, the Committee of Twenty were considering the fundamental reform of the system.[7] But crisis conditions during peacetime were not conducive to producing wholesale reform or a grand redesign; rather they were conducive to a search for 'immediate steps'.

It was evident that there was a general desire for reform, but not for change which imposed costs (see Tew, 1977; Williamson, 1977b). By 1974 the oil crisis had reduced the negotiators' expectations, and the search was for an evolutionary approach to the restoration of monetary order. The fear of course with such an *ad hoc* approach was that political compromises would produce inconsistencies, and hence an unstable system.

At the outset of the negotiations there was a strong presumption that there would be a return to an adjustable peg system of exchange rates. The removal, however, of floating exchanges was not only dependent upon the reduction of inflation, it was dependent also on dealing with the inherited problems, or legacies, of the Bretton Woods system. The early negotiations of the Committee of Twenty (C-20) included, for example, discussion about the possible adoption of 'reserve indicators'. These were seen as a means of signalling the need for adjustment policies, and therefore of reducing adjustment rigidities and asymmetries. A settlements system had also to be ironed out if a return to pegged exchange rates was to be possible. The stability of such a system would be dependent upon resolving the problems of dollar inconvertibility and the consolidation of existing dollar holdings. Similarly, the control of liquidity under any future standard could not be divorced from a consideration of the less developed countries (LDCs). However, affirmation of the commitment to the SDR principle, by the Board of Governors of the IMF in 1972 was in principle only.

The legacies of Bretton Woods

The legacies of the Bretton Woods system included therefore the persistence of payments imbalances, the presence of large and inconvertible[8] dollar balances in reserve holdings, and the uncertain position of gold as a monetary asset.

Given the desire to move away from capital controls and to avoid trade restrictions, the US proposals in 1972 to the C-20 for a return to stable exchange rates and currency convertibility were based upon the need to prevent the demand for reserves exceeding the supply. Signals for adjustment, in the form of 'reserve indicators', would maintain the balance between acceptable levels of imbalance and the availability of reserves to finance that imbalance. Countries' reserve norms could be established in line with global reserve availability. Indicator points would provide a signal that policy measures to correct surplus or deficit were required when reserves diverged from these norms. The activation of policy, for reserve gain especially, would be likely of course to require more than a system of signals. The sanction against the surplus countries, in the US proposal, came in the form of a non-convertibility point as reserves grew to a certain level. Growth of a country's reserves above this point would result in the loss of the right to demand conversion of further acquisitions into the primary reserve asset. Ironically, an adjustment system based on a convertibility–reserve change link, corresponds closely to the views expanded much earlier by Keynes, that convertibility alone was an asymmetrical tool which operated against the deficit countries only.

European countries opposed reliance on a simple single indicator for policy adjustment and the limitation on convertibility. They accepted that the burden of proof did lie on the country in payments imbalance, but were resistant to imposing the constraint on domestic policies of automatic rules. Awareness, however, of the constraint that assessment also imposed on the removal of surpluses and deficits, led to the French proposal for a system of 'graduated pressures'. As an alternative to loss of convertibility, they proposed that beyond certain levels of reserve accumulation, surplus countries would be required to deposit additional reserves with the IMF. Such deposits could be made subject to a **negative** rate of interest. (Again this idea corresponds closely to those of Keynes, which prompted the US concession to include a 'scarce currency clause' within the IMF charter.) Thus full asset settlement was to be retained under the French proposal, since the deficit countries would still be faced with convertibility obligations as the surplus countries acquired their currencies. But into what asset(s) were currencies to be convertible for settlement purposes?

Following the suspension of convertibility, the dollar was potentially an international currency *par excellence*. Europe was however unwilling to accept dependence on the dollar and the seigniorage benefits that accrued to the US. In any case, as large holders of dollar assets, Europe was anxious to restore full/multilateral **asset** convertibility, whether it be into US gold holdings or an alternative primary reserve asset such as the SDR. From the viewpoint of the US in particular, given its assets/potential liabilities ratio, the restoration of dollar convertibility was dependent upon the elimination, or sharp reduction of outstanding balances, i.e. the 'dollar overhang', by consolidation or funding.

As far as funding was concerned, there seemed little desire on the part of Europe to convert existing dollar holdings into long-term non-liquid liabilities against the US. Despite the enormous growth of liquidity, especially of dollar holdings during the 1970–73 period, Europe apparently did not feel that liquid reserves were excessive. In any case many countries, including LDCs, were anxious to retain freedom of choice in the composition of their reserves. The reformers were in fact faced with the problem of reconciling pressure for a multi-currency intervention system with the long-term commitment to the SDR as the principle reserve asset.

As an alternative to funding, existing dollar balances could be consolidated, compulsorily or voluntarily, through a substitution account at the IMF. The exchange of dollars for SDRs through such a substitution account required that privately held dollars could be prevented from moving into official reserves, if an inflationary growth of SDRs was to be avoided. This was especially the case if the scheme was compulsory. The opting for a voluntary scheme would allow countries freedom of reserve choice, but would also mean that there was a chance that claims on the US would increase rather than decrease.

Since interest-rate obligations would attach to dollars consolidated at the IMF as SDRs were issued, naturally the US favoured a low interest rate on SDRs. A low interest rate, especially if the consolidation was voluntary, was not viewed, however, by some countries to encourage the development of the SDR as the principal reserve asset. Paradoxically, the developing countries, whilst favouring the promotion of the SDR, were prospective net-users of SDRs and preferred therefore a low rate of interest in the face of an already mounting burden of debt. In any case, these countries saw the consolidation of the dollar into SDRs as a constraint on further SDR creation, since consolidation would substantially increase the industrialised countries' SDR holdings.

The commitment to the management of the volume of world liquidity, presumably through the control of the SDR, would appear therefore to have been somewhat incompatible with the pressures for voluntary consolidation and a multicurrency intervention system. The experience of the Bretton Woods system had shown the problems of regulating the size of the US deficit, or the key-currency countries' deficits, in line with global liquidity requirements. To some extent the dilemma stemmed from the need to reconcile immediate requirements with long-term objectives. Late 1973 for instance saw the beginning of the oil crisis, and oil-deficit countries were anxious to acquire reserve currencies, including the dollar, to finance their deficits. Control of liquidity therefore required the adoption of rules about reserve currency holding and SDR substitution, at a time when new circumstances encouraged the opposite development.

The establishment of an SDR standard also involved breaking its link with gold, i.e. its valuation in terms of gold. The consolidation of gold holdings, however, presented special problems to the negotiators. During 1973 the free market price of gold rose to $120 per ounce. This was so far in excess of the official price of $42.22 per ounce, that central banks were reluctant to sell gold to each other. The European central banks were clearly concerned by this 'immobilisation' of their gold reserves (which had been increasing since the formation of the two-tier system), and it was unlikely that they could be prevented permanently from applying realistic prices to a commodity of which they possessed enormous quantities. (The French for example began to attach market-related values to their official gold holdings in 1975.) The removal of the official price regulation, however, threatened to enhance the monetary role of gold, rather than encourage its gradual phasing out. By effectively increasing the value of the gold holding in countries' reserves, these countries may have become less inclined to support the creation of additional SDRs and to exchange gold for SDRs, if they anticipated further increases in the market value of gold.

The LDCs were of course resistant to any proposal for the removal of the 'official' price of gold, since they were anxious to increase the importance of the SDR in the system, and to link it with a regular and increasing flow of real resources from the industrial countries to the developing world. From the industrialised countries' viewpoint, however, the aid-link question was not central to negotiating the restoration of monetary order. As such, the development problem did not receive much attention from the industrialised countries. In fact, during a period that has witnessed rapid inflation, the 'oil crisis' and a recession in production and employment, the real value of development aid has tended to fall rather than increase.

It is to a consideration of the climate in which the reform discussions were conducted that we must now turn our attention.

Inflation and recession

Table 8.1 demonstrates the emergence of world inflation after 1972. West Germany and the US have been the only countries to keep annual inflation to single figures during this period. This contrasts with the 1960–70 period, when the average annual rate of price increase for all the industrial countries was 3.4 per cent. World inflation at unprecedented rates was, as we have seen, the immediate cause of the breakdown of the pegged exchange rate system. Inflation had of course been present throughout the post-war period. But relatively modest rates of inflation, within a relatively small range of values, were compatible with a pegged system, given the surplus countries' willingness to lend to the deficit countries.

The possible causes of the sudden acceleration in prices during 1972–3 are numerous and the subject of much debate. We have already referred to the inflationary financing of the Vietnam War. The very large US deficits during 1970–2 give support to the international liquidity–monetarist explanation of inflation (Heller, 1976). Heller

Table 8.1 Annual percentage rates of inflation (GNP deflators) in selected countries, 1971–6

	1971	1972	1973	1974	1975	1976
Canada	3.1	5.0	9.1	14.9	11.2	9.5
US	5.1	4.1	5.8	9.7	9.6	5.3
Japan	4.4	4.8	11.5	20.7	7.4	6.4
France	5.6	6.1	7.6	11.6	12.9	9.7
Germany (West)	7.9	5.9	6.1	6.9	7.1	3.1
Italy	7.1	6.2	11.9	17.7	17.3	17.8
UK	8.9	8.0	7.6	13.6	28.3	15.1

Source: IMF Annual Reports, 1976, Table 2, p. 6; and 1977, Table 1, p. 3

argues that the enormous growth of reserves during this period restricted the ability of the authorities to control domestic money supplies. Certainly the period witnessed expansionary monetary policies. However, the major recipient of these reserves was West Germany, the country as we have seen, which was most successful in constraining inflationary pressures.

The contribution of monetary forces remains the subject of debate. The year 1972 did however witness a unique (or at least unusual) combination of factors that we might view as contributory to world inflation. The upturn in economic activity in the US in 1972 was, for instance, accompanied by a remarkably synchronised upturn in all the major industrial economies (see Table 8.3). The breakdown of the 'normal' labour demand–wage increase relationship in the late 1960s in many countries, meant that the expansion phase of this business cycle was accompanied by large wage increases at much lower levels of capacity utilisation. In addition, the rapid increase in production was accompanied by an unprecedented explosion in world prices of industrial raw materials and food. (On a base 1970 = 100, the London Economist index of world raw material prices rose from 119 to 249, between the second quarter of 1972 and the second quarter of 1974.) Excluding the oil price rises that came at the end of this period, the explanations offered for these cost increases to the industrialised countries include: the synchronisation of the upturn in demand for raw materials, supply deficiencies (including exceptional crop failures) and some speculative stockpiling. The 'imported inflation' argument became popular, especially in a country like the UK, where the depreciation of sterling exaggerated the effects of these price increases. The marked variation in inflation rates between countries shown in Table 8.1, and a corresponding sharp movement in exchange rates between 1973 and 1975 (see Fig. 8.1), suggest however, that the 'imported inflation' argument was not general.

The 'oil crisis'

Further and dramatic impetus was given to inflation rates by the quadrupling of the price of oil at the end of 1973. The oil embargo following the Arab–Israeli war in October 1973, and the subsequent announcement of spectacular increases in the price of oil by OPEC helped to assure the continuation of a system of floating rates.

Table 8.2 Current balances* of selected industrial countries, 1973–6

	($ billion) 1973	1974	1975	1976
US	2.5	1.4	15.5	3.1
UK	−1.2	− 7.8	− 2.8	−1.1
Canada	0.1	− 1.6	− 4.7	−4.2
France	−0.1	− 4.8	1.1	−5.0
Germany (West)	6.7	12.3	7.5	6.8
Italy	−1.2	− 6.6	0.9	−1.7
Japan	0.1	− 4.5	− 0.4	3.9

*Excludes official transfers
Source: *IMF Annual Report,* 1977, Table 8, p. 16

Besides the boost given to inflation, the oil price rises were to have a considerable impact on countries' payments positions and on income and employment levels (see Corden and Oppenheimer, 1974). Table 8.2 demonstrates the sharp movement into current-account deficits in the oil import-dependent countries of Western Europe, and Japan. Because of the oil-producing countries' inability to spend all of their increased oil revenues on the exports of the industrialised countries, the withdrawal of income from the industrial countries in the form of increased import bills was to have significant deflationary effects on production and employment.[9] Table 8.3 illustrates the suddenness of the collapse of buoyant global conditions between 1973 and 1974. This movement into recession in 1974 was also to have depressing effects on the developing countries, who were dependent on industrial markets for the sale of their primary products.

Table 8.3 Annual percentage changes in real output in selected countries, 1971–6

	1971	1972	1973	1974	1975	1976
Canada	6.5	5.9	7.5	3.7	1.1	4.9
US	3.0	5.7	5.5	−1.4	−1.3	6.0
Japan	7.3	9.1	9.8	−1.3	2.4	6.3
France	5.3	5.7	5.4	2.3	0.1	5.2
Germany (West)	3.0	3.4	4.9	0.4	−2.5	5.7
Italy	1.6	3.1	6.9	3.9	−3.5	5.6
UK	2.0	3.1	6.1	−0.1	−1.6	1.5

Source: *IMF Annual Reports,* 1976, Table 1, p. 5; and 1977, Table 1, p. 3

In addition to attempting to minimise their oil payments by obtaining privileged bilateral contracts with members of OPEC (and there were many such agreements made during 1974), or by reducing their demand for oil by energy-saving methods, or by further slowing down the rate of economic activity, the non-oil industrial countries were faced with two extreme possibilities for 'paying' for the increased oil bill. Payment could be made with real resources, including the transfer of property rights, or in monetary assets, i.e. a variety of types of financial claims (see Willet, 1975).

In the extreme, the first alternative required the oil producers to spend all their oil receipts on current imports of goods and services. The oil-importing countries did not, however, have the productive capacity, or the willingness to release such resources through the reduction of domestic absorption, and neither did the oil producers have the industrial capacity, or lack of foresight, to bring about a total transfer in real terms largely for current consumption. Certainly there has been additional expenditure on imports by the oil-producing countries, which has reduced the net effect of the oil price increases on the current payments positions of the industrial countries. In Table 8.4, the decline in the current surplus of the oil-exporting countries after 1974 was due largely, however, to the recession and the downturn in oil demand, rather than to the growth of exports to the oil producers. These self-adjustment forces will nevertheless increase over time as the oil-exporting countries' absorptive capacity increases.

Table 8.4 A summary of current balance situations, 1973–6

	($ billions)			
	1973	**1974**	**1975**	**1976**
Major oil exporters	+ 6.2	+67.4	+34.7	+41.0
Industrial countries	+11.1	−11.2	+18.6	− 1.4
Non-oil primary producers				
More developed	+ 1.3	−14.3	−14.8	−14.3
Less developed	−10.9	−29.5	−38.2	−25.8

Source: IMF Annual Report, 1977, Table 7, p. 15

An alternative method of making a 'real' payment was to encourage the oil producers to reinvest their oil revenue in the oil-importing countries. The oil producers could acquire property rights in importing countries' industries, and the importers' current oil deficits in the extreme situation would be totally offset by an equal inflow of long-term capital. Ignoring the dangers of the loss of property rights, this was an attractive alternative to the oil-importing countries. Although some 'recycling' of the oil surpluses has taken this form, the oil producers have been reluctant to hold their assets in illiquid forms. Given also that activity rates have been depressed and short-term interest rates high in the industrial countries, the oil producers have preferred to hold their wealth in short-term balances or other liquid claims.

The deferral of payment in real terms, by providing oil producers with monetary assets with which they could make claims on the future production of the importing countries, was more of a problem for individual countries than for the non-oil producers as a whole. In aggregate terms, there was no financing problem, since if the oil producers were unable to receive payment fully in resource terms, or by claims on property, then they had to accumulate the monetary assets of the deficit countries. The problem for the individual country was whether the oil producers were willing to accept payment in the particular country's currency, or preferred instead payment in some other currency or reserve asset.

The 'weak'-currency countries were forced to attract short-term funds by offering relatively high interest rates, to compensate for the possibility of purchasing-power loss from currency depreciation. (Reference back to Table 5.2 on p. 138 will show that the UK for instance was able to finance a significant amount of its current deficit in 1974 by increasing sterling liabilities.) Such funds were likely to be very sensitive to exchange-rate and interest-rate variations, and posed a speculative threat against the weaker currencies. To avoid the threat to existing reserves, the deficit countries needed to earn, or borrow, additional reserve currencies, especially dollars.

Collectively the first alternative required either that industrial countries attempted to increase their current surplus with the US, or with the non-oil-producing developing countries. We have already made reference to the paradoxical pressure on the US to continue to run a payments deficit, which would provide dollars to finance oil deficits. The European countries made considerable exhortation to the US to avoid deflationary policies, which helped to protect their current payments position. In the event, the US ran a surplus on goods and services during the 1973–6 period, and thereby heightened the deflationary threat of the oil deficits. Table 8.3 shows that the global recession in fact deepened in 1975. However, the payments position of the industrialised countries as a whole significantly improved as the demand for oil and raw materials from the developing countries fell. Table 8.4 shows that the industrial countries moved into current-account surplus by 1975 (though the surplus was largely earned by the US and West Germany), as the industrial countries' surplus with the developing countries increased. The continued current-account deficits of the UK, and many of the smaller industrial countries in 1975, and the masking of the oil problem by the downturn in activity rates, meant nevertheless that the danger still existed that some deficit countries might try to earn their additional dollar requirements from other industrial countries, through protectionist policies.

To avoid this threat of the growth of protectionism, and of further recessionary pressures, the deficit countries had to be able to borrow funds. Private capital markets have been fairly successful in borrowing from the international community in general for the deficit countries, and in 'recycling' petro-dollars in particular. Examination of Table 5.3 on p. 139–40 shows that the US remained a net exporter of capital throughout the period, and in countries like the UK the money markets have been able to arrange substantial loans through the intermediary of the Eurocurrency market, for instance. However, the desire for a more reliable means of recycling petro-dollars, given the oil producers' continued preference to lend short-term and the deficit countries' preference to borrow long-term, and given also the difficulties of the developing countries in finding access to private credit, led to pressure for official recycling schemes. As a result, an 'oil facility' at the IMF was arranged for 1974 and 1975. Under this scheme, the IMF borrows directly from the oil producers, and other surplus countries, and lends these funds to the deficit countries. (The Bank for International Settlements also offers official help in various forms, through the OECD's Financial Net scheme.)

By the end of 1975, the 'crisis' appeared to have been weathered as inflationary pressures abated. Further reductions of inflation rates were essential if OPEC was to be prevented from justifying further large price increases to maintain the real value of their oil surpluses. Some of the masking of the problems would be removed, however, if a recovery of world income and trade restored some of OPEC's lost bargaining power.

There has of course been a series of attempts in recent years to repeat the success of OPEC by other commodity groups. The oil experience is, however, unlikely to be repeated across a wide range of commodities (for reasons discussed in Chapter 4). As far as the industrialised countries are concerned, the severity of the recession has been restricted by the efficiency of international capital markets, and the realisation on the part of governments of the need to cooperate and avoid protectionist policies. At the end of 1975 the industrial countries, however, urgently needed to restore credibility to domestic management policies, if they were to reconcile the adjustment costs of higher oil prices with a recovery of production and employment at reduced rates of inflation, and if they wished to maintain relatively stable exchange rates (see Letiche, 1977).

The managed floating experience

Despite the diversity of arrangements (currencies officially floating were often managed and those with a formal peg had been subject to frequent adjustment), by mid-1976 the major industrial countries had been operating under a more flexible exchange-rate system for a period of over three years.[10] Academic and official concensus was that floating rates had in fact worked better than expected. The collapse of the adjustable peg system had been disorderly, and it is possible to interpret the 1973–5 period, which witnessed substantial long-term swings and short-term fluctuations in exchange rates, as part of a learning process.

The longer-term swings have however tended to reflect the marked

Fig. 8.1 Exchange rates against the US dollar, January 1974–June 1976. (Source: *IMF Annual Report,* 1976, Chart 8, p. 26)

differences among national economies, with respect to rates of inflation, interest rates and balance-of-payments positions (see Fig. 8.1). Such movements have in fact contributed significantly to payments adjustment, and thereby discouraged possibly the spread of protectionist attitudes. Any tendency to over-correct on the part of currency markets does not in any case appear to have had detrimental effects on world trade. We argued in Chapter 5 that conclusions are difficult to draw from the evidence, but the downturn in world trade between

1973 and 1975 appears to be consistent with, and explained by, the downturn in world output.

Speculative and destabilising capital flows in the shorter run may well have been caused by the erratic nature in which the authorities have managed exchange rates during this learning period, and by the differences between countries in the degree to which they have intervened on currency markets. Intervention by the US for instance, had until 1977 been infrequent and in small amounts. Other countries, who have attempted to manage the development of their exchange rate through heavy reserve use for periods, have at times had to allow their rate to change substantially under speculative pressures. The managed rate was not judged by the market to be consistent with the underlying conditions. Experience has also shown that the maintenance of stable exchange rates is difficult when underlying economic and financial policies of countries are not coordinated.

By 1976 it was becoming increasingly apparent that the stability of exchange rates did not require the official pegging of exchange rates. Indeed, 1975 and 1976 witnessed further moves towards greater diversity in exchange-rate practices among countries. For example, a number of countries who had previously pegged to the floating pound switched to a peg on the SDR, or a trade-weighted basket of currencies. Alternatively, several countries showed greater willingness to adjust their pegs. Despite these divergent developments, however, there was a growing awareness of the need to direct domestic policies towards the pursuit of a reasonable level of exchange stability. In fact IMF pressure for the adoption of specific principles for the guidance of policy, and for Fund surveillance of exchange-rate policies, had been indicated by the decision of the Fund's Executive Board in June 1974 to adopt 'guidelines for the management of floating exchange rates'.

Recent developments

In April 1976 the Board of Governors of the Fund approved proposals to amend the Articles of the Fund's Charter in such a way as to legalise the prevailing varied exchange-rate policies. A new Article IV of the Charter was in fact accepted by the annual conference of the IMF at Jamaica, later in 1976. The new 'obligations regarding exchange arrangements' stated that exchange arrangements may include:

1. the maintenance by a member of a value for its currency in terms of the special drawing right or another denominator other than gold, selected by the member; or
2. cooperative arrangement by which members maintain the value of their currencies in relation to the value of the currency or currencies of other members; or
3. other exchange arrangements of a member's choice.

(See Gold, 1976, and 1977.)

Article IV was a compromise between the opposing French and American points of view (de Vries, 1976). However, the US conversion to a belief in 'free market forces' (however ill-defined) meant, given their effective veto power under existing voting rules, that the agreement had established subject to ratification an effective barrier to the re-introduction of a widespread system of par values. Whatever their beliefs, the US was in any case unlikely to agree to a return to a par-value system until new convertibility rules were formulated. (The Jamaica agreement had in fact left the convertibility obligations of Article VIII of the Fund's Charter untouched.)

The Jamaica agreement made little progress on the issue of liquidity control and of rules about reserve currencies – other than to affirm the abolition of the official price of gold. This was despite the fact that the existing articles of the Fund continued to forbid monetary authorities from buying gold at a price above the official one. The new gold arrangements had been agreed among the EEC ministers in 1974, and formalised in August 1975 by the finance ministers of the US, France, West Germany, the UK and Japan. Under these arrangements, monetary authorities were now able to engage in transactions in gold at any price they wished. Although the Group of Ten agreed not to increase their total holdings of gold, and to eliminate all obligations to use gold in transactions with the Fund (which was also to sell one-third of its gold holdings[11]), the agreement was to be reviewed at the end of a two-year period. After then it would be possible to terminate these arrangements.

While the unpegging of the official gold price was in principle likely to encourage the phasing out of its monetary role (which in the long run appeared inevitable), by turning it into a commodity with an unstable price, the two-year proviso made its immediate phasing out less certain. The revaluation of official gold holding would substantially increase international liquidity, and in favour of the gold-holders, especially Europe. The US pressure for the demonetisation of gold had been resisted by the European countries, who if they required could use their up-valued gold holdings as a competitor to the dollar. Rather than taking gold out of the system, by centralising it at the Fund and substituting SDRs for it, the IMF was selling off part of its gold holding. Even though the LDCs obtained an increase in their voting strength at the Fund, and an increase in total IMF quotas from SDR 29 to SDR 39 billion, from the conference, the commitment on paper to the SDR as the principal reserve asset was given little operational significance.

On the one hand, the reform developments up to the end of 1976 can be interpreted as merely an *ex post* legalisation of monetary disorder. IMF surveillance of exchange-rate policy was of little importance in the absence of agreed rules concerning the management of flexible rates. Similarly, the future monetary role of gold remained uncertain and no rules on reserve-currency convertibility had been established. On the other hand, the Jamaica agreement can be viewed as the starting point for an *ad hoc* restoration of monetary order, based on international cooperation and IMF supervision. Whichever interpretation is most appropriate, the international community had left its options open.

8.5 The reform options

There has of course been a myriad of proposals for monetary reform, which involve a greater or lesser degree of restructuring of the international monetary system. In reality however, the possibilities are restricted by the legacies of the past, and by political constraints. We have already shown that expectations are now geared to *ad hoc* rather than wholesale reform. Our final task is therefore to discuss the feasibility of, and arguments for moving towards common exchange-rate policies, supranational monetary control and a single fiat currency.

This, and earlier chapters, have emphasised the interrelationship between the problems of liquidity and adjustment. The reform discussions have, and continue in fact to be, burdened by apparently contradictory pressures. Although exchange-rate flexibility, increasingly preferred on philosophic and practical grounds, tends to reduce adjustment rigidities, it also provides conditions which may discourage the development of a single world currency and world central bank. The variability of exchange rates tends to encourage countries to add to their reserves the currency or currencies which have the most advantages and attractions. Similarly, the ability of countries to increase their insulation from external influences by allowing the exchange rate to vary, reduces the efficiency of collective or central control.

There is presumably, however, some 'optimal' (in global terms) trade-off between the adjustment and liquidity targets, which satisfies also the confidence and stability requirements. Reconciliation of alternative national viewpoints will however be a lengthy process, for as Solomon argues:

> *The central questions for the future of the international monetary system have to do with reconciling the fact that economic policy is made by politically independent governments, with the fact that economic welfare of the people over which these governments preside has become increasingly dependent on events and policies in other countries.*
>
> (Solomon, 1977, p. 322)

Future exchange-rate policy?
We have seen how the present 'mixed' exchange-rate system was a response to the problems of interdependence (in inflationary and recession conditions), rather than a deliberate means of achieving balance-of-payments adjustment. Instead of seeking some insulation

from external influences, through capital and trade restrictions, the world has evolved a more flexible arrangement of exchange rates. A common policy is, however, absent. Increasing awareness of the problems of interdependence, and of persistent payments deficits and surpluses, means that politically independent nations are unlikely to return to a rigid system of pegged rates. (After a significant period of relative domestic and exchange stability, interest may however be revived in some form of 'managed flexibility', e.g. gliding parities.) However, governments are unlikely to relinquish completely the right to manipulate the exchange rate for domestic and external policy purposes. The choice is therefore between continuing the present varied system or extending the concept of managed floating by introducing common rules for adjustment and the nature of intervention (see Ethier and Bloomfield, 1975). This latter alternative appears highly attractive, since a common framework would discourage the pursuit of (possibly self-defeating) national self-interest, discourage destabilising capital flows and redistribute the adjustment burden between deficit and surplus countries. It is also the more difficult option to achieve. Such multilateral surveillance, which includes for example the adoption of target rates of exchange for countries by the IMF, and which is only a loose commitment to take unspecified measures, is unlikely to achieve optimal results.

National governments are, however, reluctant to submit themselves to automatic rules and penalties (e.g. loss of convertibility or graduated interest charges) in the face of reserve gain or loss. Besides political resistance, governments feel that discretion is required in distinguishing between erratic movements and more systematic changes in payments and reserve positions. (There are also technical difficulties in distinguishing between trend and cyclical movements in payments positions and in deciding how to react to cyclical movements.) The avoidance of alternative interpretations requires, of course, the unlikely willingness of national policy-makers to submit themselves to supranational control. Willingness, however, may be greatest where common exchange-rate policies can be arranged on a regional basis, and where commitment to political harmony is greatest. The European experience nevertheless has shown (with the termination of the special arrangement between the Benelux currencies in March 1976, and the departure of the French franc from the 'snake' in January 1974), that national tensions are likely to emerge in the face of uncertainties whenever supranational authority is absent. In global terms therefore, there are rational economic criteria for extending to the world economy the principles of national economic management.

Fund or banker?

Thus far the IMF has fulfilled some, but only some, of the functions of a world central bank. It has offered to some extent the facility of lender of the last resort to individual countries in the event of liquidity crisis. Its resources for this function have however been limited, and we have seen in practice how large-scale support lending has often come from a consortium of major national central banks. (The establishment of an Oil Facility at the IMF was perhaps indicative, however, of the Fund's willingness to supplement its direct lending power, by acting as a vehicle for recycling surpluses towards the deficit countries.)

Nevertheless, the political determination of the IMF's liquidity-creating capacity has meant that the Fund has been unable to fulfil the central-reserve-bank function. It has been unable to control, through its own lending activities, either the desired trend or counter-cyclical growth of global liquidity. Not of course that the desired growth of liquidity could be easily determined by a world central bank. National cycles are frequently out of phase with each other, and there are marked variations in national growth and inflation rates, which would impose divergent demands on the central policy-maker. It is indeed for this reason that countries are unlikely to be willing to relinquish their sovereignty over domestic economic policy. If a single world currency under the control of the IMF, or of some reformulated central body, was established, a common monetary policy to be fully effective would require the coordination of fiscal and other policies. Such a development at present seems highly unlikely, since it would require the breakdown of national government, and the global centralisation of political control.

There have however been proposals for central control of the inter-national monetary system, and therefore for a move towards the establishment of a world bank. The Triffin plan was an example of a fairly extreme formulation of such proposals. Whilst taking the IMF as the frame of reference, and calling initially only for the centralisation of world reserves as deposits at the Fund, it ultimately sought to empower the Fund to engage in open-market operations. This reserve-creation power, i.e. buying of financial assets in the open capital markets, would allow the 'Fund' to regulate the supply of international liquidity. The earlier Keynes plan was more modest. It sought the creation of a new international currency and the centralisa-tion of the clearing-union function. The basic assumption of the plan was that external balance was of a short-term cyclical nature. Such imbalances could be financed via the clearing union, which would recycle funds from the surplus to the deficit countries. The use of interest charges to penalise quota use and acquisition was seen by Keynes as a means of encouraging countries to adopt suitable expenditure-reducing and switching policies, or of encouraging equilibrating capital flows (i.e. direct borrowing by deficit countries from surplus countries).

The Triffin plan therefore emphasised the reserve-creation function of a central bank and the Keynes plan the lending function. Even on an SDR standard the IMF is only likely to fulfil the former function with the support of majority national opinion. The latter function, by con-trast, would no doubt increase with the further expansion of centrally created reserve assets. Countries are, however, likely to be reluctant to move towards a single, centrally created reserve, whose use or acquisition (in Keynesian fashion) is subject to penal charges. More automatic and regular adjustment of exchange rates should of course reduce the problem of excessive reserve gain or loss. But equally, more flexible exchange rates would reduce the monetary discipline that the IMF could impose on national economies.

Despite floating exchange rates, however, the commitment to reform, via the vehicle of the IMF since 1972, has been accompanied by an apparent and greater determination to extend central influence over national policies. Increased experience of management of the world economy and increased awareness of the need for international cooperation perhaps accounts for this increase in status for the IMF. Whether this reflects a move towards the establishment of a world bank in the long term remains, of course, the subject of conjecture.

SDR or multiple currency standard?

It was in order to restore discipline over domestic policies that some conservative economists advocated, during the 1950s and 1960s, a return to a gold standard and a system of rigidly fixed exchange rates. To overcome the liquidity deficiencies of a system based on gold, Harrod (1961) proposed a raising of the price of gold. The recent removal of an official restriction on the price of gold threatens temporarily to restore gold's attraction to some European central banks. However, the unsuitability of the gold-standard adjustment mechanism to modern conditions, and the anachronism of a commodity standard point to its ultimate demise.[12]

The rational extension of the fiat-currency principle to the international monetary system has received academic support throughout the post-war period. Both the Keynes and Triffin plans had argued for centrally created reserves as a means of overcoming what they saw as the long-term liquidity deficiencies of the Bretton Woods system. Both proposals envisaged the initial retention of gold alongside the new fiat currency. However, the restriction by Keynes that the fiat currency could not be used to purchase gold, indicated awareness of the long-term confidence problem of any system based on more than one asset. Triffin also wished to remove the confidence problem by empowering the IMF to require reserve holdings of foreign currency (dollars) and to gradually liquidate them.

The extent of the growth of dollar reserve holdings during the late 1960s and early 1970s makes the centralisation of such reserves at the IMF a more difficult procedure now. Floating exchange rates have, in any case, encouraged the multiplication of reserve currencies (i.e. the holding of 'strong' currencies other than the dollar), and thereby placed a constraint on the further movement towards an SDR standard. A multiple (key) currency standard (e.g. the Zolotas plan) would of course help to reduce the speculative threat against any one currency and reduce the dependence on a US deficit for liquidity growth.

The threat of destabilising shifts out of weaker into stronger key currencies would remain, and the aggregate deficit of the key-currency countries would still not guarantee the desired stable expansion of global liquidity. It is to remove the second-class currency problem and to permit a planned and stable growth of liquidity, that an SDR standard has been advocated.

On pragmatic grounds, the transition to a wholly fiat standard, given outstanding dollar balances (and to a lesser extent gold holdings), is likely to be a lengthy procedure. Support for further major allocations of SDRs is likely to be dependent on a formalisation of a fiat-exchange principle, i.e. an SDR-dollar standard, as a basis for the long-term centralisation and amortisation of the foreign-exchange element (de Vries plan, 1972). Successful funding of sterling balances, for instance, could provide a climate favourable to the liquidation (through funding or SDR substitution) of other non-SDR reserve holdings.

The international community, or the IMF, would then have to decide upon how many reserves to create and how to distribute them. Political bargaining or technical rules, based on existing trade levels, are likely to gear the development of an SDR system to the needs of the industrialised nations.

An aid link?

It is for this reason that there have been several proposals to link the creation of an international fiat money with the need to channel resources to the less developed countries, e.g. the Stamp plan (Stamp, 1958). The weighting of SDR distribution in favour of the less developed countries, would allow these countries to finance their balance-of-payments deficits, and therefore their development programmes. The industrialised nations would, in turn, receive SDRs in payment for the real resources exported to the LDCs and add them to their reserves.

The LDCs would have, of course, a vested interest in a rapid (and inflationary) expansion of international liquidity under such an arrangement. During a period of inflation and recession, the industrialised countries are likely to be resistant to inflationary liquidity growth, and the automatic and multilateral transfer of real resources to the LDCs. They are likely to continue to prefer bilateral arrangements, which tie aid to their own exports. Liquidity-aid link proposals are therefore dependent on the establishment of benign supranational control.

The development problem is, in any case, logically separate from the issues of international monetary reform. Decisions regarding the global distribution of income can be made within or outside the monetary framework. In the immediate future, the liquidity-aid link issue would appear to place an additional constraint on an already complex picture. The LDCs can not afford to hinder monetary reform and the recovery of production in the industrialised countries. By doing so they are likely only to restrict the growth of their own exports. Nevertheless, the indebtedness of the less developed countries has been seriously increased by the rise in oil prices, and subsequent recession in the industrialised world. In the longer term therefore, the criteria for SDR allocation will need to be steadily and progressively revised in favour of the LDCs. The LDCs have a low propensity to hold reserves, and allocations in their favour need not be inconsistent with a strategy for planned expansion in the developed world.

Notes

1. The actual financing of reconstruction was not the concern of the Bretton Woods designers. See Scammell (1961) for a consideration of the Marshall plan and of the events leading up to the restoration of general convertibility amongst European currencies in 1959.
2. For a discussion of the attempt to return to the gold standard in the 1920s, and of the events surrounding its final collapse, see Yeager (1966).
3. Keynes used the term 'bancor' to describe the proposed international money, which the clearing union would issue.
4. 'Europe' was traditionally more inclined to hold gold and to use these holdings as a political tool against the US. The French, in particular, had ambitions to return to a gold standard. The Scandinavian countries and Japan, by contrast, were more inclined to hold interest-bearing dollars.
5. A second dollar devaluation of 10 per cent to $42.22 per ounce of gold, to supplement the Smithsonian realignment, occurred in February 1973.
6. Germany had for example imposed restrictions in March 1972 on foreign borrowing by German business.
7. This was a committee of the Board of Governors of the IMF, set up in spring 1972, to consider the reform of the international monetary system.
8. 'Market' convertibility of the dollar had of course remained throughout the period, inasmuch as the dollar was convertible into other currencies at the prevailing market rate of exchange.
9. Solomon (1977) uses the term 'oil tax'. The oil price rise during 1974 was in fact analogous to a rise in indirect taxation of about $1\frac{1}{2}$ per cent of the GNP of the OECD countries. The proportion for the oil-dependent European economies was even larger.
10. Although a majority of countries continued to peg their currencies in some fashion, those countries whose currencies were allowed to float dominated world trade and financial transactions.
11. One-half of this gold was to be restituted at the old official price to Fund members in proportion to the members' quotas. The other half was to be sold on the free market and the profits were to be directed towards the LDCs.
12. For a consideration of the constraints on a remonetisation of gold, see Williamson (1977a), and refer back also to Chapter 6.

References

Agarwal, M., Askari, H. and Corson, W. (1975) 'A testing of the Ricardian theory of comparative advantage', *Economia Internazionale*, **28**, 341–52.

Alexander, S. S. (1952) 'Effects of a devaluation on a trade balance', *IMF Staff Papers*, **2**, 263–78. Reprinted in Caves and Johnson (1968).

Alexander, S. S. (1959) 'Effects of devaluation: a simplified synthesis of elasticities and absorption approaches', *American Economic Review*, **49**, 22–42.

Aliber, R. Z. (1973) *The International Money Game*, Macmillan, London.

Balassa, B. (1961) *The Theory of Economic Integration*, Irwin, Homewood, Illinois.

Balassa, B. (1963) 'An empirical demonstration of classical comparative cost theory', *Review of Economics and Statistics*, **45**, 231–8.

Balassa, B. (1965) 'Tariff protection in industrial countries: an evaluation', *Journal of Political Economy*, **73**, 573–94.

Balassa, B. (1967a) *Trade Liberalisation Among Industrial Countries*, McGraw-Hill, London.

Balassa, B. (1967b) 'Trade creation and trade diversion in the European Common Market', *Economic Journal*, **77**, 1–21, reprinted in Robson (1972).

Balassa, B. (1971) *The Structure of Protection in Developing Countries*, Johns Hopkins Press, Baltimore.

Balassa, B. et al. (1974) *European Economic Integration*, North-Holland, Amsterdam.

Baldwin, R. (1971a) 'Determinants of the commodity structure of US trade', *American Economic Review*, **61**, 126–46.

Baldwin, R. (1971b) *Non-tariff Distortions of International Trade*, Brookings Institute, Washington.

Barker, P. (1977) 'International cartels in primary commodities', in Maunder, P. (ed.), *Case Studies in International Economics*, Heinemann, London.

Basevi, G. (1966) 'The United States tariff structure: estimates of effective rates of protection of United States industries and industrial labour', *Review of Economics and Statistics*, **48**, 147–60.

Bauer, P. (1973) 'Inflation, SDR's and aid', *Lloyds Bank Review*, No. **109**, 31–5.

Baumol, W. B. (1957) 'Speculation, profitability and stability', *Review of Economics and Statistics*, **39**, 263–71.

Becker, G. (1964) *Human Capital*, Columbia University Press, New York.

Bernstein, E. M. (1956) 'Strategic factors in balance of payments adjustment', *IMF Staff Papers*, **5**, 152–9.

Bhagwati, J. (1958) 'Immiserizing growth: a geometric note', *Review of Economic Studies*, **25**, 201–5, reprinted in Caves and Johnson (1968).

Bhagwati, J. (1964) 'The pure theory of international trade: a survey', *Economic Journal*, **74**, 1–84.

Bhagwati, J. (1968) *The Theory and Practice of Commercial Policy*, Princeton University Press, Princeton.

Bhagwati, J. (ed.) (1969a) *International Trade*, Penguin, Harmondsworth.

Bhagwati, J. (1969b) 'On the equivalence of tariffs and quotas', in Bhagwati, J., *Trade, Tariffs and Growth*, Weidenfeld and Nicolson, London.

Bhagwati, J. (1973) 'The theory of immiserizing growth: further applications', in Connolly and Swoboda (1973).

Bhagwati, J. and Ramaswami, V. K. (1963) 'Domestic distortions, tariffs, and the theory of optimum subsidy', *Journal of Political Economy*, **71**, 44–50.

Bharadwaj, R. (1962a) 'Structural basis for India's foreign trade', *Series in International and Monetary Economics*, **No. 6**, University of Bombay, Bombay.

Bharadwaj, R. (1962b) 'Factor proportions and the structure of Indo-US trade', *Indian Economic Journal*, **10,**105–16.

Brittan, S. (1969) *Steering the Economy*, Secker and Warburg, London.

Caves, R. E. and Johnson, H. G. (eds) (1968) *Readings in International Economics*, Allen and Unwin, London.

Chrystal, K. A. (1977) 'Demand for international media of exchange', *American Economic Review*, **67**, 840–50.

Clark, P. B. (1970) 'Optimum international reserves and the speed of adjustment', *Journal of Political Economy*, **78**, 356–76.

Coffey, P. (1975) 'The Lomé Agreement and the EEC: implications and problems', *Three Banks Review*, **No. 108**, 44–56.

Coffey, P. and Presley, J. R. (1971) *European Monetary Integration*, Macmillan, London.

Cohen, B. J. (1966) 'Adjustment costs and the distribution of reserves', *Essays in International Finance*, **No. 18**, Princeton University, Princeton.

Cohen, B. J. (1969) *Balance of Payments Policy*, Penguin, Harmondsworth.

Common, M. S. (1976) *Basic Econometrics*, Longman, London.

Connolly, M. B. and Swoboda, A. K. (eds) (1973) *International Trade and Money*, Allen and Unwin, London.

Cooper, C. A. and Massell, B. F. (1965) 'A new look at customs union theory', *Economic Journal*, **75**, 742–7, reprinted in Robson (1972).

Cooper, R. N. (1966) 'The balance of payments in review', *Journal of Political Economy*, **74**, 379–95.

Cooper, R. N. (ed.) (1969) *International Finance*, Penguin, Harmondsworth.

Cooper, R. N. (1972) *Sterling, European Monetary Unification, and the International Monetary System*, British North-American Committee.

Corden, W. M. (1956) 'Economic expansion and international trade: a geometric approach', *Oxford Economic Papers*, **8**, 223–8.

Corden, W. M. (1970) 'The efficiency effects of trade and protection', in McDougall, I. A. and Snape, R. H. (eds), *Studies in International Economics*, North-Holland, Amsterdam.

Corden, W. M. (1971) *The Theory of Protection*, Clarendon Press, Oxford.

Corden, W. M. (1974) *Trade Policy and Economic Welfare*, Clarendon Press, Oxford.

Corden, W. M. (1975) 'The costs and consequences of protection: a survey of empirical work', in Kenen (1975).

Corden, W. M. and Oppenheimer, P. M. (1974) 'The basic implications of the rise in oil prices', *Moorgate and Wall St Journal*, **Autumn,** 23–38.

Currie, D. A. (1976) 'Some criticisms of the monetary analysis of balance of payments correction', *Economic Journal*, **86**, 508–22.

Curzon, G. and V. (1971) *Hidden Barriers to International Trade*, Trade Policy Research Centre, London.

Dasgupta, A. K. (1974) *Economic Theory and the Developing Countries*, Macmillan, London.

Dasgupta, A. K. and Hagger, A. J. (1971) *The Objectives of Macro-Economic Policy*, Macmillan, London.

Denison, E. F. (1962) *The Sources of Economic Growth in the US and the Alternatives Before Us,* Committee for Economic Development, New York.

Denison, E. F. (1967) *Why Growth Rates Differ: Post War Experience in Nine Western Countries*, Brookings Institute, Washington.

de Vries, T. (1972) 'Agenda for monetary reform', *Essays in International Finance*, **No. 95**, Princeton University, Princeton.

de Vries, T. (1976) 'Amending the fund's charter: reform or patchwork', *Banca Nazionale del Lavoro Quarterly Review*, **29**, 272–83.

Diaz-Alejandro, C. F. (1975) 'Trade policies and economic development' in Kenen (1975).

Dreyer, J. S. (1975) 'The mechanics of alternative valuations of the special drawing right', *Banca Nazionale del Lavoro Quarterly Review*, **28**, 268–83.

Eastman, H. C. and Stykolt, S. (1967) *The Tariff and Competition in Canada*, University of Toronto Press, Toronto.

EFTA Secretariat (1969) *The Effects of EFTA on the Economies of Member States*, EFTA, Geneva.

EFTA Secretariat (1972) *The Trade Effects of EFTA and the EEC 1959—1967*, EFTA, Geneva.

Elkan, W. (1974) *An Introduction to Development Economics*, Penguin. Harmondsworth.

Erb, G. F. and Schiavo-Campo, S. (1969) 'Export instability, level of development and economic size of less developed countries', *Bulletin of the Oxford Institute of Economics and Statistics*, **31**, 263–83.

Ethier, W. and Bloomfield, A. I. (1975) 'Managing the managed float', *Essays in International Finance*, **No. 112**, Princeton University, Princeton.

Fand, D. I. (1975) 'World reserves and world inflation', *Banca Nazionale del Lavoro Quarterly Review*, **28**, 347–69.

Fausten, D. K. (1975) *The Consistency of British Balance of Payments Policies*, Macmillan, London.

Findlay, R. and Grubert, H. (1959) 'Factor intensities, technological progress and the terms of trade', *Oxford Economic Papers*, **11**, 111–21, reprinted in Bhagwati (1969a).

Flanders, M. J. (1971) 'The demand for international reserves', *Studies in International Finance*, **No. 27**, Princeton University, Princeton.

Fleming, J. M. (1971) 'The SDR: some problems and possibilities', *IMF Staff Papers*, **18**, 24–45.

Frenkel, J. and Johnson, H. G. (eds) (1976) *The Monetary Approach to the Balance of Payments*, Allen and Unwin, London.

Friedman, I. (1973) 'International monetary system: 1973 reforming in a hurricane', *Banca Nazionale del Lavoro Quarterly Review*, **26**, 352–74.

Friedman, M. (1953) 'The case for flexible exchange rates', in *Essays in Positive Economics*, University of Chicago Press, Chicago, reprinted in Caves and Johnson (1968).

Gehrels, F. (1956–7) 'Customs unions from a single country viewpoint', *Review of Economic Studies*, **24**, 61–4.

Gold, J. (1976) 'Floating currencies, gold and SDRs: some recent legal developments', *IMF Pamphlet Series*, **No. 19**, IMF, Washington DC.

Gold, J. (1977) 'Floating currencies, SDRs and gold: further recent developments', *IMF Pamphlet Series*, **No. 22**, IMF, Washington DC.

Graham, A. W. M. (1977) 'Objectives and instruments', in Morris, D. (ed.), *The Economic System in the UK*, Oxford University Press, Oxford.

Greenaway, D. (1979) Intra-Industry Trade and Inter-Industry Trade, *Economics*, Winter.

Greenaway, D. and Milner, C. R. (1978) 'International liquidity, retrospect and prospect', *National Westminster Bank Review*, **May**, 48–56.

Grubel, H. G. (1964) 'The benefits and costs of being the world banker', *National Banking Review*, **December**, 189–212.

Grubel, H. G. (1971) 'The demand for international reserves: a critical review of the literature', *Journal of Economic Literature*, **9**, 1148–66.

Grubel, H. G. (1977) *International Economics*, Irwin, Homewood, Illinois.

Grubel, H. G. and Johnson, H. G. (1971) *Effective Tariff Protection*, GATT, Geneva.

Grubel, H. G. and Lloyd, P. J. (1975) *Intra-Industry Trade*, Macmillan, London.

Haberler, G. (1949) 'The market for foreign exchange and the stability of the balance of payments: a theoretical analysis', *Kyklos*, **3**, 193–218, reprinted in Cooper (1969).

Haberler, G. (1950) 'Some problems in the pure theory of international trade', *Economic Journal*, **60**, 223–40, reprinted in Caves and Johnson (1968).

Halm, G. N. (1970) *Approaches to Greater Flexibility of Exchange Rates*, Princeton University Press, Princeton.

Harcourt, G. C. (1969) 'Some Cambridge controversies in the theory of capital', *Journal of Economic Literature*, **7**, 369–405.

Harris, J. R. and Todaro, M. P. (1970) 'Migration, unemployment and development; a two-sector analysis', *American Economic Review*, **60**, 126–42.

Harrod, R. F. (1951) *Life of John Maynard Keynes*, Macmillan, London.

Harrod, R. F. (1961) *Alternative Means of Increasing International Liquidity*, European League for Economic Cooperation, Brussels.

Hawkins, E. K. (1970) *The Principles of Development Aid*, Penguin, Harmondsworth.

Heckscher, E. (1919) 'The effects of foreign trade on the distribution of income', in Ellis, H. and Metzler, L. A. (eds) (1948), *Readings in the Theory of International Trade*, Irwin, Homewood, Illinois.

Helleiner, G. K. (1972) *International Trade and Economic Development*, Penguin, Harmondsworth.

Helleiner, G. K. (1973) 'Manufactured exports from less-developed countries and multinational firms', *Economic Journal*, **84**, 21–47.

Heller, R. (1976) 'International reserves and world wide inflation', *IMF Staff Papers*, **23**, 61–87.

Hicks, J. R. (1953) 'An inaugural lecture', *Oxford Economic Papers*, **5**, 117–35, reprinted in Caves and Johnson (1968) as 'The long run dollar problem'.

Hirsch, F. and Higham, D. (1974) 'Floating rates – expectations and experience', *Three Banks Review*, No. 102, 3–34.

Houthakker, H. and Magee, S. (1969) 'Income and price elasticities in world trade', *Review of Economics and Statistics*, **51**,

Hume, D. (1752) 'Of the balance of trade', excerpts reprinted in Cooper (1969).

Humphrey, D. D. and Ferguson, C. E. (1960) 'The domestic and world benefits of a customs union', *Economia Internazionale*, **13**, 197–213.

International Monetary Fund (1974, 1976) *Annual Report*, Washington.

Iyoha, M. A. (1976) 'Demand for international reserves in less developed countries', *Review of Economics and Statistics*, **58**, 351–5.

Johnson, H. G. (1955) 'Economic expansion and international trade', *Manchester School*, **23**, 95–112.

Johnson, H. G. (1958a) 'The gains from freer trade in Europe: an estimate', *Manchester School*, **26**, 247–55, reprinted in Robson (1972).

Johnson, H. G. (1958b) 'Towards a general theory of the balance of payments', reprinted in Caves and Johnson (1968) and Cooper (1969).

Johnson, H. G. (1959) 'Economic development and international trade', reprinted in Caves and Johnson (1968).

Johnson, H. G. (1961) *International Trade and Economic Growth*, Harvard University Press, Cambridge, Mass.

Johnson, H. G. (1962) 'Economic development and international trade', in Johnson, H. G., *Money, Trade and Economic Growth*, Harvard University Press, Cambridge, Mass., reprinted in Caves and Johnson (1968).

Johnson, H. G. (1965a) 'Optimal trade intervention in the presence of domestic distortions', in Baldwin, R. *et al.*, Trade, Growth and the Balance of Payments: Essays in Honour of Gottfried Haberler, Rand-McNally, New York.

Johnson, H. G. (1965b) 'An economic theory of protectionism, tariff bargaining and the formation of customs unions', *Journal of Political Economy*, **73**, 256–83, reprinted in Robson (1972).

Johnson, H. G. (1966) 'The welfare costs of exchange stabilisation', *Journal of Political Economy*, **74**, 512–18.

Johnson, H. G. (1967a) *Economic Policies Towards Less Developed Countries*, Unwin University Books, London.

Johnson, H. G. (1967b) 'Theoretical problems in the international monetary system', *Pakistan Development Review*, **7**, 1–28, reprinted in Cooper (1969).

Johnson, H. G. (1969) 'The future of gold: the gold rush of 1968 in retrospect and prospect', *American Economic Review*, **59**, 344–8.

Johnson, H. G. (1970) 'A new view of the infant-industry argument', in McDougall, I. A. and Snape, R. H. (eds), *Studies in International Economics,* North-Holland, Amsterdam.

Johnson, H. G. (1971) 'Tariffs and economic development: some theoretical issues', in Johnson, H. G., *Aspects of the Theory of Tariffs,* Allen and Unwin, London.

Johnson, H. G. (1972) 'The Bretton Woods system, key currencies and the dollar crisis of 1971', *Three Banks Review,* **No. 94,** 3–22.

Johnson, H. G. (1973) 'The monetary approach to balance of payments analysis' in Connolly and Swoboda (1973).

Johnson, H. G. (1975) 'World inflation and the international monetary system', *Three Banks Review,* **No. 107,** 3–22.

Johnson, H. G. (1976) 'Money and the balance of payments', *Banca Nazionale del Lavoro Quarterly Review,* **29,** 3–18.

Johnson, H. G. (1977) 'The monetary approach to balance of payments theory and policy: explanations and policy implications', *Economica,* **44,** 217–29.

Kahn, Lord (1973) 'SDRs and aid', *Lloyds Bank Review,* **No. 110,** 1–8.

Kaser, M. (1967) *Integration Problems of the Planned Economies,* Oxford University Press, Oxford.

Kelly, M. G. (1970) 'The demand for international reserves', *American Economic Review,* **60,** 655–67.

Kenen, P. B. (1966) 'Financing and adjustment: the carrot and the stick', in Fellner, W. et al., *Maintaining and Restoring Balance in International Payments,* Princeton University Press, Princeton.

Kenen, P. B. (ed.) (1975) *International Trade and Finance: Frontiers for Research,* Cambridge University Press, Cambridge.

Kennedy, C. and Thirlwall, A. P. (1972) 'Studies in applied economics: technical progress', *Economic Journal,* **83,** 11–72.

Kindleberger, C. P. (1953) *International Economics* (5th ed. 1973), Irwin, Homewood, Illinois.

Kindleberger, C. P. (1969) 'Measuring equilibrium in the balance of payments', *Journal of Political Economy,* **77,** 873–91.

Kirkpatrick, C. H. and Nixson, F. I. (1976) 'UNCTAD IV and the new international economic order', *Three Banks Review,* **No. 112,** 30–49.

Krauss, M. B. (1976) 'The economics of the "guest worker" problem: a neo-Heckscher–Ohlin approach', *Scandinavian Journal of Economics,* **78,** 470–6.

Kravis, I. B. (1956) 'Availability and other influences on the commodity composition of trade', *Journal of Political Economy,* **64,** 143–55.

Laidler, D. W. (1974) *Introduction to Microeconomics,* Philip Allan, Oxford.

Lamfalussy, A. (1963) 'Intra-European trade and the competitive position of the EEC', paper read at Manchester Statistical Society.

Lancaster, K. (1957) 'The Heckscher–Ohlin trade model: a geometric treatment', *Economica,* **24,** 19–39, reprinted in Bhagwati (1969a).

Lederer, W. (1963) 'The balance of foreign transactions: problems of definition and measurement', *Special Paper in International Economics,* **No. 5,** Princeton University, Princeton.

Leontief, W. W. (1933) 'The use of indifference curves in the analysis of foreign trade', *Quarterly Journal of Economics,* **47,** 493–503, reprinted in Bhagwati (1969a).

Leontief, W. W. (1953) 'Domestic production and foreign trade; the American capital position re-examined', *Economia Internazionale,* **7,** 3–32, reprinted in Caves and Johnson (1968) and Bhagwati (1969a).

Leontief, W. W. (1956) 'Factor proportions and the structure of American trade: further theoretical and empirical analysis', *Review of Economics and Statistics,* **38,** 386–407.

Lerner, A. P. (1936) 'The symmetry between import and export taxes', *Economica,* **3,** 306–13, reprinted in Caves and Johnson (1968).

Letiche, J. M. (1977) 'Lessons of the oil crisis', *Lloyds Bank Review,* **No. 124,** 31–43.

Linder, S. B. (1961) *An Essay on Trade and Transformation*, John Wiley, New York.

Lipsey, R. G. (1960) 'The theory of customs unions, a general survey', *Economic Journal*, **70**, 496–513, reprinted in Caves and Johnson (1968) and Bhagwati (1969a).

Lipsey, R. G. and Lancaster, K. J. (1956–7) 'The general theory of second best', *Review of Economic Studies*, **24**, 11–32.

Little, I. M. D. and Mirrlees, J. A. (1969) *Manual of Industrial Project Analysis in Developing Countries*, OECD, Paris.

Little, I., Scitovsky, T., and Scott, M. (1970) *Industry and Trade in Some Developing Countries: A Comparative Study*, Oxford University Press, London.

Lutz, F. (1963) 'The problems of international liquidity and multiple currency standard', *Essays in International Finance*, **No. 41**, Princeton University, Princeton.

MacBean, A. T. (1966) *Export Instability and Economic Development*, Allen and Unwin, London.

MacDougall, G. D. A. (1951) 'British and American exports: a study suggested by the theory of comparative costs', *Economic Journal*, **61**, 697–724, reprinted in Caves and Johnson (1968).

Machlup, F. (1950) 'Three concepts of the balance of payments and the so-called dollar shortage', *Economic Journal*, **60**, 46–68, reprinted in Machlup (1966b).

Machlup, F. (1958) 'Equilibrium and disequilbrium: misplaced concreteness and disguised politics', *Economic Journal*, **68**, 1–24, reprinted in Machlup (1966b).

Machlup, F. (1965) 'Adjustment, compensatory correction, and financing of imbalance in international payments', in Baldwin, R. E. et al., *Trade, Growth and the Balance of Payments*, Rand McNally, Chicago.

Machlup, F. (1966a) 'The need for monetary reserves', *Banca Nazionale del Lavoro Quarterly Review*, **19**, 199–201.

Machlup, F. (1966b) *International Monetary Economics*, Allen and Unwin, London.

Machlup, F. (1970) 'The foreign exchange market: misunderstandings between practitioners and economists', in Halm (1970).

Maizels, A. (1968) *Exports and Economic Growth of Developing Countries*, Cambridge University Press, Cambridge.

Major, R. L. (1962) 'The Common Market: production and trade', *National Institute Economic Review*, **21**, 24–36.

McKenzie, G. W. (1976) *The Economics of the Eurocurrency System*, Macmillan, London.

McKinnon, R. I. (1963) 'Optimum currency areas', *American Economic Review*, **53**, 717–24, reprinted in Cooper (1969).

Mansfield, E. (1970) *Microeconomics: Theory and Applications* (2nd edn 1975), Norton, New York.

Meade, J. E. (1951) *The Theory of International Economic Policy. Volume I: The Balance of Payments*, Oxford University Press, Oxford.

Meade, J. E. (1952) *A Geometry of International Trade*, Allen and Unwin, London.

Meade, J. E. (1955) *The Theory of Customs Unions*, North-Holland, Amsterdam.

Meier, G. M. (1970) *Leading Issues in Economic Development*, Oxford University Press, Oxford.

Metcalfe, J. S. and Steedman, I. (1973) 'Heterogenous capital and the H–O–S theory of trade', in Parkin, J. M. and Nobay, A. R. (eds), *Essays in Modern Economics*, Longman, London.

Michaely, M. (1977) *The Theory of Commercial Policy*, Philip Allan, Oxford.

Mikesell, R. F. (1968) *The Economics of Foreign Aid*, Weidenfeld and Nicholson, London.

Milner, C. R. (1977) 'The growth of manufactured imports into the UK: protecting textiles?' in Maunder, P. (ed.), *Case Studies in International Economics*, Heinemann, London.

Milner, C. R. and Greenaway, D. (1979) 'Trade restrictions or trade liberalisation?', *Hobart Paper*, Institute of Economic Affairs, London.

Mishan, E. J. (1977) *The Economic Growth Debate*, Allen and Unwin, London.

Morgan, E. V. and Morgan, A. D. (1977) 'Gold or paper?', *Hobart Paper*, **69**, Institute of Economic Affairs, London.

Morton, K. and Tulloch, P. (1977) *Trade and Developing Countries,* Croom-Helm, London.

Mundell, R. A. (1960a) 'The pure theory of international trade', *American Economic Review,* **50,** 67–110.

Mundell, R. A. (1960b) 'The monetary dynamics of international adjustment under fixed and flexible exchange rates', *Quarterly Journal of Economics,* **74,** 237–57.

Mundell, R. A. (1961) 'A theory of optimum currency areas', *American Economic Review,* **51,** 509–17.

Mundell, R. A. (1962) 'The appropriate use of monetary and fiscal policy for internal and external stability', *IMF Staff Papers,* **9,** 70–9.

Mundell, R. A. (1968) *International Economics.* Collier-Macmillan, New York.

Mussa, M. (1974) 'A monetary approach to balance of payments analysis', *Journal of Money, Credit and Banking,* **6,** 333–51.

Nurkse, R. (1944) *International currency experience,* League of Nations, Geneva.

Nurkse, R. (1945) 'Conditions of international monetary equilibrium', *Essays in International Finance,* **4,** Princeton University, Princeton.

OECD (1970) 'OECD trade model: 1970 version', *Occasional Studies,* OECD, Paris.

Ohlin, B. (1933) *Inter-regional and International Trade,* Harvard University Press, Cambridge, Mass.

Panić, M. (1975) 'Why the UK's propensity to import is high', *Lloyds Bank Review,* No. **115,** 1–12.

Parkin, M. (1976) 'Monetary union and stabilisation policy in the European Community', *Banca Nazionale del Lavoro Quarterly Review,* **29,** 222–40.

Pearce, I. F. (1961) 'The problem of the balance of payments' *International Economic Review,* **2,** 1–28.

Pearce, I. F. (1970) *International Trade,* Macmillan, London.

Pearson, L. B. (1969) *Partners in Development,* Praeger, New York.

Pinder, J. (1969) 'Problems of European integration', in Denton, G. R. (ed.), *Economic Integration in Europe,* Weidenfeld and Nicholson, London.

Polak, J. J. (1971) 'Some reflections on the nature of special drawing rights', *IMF Pamphlet Series,* No. **16,** Washington DC.

Polak, J. J. (1974) 'Valuation and rate of interest of the SDR', *IMF Pamphlet Series,* No. **18,** Washington DC.

Posner, M. V. (1961) 'Technical change and international trade', *Oxford Economic Papers,* **13,** 323–41.

Prebisch, R. (1964) *Towards a New Trade Policy for Development,* United Nations, New York, reprinted in Meier (1970).

Presley, J. R. and Dennis, G. (1976) *Optimum Currency Areas: Theory and Practise,* Macmillan, London.

Pryor, F. (1966) 'Economic growth and the terms of trade', *Oxford Economic Papers,* **48,** 45–57.

Report of the Advisory Committee on the Presentation of Balance of Payments Statistics (1976), in *Survey of Current Business,* **56,** No. 6, 18–27.

Ricardo, D. (1817) *The Principles of Political Economy and Taxation.* Dent, London.

Robertson, D. (1972) *International Trade Policy,* Macmillan, London.

Robertson, D. (1973) 'Multilateral trade negotiation', *National Westminster Bank Review,* **February,** 46–58.

Robson, P. (ed.) (1972) *International Economic Integration,* Penguin, Harmondsworth.

Rueff, J. (1961) 'Gold exchange standard: a danger to the West', *The Times,* 27–29 June.

Rueff, J. (1967) *Balance of Payments,* Macmillan, London.

Rybczynski, T. M. (1955) 'Factor endowment and relative commodity prices', *Economica,* **22,** 336–41, reprinted in Caves and Johnson (1968).

Salant, W. S. (1969) 'International reserves and payments adjustment', *Banca Nazionale del Lavoro Quarterly Review,* **22,** 281–308.

Samuelson, P. A. (1948) 'International trade and the equalisation of factor prices', *Economic Journal,* **58,** 163–84.

Samuelson, P. A. (1949) 'International factor price equalisation once again', *Economic Journal,* **59,** 181–97, reprinted in Caves and Johnson (1968).

Samuelson, P. A. (1962) 'The gains from international trade once again', *Economic Journal,* **72,** 820–9, reprinted in Bhagwati (1969a).

Scammell, W. M. (1961) *International Monetary Policy,* Macmillan, London. (1st edn 1957.)

Scammell, W. M. (1974) *International Trade and Payments,* Macmillan, London.

Scherer, F. M. (1970) *Industrial Market Structure and Economic Performance,* Rand McNally, Chicago.

Scitovsky, T. (1958) *Economic Theory and Western European Integration,* Allen and Unwin, London.

Scitovsky, T. (1966) 'A new approach to international liquidity', *American Economic Review,* **56,** 1212–20.

Shone, R. (1972) *The Pure Theory of International Trade,* Macmillan, London.

Singer, H. W. (1950) 'The distribution of gains between investing and borrowing countries', *American Economic Review,* **40,** 473–85.

Singer, H. W. and Ansari J. (1977) *Rich and Poor Countries,* Allen and Unwin, London.

Södersten, B. (1964) 'Economic growth and international trade', *Stockholm Economic Studies,* New Series, **No. 5,** Stockholm.

Södersten, B. (1970) *International Economics,* Macmillan, London.

Solomon, R. (1977) *The International Monetary System 1945—76: An Insider's View,* Harper and Row, New York.

Stamp, M. (1958) 'The fund and the future', *Lloyds Bank Review,* **No. 50,** 1–20.

Stein, L. (1977) 'Export instability and development: a review of some recent findings', *Banca Nazionale del Lavoro Quarterly Review,* **30,** 279–90.

Stern, R. M. (1962) 'British and American productivity and comparative costs in international trade', *Oxford Economic Papers,* **14,** 275–96.

Stern, R. M. (1973) *The Balance of Payments: Theory and Economic Policy,* Macmillan, London.

Stern, R. M. (1976) 'World market instability in primary commodities', *Banca Nazionale del Lavoro Quarterly Review,* **29,** 175–95.

Stolper, W. F. and Samuelson, P. A. (1941) 'Protection and real wages', *Review of Economic Studies,* **9,** 58–73, reprinted in Bhagwati (1969a).

Stolper, W. F. and Roskamp, K. (1961) 'Input–output tables for East Germany with applications to foreign trade', *Bulletin of the Oxford Institute of Statistics,* **23,** 379–92.

Swan, T. W. (1963) 'Longer run problems of the balance of payments', in Arndt, H. W. and Corden, W. M. (eds), *The Australian Economy: A Volume of Readings,* Cheshire Press, Melbourne, 1963, reprinted in Caves and Johnson (1968).

Swann, D. W. (1970) *The Economics of the Common Market* (3rd edn 1975), Penguin, Harmondsworth.

Swoboda, A. K. (1973) 'Policy conflict, inconsistent goals and the coordination of economic policies', in Johnson, H. G. and Swoboda, A. K. (eds), *The Economics of Common Currencies,* Allen and Unwin, London.

Tarshis, L. (1954) 'International price ratios and international trade theory', *American Economic Review,* **44,** 120–2.

Tatemoto, M. and Ichimura, S. (1959) 'Factor proportions and foreign trade: the case of Japan', *Review of Economics and Statistics,* **41,** 442–6.

Telser, L. G. (1959) 'A theory of speculation relating to profitability and stability', *Review of Economics and Statistics,* **41,** 295–301.

Tew, B. (1977) *The Evolution of the International Monetary System, 1945—77,* Hutchinson, London.

Tinbergen, J. (1952) *On the Theory of Economic Policy,* North-Holland, Amsterdam.

Triffin, R. (1961) *Gold and the Dollar Crisis,* Yale University Press, New Haven.

Triffin, R. (1964) 'The myths and realities of the so-called gold standard', in Triffin, R., *Our International Monetary System: Yesterday, Today and Tomorrow,* Random House, New York, reprinted in Cooper (1969).

Tsiang, S. C. (1961) 'The role of money in trade balance stability: synthesis of the elasticity and absorption approaches', *American Economic Review*, **51**, 912–36, reprinted in Cooper (1969) and Caves and Johnson (1968).

Tsiang, S. C. (1977) 'The monetary theoretic foundations of the modern monetary approach to the balance of payments', *Oxford Economic Papers*, **29**, 319–38.

Tsoukalis, L. (1977) *The Politics and Economics of European Monetary Integration*, Allen and Unwin, London.

United Nations (1971) *Current Problems of Economic Integration: Agricultural and Industrial Cooperation among Developing Countries*, New York.

UNCTAD (1976) *Review of International Trade and Development 1975*, UN, New York.

Vanek, J. (1965) *General Equilibrium in International Discrimination*, Harvard University Press, Cambridge, Mass.

Veil, E. (1975) 'Surpluses and deficits in the balance of payments: definition and significance of alternative concepts', *OECD Occasional Studies*, OECD, Paris.

Vernon, R. (1966) 'International investment and international trade in the product cycle', *Quarterly Journal of Economics*, **80**, 190–207.

Vernon, R. (ed.) (1970) *The Technology Factor in International Trade*, NBER and Columbia University Press, New York.

Viner, J. (1950) *The Customs Union Issue*, Carnegie Endowment, New York.

Waelbroeck, J. (1976) 'Measuring the degree of progress of economic integration', in Machlup, F. (ed.), *Economic Integration, Worldwide, Regional, Sectoral*, Macmillan, London.

Wahl, D. F. (1961) 'Capital and labour requirements for Canada's foreign trade', *Canadian Journal of Economics and Political Science*, **27**, 349–58.

Werner Report (1970) *Report to the Council and the Commission on the Realization by Stages of Economic and Monetary Union in the Community*, European Commission, Brussels.

Westaway, A. J. and Weyman-Jones, T. G. (1977) *Macroeconomics: Theory, Evidence and Policy*, Longman, London.

Whitman, M. von N. (1975) 'Global monetarism and the monetary approach to the balance of payments', *Brookings Papers*, **March**, 491–555.

Willett, T. D. (1975) 'The oil transfer problem and international economic stability', *Essays in International Finance*, **113**, Princeton University, Princeton.

Williamson, J. (1973) 'International liquidity', *Economic Journal*, **83**, 685–746.

Williamson, J. (1976) 'International monetary disorder', in Parkin, M. and Nobay, A. (eds), *Current Issues in Economic Policy*, Allen and Unwin, London.

Williamson, J. (1977a) 'The problems of remonetising gold', *Banca Nazionale del Lavoro Quarterly Review*, **30**, 171–86.

Williamson, J. (1977b) *The Failure of World Monetary Reform, 1971–74*, Nelson, Sunbury, Middlesex.

Williamson, J. and Bottrill, A. (1971) 'The impact of customs unions on trade in manufactures', *Oxford Economic Papers*, **23**, 323–51.

Wilson, T. (1976) 'Effective devaluation and inflation', *Oxford Economic Papers*, **28**, 1–24.

Wrightman, D. (1970) 'IS, LM and external equilibrium: a graphical analysis', *American Economic Review*, **70**, 203–8.

Yeager, L. B. (1966) *International Monetary Relations* (2nd edn 1976), Harper and Row, New York.

Zis, G. (1975) 'Political origins of the international monetary crisis', *National Westminster Bank Review*, **August**, 28–43.

Zolotas, X. (1961–2) 'Towards a reinforced gold exchange standard', *Bank of Greece Papers and Lectures*, **Nos. 7 and 12**, reprinted in Grubel, H. G. (1963), *International Monetary Reform: Plans and Issues*, Oxford University Press, Oxford.

Index